Music in American Life

*A list of books in the series appears
at the end of this book.*

"THE WHOREHOUSE BELLS WERE RINGING"

AND OTHER SONGS COWBOYS SING

Collected and Edited by

Guy Logsdon

UNIVERSITY OF ILLINOIS PRESS
Urbana and Chicago

Library of Congress Cataloging-in-Publication Data

"The Whorehouse bells were ringing" and other songs
    cowboys sing.
    (Music in American life)
    Folk songs; unacc.
    Bibliography: p.
    Includes index.
    1. Cowboys—West (U.S.)—Songs and music.
2. Folk music—West (U.S.) 3. Folk-songs, English—
West (U.S.) I. Logsdon, Guy William. III. Series.
M1629.W59 1989   88-19931
ISBN 0-252-01583-5 (alk. paper)

Dedicated to the memory of

Lewis R. Pyle
and
Riley Neal

Payson, Arizona

Harry Patton of the Three Block Ranch, New Mexico, playing his fiddle in a division camp house many miles from the ranch headquarters, around 1907. (The Erwin E. Smith Collection of the Library of Congress on deposit at the Amon Carter Museum, Fort Worth.)

CONTENTS

PREFACE

Others called them "cowboys," but they call themselves punchers, cowpunchers, cowhands, cowpokes, buckaroos, wranglers, vaqueros, waddies, cowmen and other less sophisticated, but colorful, sobriquets. Rarely do they refer to themselves as cowboys, for that is the romantic title for their breed of men. The word conjures visions of dime novels, Louis L'Amour, Hollywood, television cowboys—not working men. Their own appellations reflect their work and often their home range. They use *cowboy* as a verb: he cowboys; he's cowboying on a different range; he cowboyed for that outfit for years. A Colorado ranch woman observed, "They're *men,* not boys." However, with this knowledge in mind, I have opted to follow the popular tradition of romanticizers and in this collection call the men who work with cattle and horses *cowboys.*

It is logical for me to follow this path of romantic terminology, for my interest in cowboys and their songs developed from the romantic image. It is tempting to say that as a boy in Oklahoma I grew up around cattle and would lie at night listening to the sounds of the herds and the cowboys singing and that in daytime I would see cowboys in their colorful garb ride by; but in truth, I was inspired by B-grade westerns. The Saturday afternoon heroes were, indeed, my heroes. This Hopalong Cassidy-Johnny Mack Brown inspiration was enhanced by the annual rodeo held each August in my hometown, Ada, Oklahoma, and by the glamour, excitement, and color of the rodeo parade—more than five miles of horses and riders, riding double-file, dressed in satin roundup-club shirts, and often mounted on expensive silver-trimmed nonworking cowboy saddles.

In 1948, my mother opened a western clothing store, one of the few stores in Oklahoma where western garb could be purchased. Working cowboys, rodeo cowboys, and would-be cowboys traded with us. I worked in the shop and wore western clothes. I became a *cloth* cowboy. When the shop was first opened, one of my sisters married a cowboy (rancher), and my brother started working as a rodeo clown and ultimately became a rancher. I have two other sisters who are normal.

My interest in music came from my father, an old-time fiddler who could play any stringed instrument. He taught each of us to play instruments by ear. As the youngest, I played the bass fiddle and later taught myself guitar technique. We had a family band and played western swing dances. More important, two or three nights a week, family and friends came to our house for music. In college I learned that much of our music was folk music.

My mother was an avid reader and collector of books. Driven by an obsession to learn, she maintained a lifelong quest for knowledge. While we made music, she read. She was proud of her Cherokee Indian ancestry. She was also deeply religious, a devout Methodist; I learned church singing through her influence. Thus, my father and my mother gave me my heritage through a love of music and books, slightly tainted by my obsession with cowboy culture and western Americana.

My interest in folk music during the early 1950s led me to the books of John A. Lomax and B. A. Botkin and to the phonorecordings of Burl Ives. Also, my wife's family and friends in her hometown, Okemah, Oklahoma, introduced me to the works of Woody Guthrie; this led me to Pete Seeger and the Weavers. By the time television embraced folk music with the weekly "hootenanny," I had learned that folk studies were far more than urban "folk clubs," but I was not prepared for the complexity of academic folk research.

Late one Saturday afternoon in the fall of 1957, I was in my father's furniture store trying to talk him into playing the fiddle into my newly acquired tape recorder, when Bill Long, my cowboy brother-in-law, walked in. My brother, John, suggested that I record some of Bill's cowboy songs; I didn't know he could sing. Bill started with "Zebra Dun," and I have been looking for cowboy songs ever since.

During the summer of 1962, I attended the International Folklore Institute at Indiana University, where classes taught by Richard Dorson, MacEdward Leach, and Archer Taylor were an awesome and overpowering experience that opened doors of research and knowledge that I did not know existed. Learning to distinguish "folklore" from "fakelore" eroded my popular lore foundation. But more important, one afternoon Archer Taylor, with gentlemanly professorial concern, spent a few hours leading and introducing me to research tools in the library. For him to be kind enough to use his time opening new realms of research to a student with limited experience was an inspiration, and to this day Archer Taylor remains the supreme example of the kind, compassionate teacher-scholar-gentleman. Also, during that summer, the Symposium on Obscenity in Folklore issue of the *Journal of American Folklore* arrived, and I witnessed the concern and excitement over this adventure in published folk bawdry.

I returned to Indiana University during the summer 1968 in order to study folk music with Kenneth Goldstein. In his classes I learned bibliographical methodology and explication in folk song research, which I have attempted to follow in editing this collection.

My professional career has been that of a teacher and librarian, including public-school teaching in California, Arizona, and Oklahoma. It was my Arizona experience in the early 1960s that opened my mind to the regional differences within the cowboy world. While teaching in the small mountain town of Payson, Arizona, I learned that my cowboy friends were carriers of traditions of past generations, and I collected a few songs from an old-time cowboy, forest ranger, and good friend, Lewis Pyle (see pp. 5–8). My family and I were vacationing in Payson in August 1968 when "Uncle Lew" introduced me to Riley Neal (see pp. 8–14). Two days later I had recorded fifty-six songs, and within two years Riley gave me more than 150 songs from his memory. Many were bawdy. From Riley, I learned slowly that cowboy songs are songs sung by cowboys, not just those songs with a cowboy theme or protagonist.

My research in hundreds of cowboy books and articles resulted in other conclusions different from popular and romantic concepts. First, the cowboy sings what he knows from his past and what appeals to his emotions; he is a sentimentalist. But his favorite songs are robust bawdy songs that range (as do "dirty" jokes and stories) from gross to clever humor. Sophisticated humor has never been part of the working man's daily fare. In fact, very little subtlety or double entendre can be found; the working man's bawdry usually leaves little to the imagination, as does his "on the job" language. However, I stress: *not all cowboys participated in or enjoyed bawdy songs and humor.*

Second, I learned that the cowboy loved to dance. In past generations if no dance halls and/or women were available, cowboys danced with one another. A ribbon or scarf tied around the arm designated those who had to dance the female role. Those dances were called "stag dances." After the trail-driving era, they served as an activity through which songs were often exchanged.

Another interesting aspect of cowboy songs is the folklore created about them by folklorists; I discuss this later in Part 3, "A Singing Cowboy Roundup." I hope that this attempt to provide a more thorough and accurate portrayal of cowboy songs and singing will stimulate further study and discussion of the working cowboy's tradition.

My research dispelled still another romantic concept. There were few, if any, musical instruments in cow camps. Certainly there were few, if any, guitars; it, along with the harmonica, became a twentieth-century romanticized adaptation imposed on the cowboy. The introduction and distribution of the harmonica within this country *probably* limited its availability during the trail-driving days, primarily the years between 1867 and 1890. The fiddle was the instrument most often mentioned in cowboy literature. The four-string banjo from music hall and minstrel tradition was second in popularity. In fact, cowboys needed no instruments. Like traditional singers from other regions, they usually sang unaccompanied.

Yet another conclusion I reached was that the number of cowboy poets, past and present, has been unusually high. The popular image—the John Wayne cowboy image—does not include a love of poetry. Yet, it is probable that no other industry or occupation continues to produce from its ranks as many poets as does the cattle industry and cowboying. Some of their poems, set to music, have became traditional cowboy songs. But because, contrary to popular belief and romantic image, only a few cowboys have been singers, many songs and poems were recited or performed in a song recitation style. Unfortunately, scholars have only recently begun investigating this tradition of writing and reciting poetry.

I have found many cowboy songs, but very few cowboy singers. Contrary to popular belief and to romantic image, there have never been many working cowboys who sing. The few I found slowly changed my theories about singing cowboys and their songs.

My collecting and reading along with working with relatively tame cattle also slowly dispelled—at least to my satisfaction—the belief that cowboy singing had functions other than recreational and diversionary. I am convinced that early references to singing to cattle other than night herding were for the most part to vocables or sounds that may have resembled melodic phrases, but were seldom to what is traditionally understood as song and singing. And the practice of singing while night herding arose as much to break the monotony of loneliness and silence and to hide a fear of darkness as to keep the herd still.

The generations of cowboys that wrote most of the songs based on cowboy themes unknowingly became active participants in creating the romantic cowboy myth. Even with the cowboys' propensity to enjoy and write poetry, many of their songs, including the bawdy, were merely exercises in rewriting and localizing old ballads and currently popular songs. It is impossible either to prove or to disprove authorship of most bawdry, but it is clear that cowboys carried many of the bawdy lyrics into their world from other regions and occupations.

We can identify the authors of some of our popular traditional cowboy theme songs. Curley Fletcher, the California/Nevada cowboy poet, stands above all. He wrote "The Strawberry Roan" and then, using the same model, wrote additional poems about horses and bulls including "The Castration of the Strawberry Roan." He composed other bawdy poetry as well. But we do not know how many cowboy poets or songwriters in all created their own bawdy songs or parodies. Most of the bawdry, I stress, was imported.

Through the efforts of western folklorists James Griffith, Hal Cannon, Michael Korn, and others, the first annual Cowboy Poetry Gathering was held in Elko, Nevada, in late January 1985. Hundreds of cowboys and cowgirls from the western states, invited to read or to recite both new and traditional poems, gathered as participants and observers. Three and four sessions were run concurrently in order to accommodate all of the invited poets. Open sessions were available for those who were not invited participants. Late one evening, at an open session for bawdy presentations, a large audience listened as the cowboys and cowgirls lined up waiting for a turn to sing, recite, or tell bawdy material. The participation and the audience response indicated that bawdy songs, poems, and stories are still a living tradition and that cowboys and cowgirls are still writing new bawdy songs and poems.

The second annual Gathering was held in Elko in late January 1986. More than five hundred cowboys and cowgirls submitted poems. The audience numbered into the thousands, but due to complaints by critics of bawdry, that session was removed from the program. However, a nucleus of concerned participants quietly organized a session in which more than a hundred observers and singers/poets successfully perpetuated the tradition.

My original intent was to edit and publish the songs Riley Neal had sung for me. However, after two years of bibliographical and discographical research, I began to feel that songs sung by a number of cowboys would be more valuable in documenting the general tradition than would the repertoire of one man. It has been many years since a field collection of cowboy songs (those collected from living cowboys on their own range) has been published. Moreover, no printed cowboy field collection has included bawdy songs. Collectors and compilers have alluded to them but for a variety of reasons did not make them available. Yet, my research continually revealed that cowboys enjoyed bawdry along with a wide variety of songs. So I changed directions.

The major problem was to choose songs representative of the diversity in my collection. Obviously, the bawdy songs had to be included. It was more difficult to select songs on cowboy themes. My criteria were personal preference and taste, songs that I often had heard cowboys request during informal song sessions, variants that differed significantly from the John A. Lomax texts, and songs that had seldom or never appeared in other collections. I decided not to include popular cowboy theme songs (except bawdy versions) such as "Streets of Laredo," for my texts, like most texts, obviously were derived John A. Lomax's books; using such popular, often printed songs seemed redundant. I confronted the same problem with the songs about other themes; I selected a few, such as "Lorena," mentioned in cowboy histories but not included in cowboy song collections. Again, I chose a few that have seldom or never appeared in other compilations. Finally, copyright restrictions led me to eliminate some songs from the 1920s and '30s.

Traditional singers—cowboys included—remember those songs that appeal to them; a song's age, origin, poetic beauty, and so forth, are generally unimportant. They remember and sing what they love, and sentimental songs provide a major source of singing pleasure. Songs such as "After the Ball," "Amber Tresses Tied in Blue," "Little Blossom," and "Put My Little Shoes Away," have been ignored by some field collectors, but they remain favorites of traditional singers. Riley Neal knew them, and to him they were as old and beautiful as "Barbara Allen."

The headnotes include information about my source, the origin of the song, and as much of its history as possible; a few songs require speculation. Also, I have occasionally included singers' comments that reflect their attitudes, personalities, and sense of humor.

I have searched for variants of each song and for as much information as possible, starting in G. Malcolm Laws, Jr., *American Balladry from British Broadsides* and *Native American Balladry*, and Tristram Potter Coffin and Roger deV. Renwick, *The British Traditional Ballad in North America*. I decided to use the title known by the singer and to list other titles under "Original Title" and "Alternate Titles." I searched all printed field and regional collections that I could obtain as well as the various Lomax volumes and many cowboy song collections.

The Archive of Folk Culture at the Library of Congress contains field recordings of Robert W. Gordon, John A. and Alan Lomax, and many other collectors and scholars, and the Performing Arts Division, Library of Congress, houses copies of Vance Randolph's voluminous bawdy Ozark manuscripts. I examined these collections for variants. I also used the John A. Lomax papers at the University of Texas, Austin, as well as the Austin E. and Alta S. Fife Folklore Archives, Utah State University, Logan; Barbara Walker's master's thesis, "A Folksong and Ballad Index to the Fife Mormon and Fife American Collections," is an excellent guide to the collection. Through the courtesy and kindness of D. K. Wilgus and library staff members of the Western Kentucky University Library, I obtained photocopies of the cowboy songs in the Wilgus-Western Kentucky Folk Archives.

Discographic information is hard to locate. Most of the commercial phonorecording information are from my own collection of recorded cowboy songs; this includes some 78 rpm discs but mainly long-play albums and re-issues. Friends who are knowledgeable about discography have been most generous with information.

It has been difficult to conclude this project, for as cowboys have heard about my intent to include their bawdy songs, they have told me about other poets and singers to interview. Unfortunately, I could not pursue all leads. For example, Slim Pickens, the actor and rodeo contestant and clown, died before I could arrange an interview. I was told by many of his friends that Slim did not sing, but could recite numerous songs and poems including bawdy material.

I intended to include only songs that I had recorded myself. Judith McCulloh, executive editor of the University of Illinois Press, and Glenn Ohrlin (see pp. 16–18) encouraged me to get acquainted with Dallas "Nevada Slim" Turner (pp. 18–21), however, and I decided to add a few of the songs he sent me.

And cowboys kept asking if a favorite song was to be included. An example is "Charlotte the Harlot." The first query came as I was completing my manuscript. I had never heard a cowboy sing the song, and I associated it with fraternity songs. Then in the spring of 1987, I received a copy of *Shitty Songs of Sigma Nu* and, in fact, "Charlotte the Harlot" was the eighth song in the collection. For the first time I looked at it carefully. Indeed, the protagonist is a cowboy, and Charlotte, the cowboys' favorite whore, has a rattlesnake in her vagina:

> Way down on the prairie where cow plop is thick,
> Where women are women and cowpokes cum quick;
> There lived pretty Charlotte, the girl we adore,
> The pride of the prairie, the cowpunchers' whore.
> (Chorus) It's Charlotte the harlot,
> > the girl we adore,
> > the pride of the prairie,
> > the cowpunchers' whore.

> She's dirty, she's vulgar, she spits in the street,
> Why whenever you see her, she's always in heat.
> She'll lay for a dollar, take less or take more,
> The pride of the prairie, the cowpunchers' whore.

> One day in the canyon, no pants on her quim,
> A rattlesnake saw her and flung himself in,
> Charlotte the harlot gave cowboys the frights,
> The only vagina that rattles and bites.

> One day on the prairie, while riding along,
> My seat in the saddle, the reins on my dong,
> Who should I meet but the girl I adore
> The pride of the prairie, the cowpunchers' whore.

> I got off my pony, I reached for her crack,
> The damn thing was rattling and biting me back.

I took out my pistol; I aimed for its head.
I missed the damned rattler, and shot her instead.

Her funeral procession was forty miles long,
With a chorus of cowpunchers singing this song:
"Here lies a young maiden who never kept score,
The pride of the prairie, the cowpunchers' whore."

This fraternity version is almost identical to a variant that Austin E. Fife collected from a student in 1961 (FAC I 841); the student claimed that he learned it from a sheepherder in Idaho. (I leave it to the reader to make analogies between sheepherders and Sigma Nu's.) Ed Cray gives an excellent explication in *The Erotic Muse* (pp. 96–99, 173–78).

Another song that has been mentioned as too vile to print is "The Bucking Bronco". Again, I have never collected this in either a clean or a bawdy version. N. Howard "Jack" Thorp included the polite-society version in his 1908 edition of *Songs of the Cowboys*; in his 1921 edition he wrote: "By Belle Star [*sic*], Indian Territory / Written about 1878. Song has been expurgated by me. . . . I knew her well" (p. 14). Thorp amplified his claim of friendship in *Pardner of the Wind* (pp. 35–36); he also said that Belle was a beautiful brunette, was well educated, and could play the piano. Actually, Belle Starr was ugly. It is doubtful that Jack Thorp ever met her, but he was a great storyteller and was not above stretching the truth to tell a good story. However, he was truthful when he claimed that he expunged and bowdlerized the song.

Austin E. Fife collected numerous variants under different titles, including this bawdy variant (FAC I 837) sung by the same "Charlotte the Harlot" student:

My love is a rider, wild horses he'll break,
But he's promised to give it up just for my sake.
With his foot in the stirrup, his saddle boots on
With a hop and a swing he is mounted and gone.

The first time I saw him 'twas early in spring,
He was riding a bronco, a high-headed thing,
And he laughed and he waved as along he did go
And he wished me to look at his bucking bronco.

He made me some presents, among them a ring
But the present I gave him was a far greater thing,
'Twas my young maidenhead, I'll have you all know,
He has won it by riding his bucking bronco.

'Twas near the arroyo he first laid me down,
He was dressed for the roundup and I wore a gown,
The he wiped off his chaps so the stain wouldn't show,
And he turned and rode off on his bucking bronco.

My love had a gun that was sturdy and long,
But he wore it to visit the lady gone wrong,
Though once it was strong and it shot straight and true
Now it wobbles and it buckles and it's red, white, and blue.

Young maidens, take warning, where'er you reside,
Beware of a cowboy who swings the rawhide,
He'll love you, he'll lay you, then one day he'll go
In the spring up the trail on his bucking bronco.

One of the earliest cowboy songs to be mentioned as bawdy, "The Bucking Bronco" contains numerous horseback-riding metaphors. For an excellent explication, see Austin E. and Alta S. Fife's commentary in their edition of Thorp's *Songs of the Cowboys* (pp. 121–34).

These are just two examples of the vast body of material still circulating in the cowboy world. The point is that—in theory, if not in practicality—I could have expanded this collection indefinitely.

A friend and noted western historian asked me why I have included bawdy songs, which will challenge the cowboy's romantic image. The question shocked me, for I thought all scholars sought the truth. I did not write the songs; I make no apology for the content. The desire for recreation is the motive behind all bawdy songs; while some readers will see only offensive words, others will surely discern the genius of humor. Traditional songs, bawdy and otherwise, persist because people value them. My purpose in compiling this collection has been to make available a true range of songs that have been—and remain—a significant part of cowboy culture and experience.

ACKNOWLEDGMENTS

I wish to express my indebtedness and appreciation to Archie Green and Judith McCulloh, who, as friends, have offered encouragement in a variety of projects over many years. Others, too numerous to mention, have offered encouragement for this controversial project, and although nameless in this statement, each has my gratitude. And I thank the University of Illinois Press personnel, especially Director Richard L. Wentworth, for their support and willingness to publish this manuscript.

Anonymous readers of my original manuscript offered a wide range of advice and criticism. To the best of my ability, I have incorporated their suggestions; this does not mean that no errors will be found. The readers spent much time evaluating my manuscript, and I thank them for their time and assistance.

I am indebted to Norm Cohen for taking special interest and giving valuable assistance in song explications. Norm is a friend to many and a scholar of impeccable style.

I extend sincere appreciation to those who through the years have opened collections and/or shared their knowledge: Joseph C. Hickerson and the staff at the Archive of Folk Culture, Library of Congress; John Wheat, Barker Texas History Center, University of Texas, Austin; J. Barre Toelken and Barbara Walker, Fife Folklore Archives, Utah State University; Don Reeves, National Cowboy Hall of Fame; Eleanor M. Gehres, Western History Department, Denver Public Library; Photo Archives, Museum of New Mexico; staff members of the Prints and Photographs Division, Library of Congress; and Guthrie T. Meade, Jr., Glenn Ohrlin,

Dallas "Nevada Slim" Turner, D. K. Wilgus, Charles Seemann, Keith and Kathryn Cunningham, Kenneth Goldstein, Gershon Legman, Frank Hoffmann, James Griffith, Lawrence Clayton, Jan Roush, Alan Jabbour, William K. McNeil, Lou Curtiss, Herbert Halpert, Elton Miles, Douglas C. Wixson, Jack Conroy, Hal Cannon, Kenneth Griffis, Marvin Grigsby, John I. White, Michael Korn, Raymond and Pat Cline, Barry Kinsey, David Farmer, Rennard Strickland, Leo Zabelin, Don Hale, and many other friends.

Judy McCulloh helped with the transcription for the music that appears in this book, and Mary Giles provided editorial assistance.

To J. Paschal Twyman, president of the University of Tulsa, and Brad Place, I say, "Thanks." We enjoyed five years of working cattle with Fred Lay, a great old-time cowboy. As week-end cowboys we learned much from Fred. Our friendship has been a significant part of my life.

I am eternally indebted to the interlibrary loan staff of McFarlin Library, University of Tulsa; they found many, many elusive books and articles for me. And I am thankful for the libraries around the country that shared material. Beth Freeman, reference librarian, McFarlin Library, University of Tulsa, has been most generous with her time and skills. Andy Lupardus and Lynn Holtzchu solved bibliographic problems; Richard Kearns has been a constant friend, and Sid Huttner directed me toward items in Special Collections. Two secretaries and friends—Mavis Farley and Barbara Booth—made my work easier.

My wife, Phyllis, and my daughters, Tamara, Cindy, Susan, and Nathalie, suffered through many years living with a man who has strange interests and ideas. I thank them for their love and patience, and in spite of my inattention and frequent absences, I dearly love and appreciate each one. I am indebted to Phyllis for her long hours and tedious work in typing my manuscript; without her my work would have been delayed and difficult.

And thanks to the nameless songwriters, poets and singers-reciters who not only gave life to songs and poems, but also kept them alive through the centuries.

I

THE SINGERS

The singers discussed in this section represent a variety of western states. Three never ranged far from their home. The others ranged far and wide throughout the West. Their experiences in the cow-horse agriculture world are as varied as their home states, but each one is a cowboy.

As singers, their backgrounds are similar; they had no formal musical training, so their singing styles are natural and unaffected. They were motivated by a love of singing and their songs were learned from others. Two singers, Bill Long and Lew Pyle, did not learn to play musical instruments; the others learned to play the guitar and other musical instruments by ear. Riley Neal, however, sang all of his songs unaccompanied.

A keen sense of humor is another common trait, along with a strong feeling of individuality. The romanticized cowboy image of the rugged, durable, independent man is, in truth, a common cowboy trait applicable to the singers. The value of and loyalty to friends and being able to rely on their word are also common cowboy traits possessed by these men. They represent the cowboy image well.

Bill Long

William Wade "Bill" Long, who lives and raises and trades horses and cattle southwest of Ada, Oklahoma, was my initial introduction to "real" cowboy songs and singing. Bill is my brother-in-law, and because

Bill Long, 1982. (Photo by Guy Logsdon.)

our family is never bashful and always has a tendency to play or speak when a lull in conversation, entertainment, or even prayer occurs, it was nearly ten years after he and my sister, Jean, were married before I knew that Bill sang.

Bill is, in truth, one who was born in a log cabin in 1922 near Connerville, Oklahoma. He is the youngest of ten children and according to him "all of the children except eight were boys." He grew up in central-southwestern Oklahoma, where his father ranched.

As a young boy he developed an interest in cowboy songs and learned a few from his older brother. Some of his sisters would send words of songs to him, and he learned a song or two from their boyfriends. To Bill, they were all old songs, even though songs such as "Sky Ball Paint" and "True Blue Bill" were songs of the 1930s. He recalled, "In the '30s everything was tough. 'Bout the only thing you could do on a Saturday night was sit around and sing or play a game of dominos. We used to pass songs around the neighborhood. I was about twelve when I learned most of 'em." So he learned songs from friends as well as from his relatives; most songs had cowboy themes.

When Bill was eight, his father died, so after high school graduation Bill decided to stay close to home and run the family place where his mother lived. For weekend diversion he entered the area's amateur rodeos as a bare-back bronc rider and bull rider. In 1942, he entered a rodeo at Norman, Oklahoma, and won the bull riding event; he was "asked" to join the Rodeo Cowboys Association (now the Professional Rodeo Cowboys Association) before they would pay him his winnings. However, Bill could not follow the professional rodeos and run a small ranch at the same time, so he devoted his life to raising horses and cattle.

In the summer of 1982, Bill Long was invited as an Oklahoma cowboy singer to participate in the annual Smithsonian Institution Festival of American Folklife in Washington, D.C. Taped recordings of the field interview and of his performances are in the Smithsonian Folklife Archives. As with most traditional singers, Bill Long does not know a vast number of songs; his standard repertoire is fewer than twenty.

Although I have used only one text, "Flyin' U Twister," in this collection, some other songs that Bill sings are "Crosseyed Sue"; "Empty Cot in the Bunk House Tonight"; "Empty Saddles in the Old Corral"; "Sky Ball Paint"; "Strawberry Roan"; "True Blue Bill"; "Utah Carroll"; "Who Broke the Lock on the Hen House Door"; and "Zebra Dun."

Lewis R. Pyle

"Uncle Lew," as he was affectionately known in Payson, Arizona, was not necessarily a good singer, but he was responsible for my continued interest in cowboy singing. Because not many cowboys actually sang or sing, it was not easy to find singers; Lew Pyle represented that in-between group who enjoyed a good memory but limited musical,

Lewis R. Pyle, 1962. (Photo by Guy Logsdon.)

singing skills. He sang in a half-singing, half-recitation style; his ability to move his voice outside the range of a complete octave was limited.

While living and working as a classroom teacher-librarian in Payson, Arizona, for three years (1960–63), my family and I became close friends —a part of their family—with Lew and his wife, Nan. When we first met, they had a "cathouse" (cattery) behind their home; they raised show cats. Within a short time, I was helping Lew feed each evening— more than forty cats, a goat, two burros, seven dogs, four parrots, and whatever other creatures that might have been taken in at that time. It was during those feeding sessions that I would get Lew to talk and tell stories. Unfortunately, I owned no portable tape recorder, and much information was lost because of my own limited memory.

Lew was born in Kansas in 1882, and in 1890, moved with his family to Starr Valley, a few miles east of Payson. He made his home in that north central part of Arizona until his death in 1974 at the age of ninety-two. During his early life, he and his father operated a freight line that supplied staples to the Payson area—eighteen pack burros that ran between Payson and Flagstaff in the summer and between Payson and Phoenix in the winter. While in his late eighties, he could still make burro pack-trees or saddles and show how to tie goods on a burro.

Along with the family, Lew helped operate the homestead ranch along Bonita Creek just under the Mogollon Rim; later he purchased his own ranch land. In 1905, he became the first field ranger for the National Forest Service in the newly created Tonto National Forest, a position he held until 1941; Lew continued to work on a temporary status for the Forest Service until 1945.

Many of Lew's adult years were spent as a bachelor, and for the most part he learned his material in cow camps or other cowboy settings. He was approximately eighty years old when I first heard him sing and recite; he had already forgotten many songs. Still, he had an amazing memory.

My most traumatic experience as a cowboy song collector happened while interviewing Lew. After much cajoling I was able to set an appointment to record him. My wife and I went to the Pyle's home, and while Phyllis and Nan visited, Lew sang and reminisced. At the end of the reel, I turned the tape and convinced Lew to recite obscene cowboy toasts that he knew. Finally, for he did not want the ladies to hear him, he started; fifteen minutes later when he was through, I discovered that a small button that activated the recording head had not worked—fifteen minutes of blank tape and some of the best cowboy material to be heard was lost. I had relied on the tape recorder without taking notes. Never again through many years could I persuade Lew to recite them.

Lew sang "Z-Bar Dun" instead of "Zebra Dun." He was adamant; he learned it near the turn of the century and would not change it to "Zebra." To me, his version of "Banks of My Native Australia" was a major discovery. His "Stinkin' Cow" was more recitation than song, and in 1966, at eighty-four, he sang "Joe Williams," "The Tenderfoot," and "The Red Light Saloon" for me.

Two years later in August 1968 while I was in Payson for a three-week visit, Lew asked me if I had ever recorded Riley Neal. My response was, "Who's Riley?" Lew told me that Riley knew more songs than anyone in that region of Arizona. After inquiring about singers for nearly eight years, it turned out that the best source lived only one block from where we had lived. Lew took me to meet Riley the next morning.

Riley Neal

Riley Neal was a few months away from being seventy-seven years old when Lew Pyle introduced me to him; he was a memorable man. Most of his life had been spent in Gisela, Arizona, approximately twelve miles southeast of Payson, where he ranched and cared for his mother until her death. A marriage lasted a very short time, so Riley was a bachelor for life. He referred to single men as "us stags."

Riley was born in Gisela in 1891, and for many of the years when both he and Lew were growing up, their home area was isolated. From Payson, it was approximately ninety miles each direction to Phoenix, Globe, and Flagstaff, and only small settlements of single ranch families were found along the way. To get to any of the aforementioned towns, travelers had to cross rugged mountainous terrain; therefore, the area was particularly appealing to people who wanted isolation. As late as the early 1950s, a trip by automobile from Payson to Phoenix required nearly ten hours of travel time. Many cowboys, prospectors, and other citizens drifted in for a short while before moving on. The area gained some fame as the setting for a few Zane Grey novels such as *To the Last Man* and *Under the Tonto Rim*.

When Lew and I visited Riley, I turned on the tape recorder. Riley immediately became nervous, so I put it on the floor with only a microphone left where he could see it. The change did not help, for he still—in traditional style—sat straight with his head slightly tilted back and eyes focused on the opposite ceiling corner. His nervousness made it difficult for him to pitch his songs naturally, and he often had to start over. Because I had asked him for cowboy songs, he started with "Charlie Rutledge" and "Little Joe, the Wrangler." I knew that he was going to have many songs, but I had no idea how good his memory was. Also, during that first session Lew would occasionally sing along with him, indicating that Lew actually had known more songs than he could recall.

After singing his third song, "Billy Vanero," Riley sang a bawdy song, "The Morman Cowboy." When he finished, the three of us laughed, and

Riley Neal, 1968. (Photo by Guy Logsdon.)

Riley asked, "You don't want that kind do you? It's an *ugly* song." My immediate reaction—"Yes!"

"Well, I know some awfully ugly ones," he said, and sang eight more —one right after another; eventually he provided more than thirty of the "ugly" songs in this collection.

During that first three-hour session Riley sang "ugly" songs, cowboy songs, older *folk* songs along with many nineteenth- and turn-of-the-century sentimental songs. It was then when I slowly started to realize that a cowboy song is a song that cowboys sing, as opposed only to songs about cowboys. Also, before the session ended, Riley played the harmonica and the piano; his piano style had a strange, heavy, left-hand sporadic rhythm. He apologized for not playing the guitar anymore. Later, I learned that Riley, along with relatives and friends, had played at dances in Gisela for many years, and his piano rendition of "My Pretty Quadroon" and other tunes had made many dancers get to their feet. Lew and I had to leave, but only after a time had been set to return the next day.

That evening as we visited with different friends around town, I told them of my excitement in finding Riley. Almost to the person, they said, "Was he drinking? If you go back tomorrow and he's drinking, get out of there fast." No one accused Riley of being mean, only tough and ornery when he was drunk. He was a big man who obviously had worked hard all of his life—he could take care of himself and others, too. But to me the comments were a challenge, and Riley and I became friends.

The next morning Riley continued, and, when I left, he had sung fifty-six songs, many of which I have used in this collection. Some of those not included are "Old Joe Clark," "The Gypsy's Warning," "Reply to the Gypsy's Warning," "Amber Tresses Tied in Blue," "The Daughter of Samuel O'Connell," and "The Blind Girl." He loved sentimental songs and wiped tears away as he sang; he considered them to be old songs because he had learned them from others.

Riley agreed to "write out" all of the songs that he knew, so back in Tulsa I sent pencil, paper, envelopes, and stamps. A friendship through letters developed, with Riley doing most of the writing.

> My father was a singer and I suppose that I inherited it from him. I can't remember when I couldn't sing or whistle a tune. I used to hear a song twice and know it all after that. (December 1, 1968)

> I sometimes think that I am kind of simple minded, farten (*sic*) around with those old songs when nobody cares anything about them anyway except me. (May 5, 1969)

> A person like me who's been raised out in the sticks never gets lonely out on the range though he may not see a soul for weeks but in a town full of people and don't know any of them he gets lonesome as hell. (October 20, 1969)

The songs that he sent changed after March 1969. Later I learned that he had become so interested in writing out the songs that he found a copy of Lomax's *Cowboy Songs* and copied those he knew. But I still received many that were not in Lomax; they were from his memory. In May 1970 he wrote:

> Every one always said that I had a wonderful memory for remembering stock, and I have. No two cows or calves ever looked the same exactly to me and I see a cow once I never forgot her and steers and bulls the same. I can get out on the range and do anything I have to do and do it well but I can do it better if no one is watching me. Lord, Man, I have branded a whole corrall (*sic*) full of calves by myself lots of times but I have always had an inferiority complex and can't do so well if anyone is watching me. . . .

He had a great memory for songs as well as stock, and he was excited about my return visit in August 1970. In fact, in order to combat throat problems and nervousness he purchased a bottle of Jim Beam, although he had not taken a drink of whiskey in six years. During that trip I could only spend two days in Payson and wanted to get at least the melody line for each song that he knew. We started at the top of the list, but we did not make it all the way through the songs.

After a few hours not only did Riley's voice give out, but a sizable portion of the bottle was also gone. Riley was feeling no pain. The next morning we continued where we had left off, on the songs and the bottle. By early afternoon it became obvious that Riley could go no further. While he only drank a swallow every now and then to "clear his throat," it got to him. Later he wrote that he did not even remember the afternoon. And as he drank, one sad emotion intensified; Riley was an extremely lonely man who loved any song of sadness and who had decided that the only thing that he could leave to show that he had been alive was his collection of songs. Later he was pleased to know that copies of his tapes were in the Archive of Folk Culture at the Library of Congress, however he always wanted them to be published.

I persuaded Riley to write his life story. Eventually a thirty-page handwritten manuscript arrived. Riley told that when he was thirteen he saw his father drown; he told about goat ranching, about cattle drives to Phoenix and to Holbrook, and about his life around Gisela. It was an interesting straightforward narrative that I edited with the intention of using as an introduction to Riley's songs had I continued with his songs only.

Our correspondence slowed, which was my fault. I was working on my dissertation, which was followed by involvement in building a major addition to McFarlin Library at the University of Tulsa. Also, three university press directors told me that there was no chance of Riley's songs being published as long as the bawdy songs were included. I shelved the collection and devoted my energies to the other projects. Riley was disappointed, but until 1975 would write occasionally—at least, I always responded.

It was a few years before I could return to Payson, but my wife made trips there during that time and through our friends, Raymond and Pat Cline of Starr Valley, I would keep up with Riley. In 1975, he moved into the Arizona Pioneers' Home in Prescott, where he lived until his death in January 1983. By the time of his birthday, November 20, 1982, I had resumed working on his collection and wanted him to know, so I called the Pioneers' Home. Although I could not talk to him, an attendant assured me that she would tell Riley that his songs would be published. I hope that he heard and understood.

Riley's memory for songs was, indeed, amazing. He sang thirty-seven songs for me during the first interview; they are listed in sequence as he recalled them during our conversation (those marked* are in this collection); I have used Riley's titles:

1. "Charlie Rutledge"*
2. "Little Joe, the Wrangler"*
3. "Billie Vanero"*
4. "Mormon Cowboy"*
5. "Old Tom Cat"*
6. "Joe Williams"*
7. "London Town"*
8. "Whorehouse Bells Were Ringing"*
9. "One-Eyed Riley"*
10. "Buttons on His Pants"*
11. "Keyhole in the Door"*
12. "Banks of My Native Australia"*
13. "Cowboy Jack"*
14. "Old Bachelor's Lament"
15. "Wedding Bells Will Never Ring for Me"
16. "Rosie Nell (Swingin' in the Lane)"
17. "Buckskin Shirt"*
18. "Frog Went a Courtin'"
19. "California Joe"*
20. "Little Mohea"*
21. "Preacher and the Bear"
22. "Gambling on the Sabbath Day"
23. "The Blind Girl"
24. "Saddest Face in the Mining Town"*
25. "Amber Tresses Tied in Blue"
26. "Naomi Wise"
27. "Daughter of Samuel O'Connell"
28. "The Boogaboo"*
29. "Little Black Mustache"

30. "Old Maid and the Burgler"
31. "Sweet Betsy from Pike"*
32. "Bad Companions"*
33. "Joe Hardy"
34. "Rattlesnake Song"
35. "Kitty Wells"
36. "Cast Aside"
37. "Spurned Suitor"

He continued on the second day with:

38. "The Shadow of the Pines"
39. "Texas Ranger's Lament"*
40. "Whistling Rufus"
41. "Old Joe Clark"
42. "Skewbald Black"*
43. "Young Man Who Wouldn't Hoe Corn"
44. "Picture from Life's Other Side"
45. "After the Ball"
46. "Haunted Falls"*
47. "The Irishman"*
48. "Red Wing" (also, bawdy version)*
49. "My Hula Hula Love"
50. "My Pretty Quadroon"
51. "Little Blossom"
52. "Convict and the Rose"
53. "Prison Song"
54. "Little Brown Jug"
55. "Gypsy's Warning"
56. "Answer to the Gypsy's Warning"

Riley sent words to the following additional songs (I recorded a melody line for most of them):

"All Night Long"*
"Barbara Allen"
"Big Rock Candy Mountain"
"Billie Boy"
"Billie the Kid"
"Blue Ridge Mountain Blues"
"Bonnie Black Bess"
"Boring for Oil"*
"Boy's Best Friend"
"Brigham Young"
"Bucking Bronco"
"Child's Prayer"*
"Cole Younger"
"Come All You Fair and Tender Ladies"
"Country Girl"*
"Cousin Harry"*
"Cowboy's Dream"
"Cowboy's Lament"
"Joe Bowers"
"Jolly Baker"*
"Juanita"*
"Just Before the Last Fierce Charge"
"Just Tell Them That You Saw Me"
"Lane County Bachelor"
"Letter Edged in Black"
"Little Blossom"
"Little Mary Phagan"
"Lorena"*
"May I Sleep in Your Barn Mister"
"Mollie Darling"
"Mormon Bishop's Lament"
"Mormon Immigrant Song"
"Mountain Meadows Massacre"
"My Lucy Love"
"My Lula Gal"*
"My Marguerite"

"Cowboy's Meditation"
"Crooked Trail to Holbrook"*
"Cuckoo's Nest"*
"Days of Forty-Nine"*
"Devilish Mary"
"Don't Marry a Man if He Drinks"
"Down Derry Down"*
"Dreary Black Hills"
"Dying Cowboy"
"Dying Nun"
"Four Thousand Years Ago"
"Frankie and Albert"
"Gay Caballero"*
"Gypsy Davie"
"Girl I Left Behind"
"Goldarn Wheel"
"Half Wit's Song"
"Hang Town Gals"
"Her Mantle So Green"
"Her White Bosom Bare"
"Home on the Range"
"Home Sweet Home"
"I Ain't Got No Use for the
    Women"
"Imbecile's Delight
    (Miscellaneous Verses)"
"I Once Had a Sweetheart"
"I'll Be all Smiles Tonight"
"In the Baggage Coach Ahead"
"I've Just Come Back to Say
    Goodbye"
"Jessie James"
"Jess's Dilemma"
"Jimmy Tucker"*

"Oaks of Jimderia"*
"Old Black Joe"
"Old Black Steer"*
"Old Horny Kebri-o"*
"Old Zebra Dun"*
"Poor Girl on the Town"*
"Pretty Polly"
"Prisoner for Life"
"Put My Little Shoes Away"
"Red River Valley"
"Root, Hog, or Die"*
"Rye Whiskey"
"Sam Bass"
"School Ma'am on the Flat"*
"Sea Crab"*
"She Was Bred in Old Kentucky"
"Silver Dagger"
"Sioux Indians"
"Soughrty Peaks"*
"Spent It for Coal"
"Sunny Tennessee"
"Sweet Evalena"
"Sweet Sixteen"*
"They're Down and They're
    Down"*
"Three Men Hunting"
"When the Work's All Done
    This Fall"
"Where the River Shannon Flows"
"Wild Rippling Water"
"Will You Love Me When I'm Old"
"Wreck of Old Ninety-seven"
"Young Charlotte"
"Young William and Mary"

Baxter Black

Baxter Black was born in 1945 and grew up in New Mexico; he is a veterinarian by training and a cowboy humorist, philosopher, and poet

Baxter Black, 1985, with his cow dog, Boller. (Photo by Steve Black; courtesy of Coyote Cowboy Company, Brighton, Colorado.)

by choice. He now lives and works out of Brighton, Colorado. Baxter's father was an Oklahoman, and many of his relatives in and around Noble, Oklahoma, are traditional fiddlers and old-time musicians. His musical background lies in family music; his songwriting ability and his humor are from his own wit and creativity. For nine years in the 1970s he worked as a veterinarian for two large cattle and sheep companies, and his responsibilities took him to large and often isolated ranches in six western states, where he became friends with many old-timers and modern cowboys and learned their philosophy and some songs. But Baxter's poetry and philosophical cowboy humor made him sought-after as a speaker, so he gave up his vet practice and now travels throughout the United States and Canada as an after-dinner entertainer.

Baxter writes a column, "On the Edge of Common Sense," that appears weekly in numerous newspapers and in livestock journals. And he has six collections of poetry and columns: *The Cowboy and His Dog or "Go Git in the Pickup!"* (1980), *A Rider, A Roper and a Heck'uva Windmill Man* (1982), *On the Edge of Common Sense* (1983), *"Doc, While You're Here . . ."* (1984), *Buckaroo History* (1985), and *Coyote Cowboy*

Poetry (1986), all published by his Coyote Cowboy Company in Brighton, Colorado. He writes cowboy and country songs, one of which, "Honky Tonk Asshole," is included in this collection. Also, two other traditional song variants that I collected from him are included: "Castration of the Strawberry Roan" and "Oh! My! You're a Dandy for Nineteen Years Old."

I met Baxter in August 1982 at the Arizona Cattle Growers' annual convention in Payson, where my fiddling daughter, he, and I picked and sang for a few nights. Then in November he came through Tulsa and spent the night, and I recorded a few songs, both traditional and his own. We met again for more picking and singing at the wedding of Jacque Cline and John Griffin at Starr Valley, Arizona, in August 1983—a genuine Arizona cowboy-cowgirl wedding. The following month he and my daughter, Cindy, were married.

Baxter knows hundreds of songs and also writes excellent songs, usually using a cowboy theme.

Glenn Ohrlin

Glenn Ohrlin and I became acquainted at the 1972 traditional music festival at the University of Illinois. When I saw Glenn as he sat in Levi's, plain work shirt, and hat, I first thought that he might be just another folk song revivalist playing the affectation game. After his first song, my apprehensions were put to rest; Glenn Ohrlin sings with the plain honesty of a genuine cowboy. While visiting later, I learned that he and I had a mutual friend, Charlie Beals. Charlie has been a legend among rodeo cowboys as the top hand at making bareback bronc and bull riding rigging; he is also one of the great saddle makers, having been taught the craft by his father-in-law, Monroe Veach. Glenn and Charlie rodeoed together and have remained friends through the years. Although Glenn's singing, stories, and personality have placed him forever among our nation's great folk artists, I admired him even more for his friendship with Charlie.

Glenn was born in 1926 in Minnesota. His father was a Swedish immigrant and his mother was of Norwegian heritage—possibly the most unlikely background for a twentieth-century cowboy. But the appeal that attracted earlier generations of young cowboys from unlikely sources also moved Glenn. He was fourteen when the family moved to California, and, shortly afterward, he ventured into Nevada to start cowboying, or as it is termed in Nevada, to become a buckaroo. In the drifting cowboy

Glenn Ohrlin on Taco, 1986. (Photo by Norman Deane; courtesy of Glenn Ohrlin.)

tradition, Glenn did not stay long at any particular ranch, and in 1943 entered his first rodeo competition. As with most individuals who finally get crowd appreciation for a performance, Glenn directed his talent to the entertainment profession—rodeoing. And his interest in the songs and stories of the cowboys traveled with him.

As with all professional sports, age makes it necessary to consider alternatives; Glenn's decision in 1954 was to purchase 166 acres near Mountain View, Arkansas. His reason for such an unlikely area to establish his ranch was simple—land was cheap. In reality, the area was not an unlikely site for a ranch. Indians and others have raised cattle in the Ozarks for decades, although the romantic image of the cowboy lies within the Plains region, not the Ozarks. Glenn continued to rodeo "off and on" through 1965, when he decided he was "a slowed up wreck fixing to happen" and ended his rodeoing career.

Glenn has successfully ranched while combining folk festival appearances with writing, drawing, and painting. He sang at the Rackensack Folklore Society Festival held at Mountain View, Arkansas in 1963, and his popularity has risen steadily. He maintains the same integrity and honesty that is associated with cowboy individualism. For a more complete coverage of Glenn Ohrlin's life and career, see Archie Green's foreword in Glenn Ohrlin's *The Hell-Bound Train*.

Glenn is active in documenting rodeo history, and in recognition of his perpetuating the songs of the rodeo cowboys and their histories, the Cowboy Hall of Fame and the Rodeo Historical Society awarded a medal to Glenn as the rodeo historian for the year of 1983. Glenn was also a participant in planning the first Cowboy Poetry Gathering in Elko, Nevada.

A sampling of Glenn's songs is available in *The Hell-Bound Train* and on a variety of recordings, but for this collection his contributions are found in "The Wild Buckaroo" and "The Open Book."

Dallas "Nevada Slim" Turner

"Slim" Turner is one of the most amazing men I have ever met; even though I had spent many years looking for cowboy songs, he was a singer and recording artist who had slipped by me until Glenn Ohrlin and Judith McCulloh encouraged me to contact him. In fact, Glenn's praise of Dallas was extremely high, mixed with regret that folk-song collectors and scholars have paid relatively little attention to this man who, for

Dallas "Nevada Slim" Turner, 1986. (Courtesy of Dallas Turner.)

performances and writing, uses the name "Nevada Slim." D. K. Wilgus expressed the same sentiments as Glenn. They were correct; Dallas is a walking encyclopedia of songs, their histories, cowboy song writers, B-westerns, border radio stations, and cowboy culture in general.

I first wrote to Dallas in the fall of 1983; he replied by sending lyrics of bawdy songs that he had learned from his mother. In early 1984, he turned to sending cassette tapes instead of letter writing, and the information was extensive. Later, a long telephone conversation added to my knowledge about him. When in early May 1986, I interviewed Dallas in Reno, he was extremely generous with his time and knowledge.

Dallas Turner was born November 27, 1927, in Walla Walla, Washington; according to Dallas, his natural mother gave him to a nurse who was attending her. When he was a few days old, the nurse, a "religious fanatic," took Dallas and left Washington, headed east. In Elko, Nevada, she met the couple who later became his foster parents, and with a "squalling baby" in her arms, asked them for a job. They hired her as a cook, and at the ranch near Burns, Oregon:

> she refused to fry bacon for the cowboys and made pies with tallow. So, they fired her two days later. She threw me on the floor and said, "Here, this damn bastard baby is yours!" They were stuck with me; they finally found my real mother and adopted me. I *knew* I was loved; I had the most wonderful foster parents.
>
> My mother—and I miss her—was a real bronc stompin' cowgirl. She could roll a cigarette with one hand; she had a heart of gold, and I would watch her ride buckin' horses when I was a little boy. She knew so many songs. . . . She used to love to sing the vulgar songs for the cowboys and was quite a song writer in her own right. My dad was quite a bit the opposite; he never did appreciate the fact that my momma collected these bawdy songs. But I've looked out the ranch house door when I was a little boy, and I have seen five or six cars pull up —an' then it was my job to take the guitar and second her as she would sing these bawdy songs for the cowboys and their wives. She didn't care about mixed company and that's why everybody came to hear her sing. . . . She was the only mother I ever knew. [In recent years he has become acquainted with his natural mother.]

When Dallas was "six or seven" years old, his parents took him to the Pendleton (Oregon) Roundup; there he saw Jack "Powder River" Lee and Kitty Lee. They were singing the old-time songs on the street and had a table from which they were selling their song books. After listening to them, Dallas said, "I can sing 'Tyin' a Knot in the Devil's Tail' "; he had learned it from their recording. They put him on the table, and while Kitty Lee played the guitar, Slim sang the song. Through the rest of their lives, he maintained a friendship with them, along with a strong loyalty to them; it is Slim's firm belief that Jack Lee, not Gail Gardner, wrote "Tyin' a Knot in the Devil's Tail."

With a strong background in traditional music and cowboy culture, as a teen-ager Slim turned to radio broadcasting as a career. And it was his childhood idol, Cowboy Slim Rinehart, who encouraged him to try to find a job at the Mexican border stations. It was a successful move; Slim worked all of the border stations for more than thirty years. He used many different names, among them, Nevada Slim, Cowboy Dallas Turner, Yodeling Slim Dallas, Texas Slim, Cowboy Gene, and Tex Vernon. He also announced for border station evangelists such as A. A. Allen and the Jessup Brothers, as well as serving as the pitchman for many products sold over the stations. Students of border radio history claim that under different names he was the greatest of the border station pitchmen. His accomplishments include recordings for Rural Rhytmn, Rich 'R-Tone, and other labels, and he has written more than one thousand songs, some of which have been recorded by well-known country-western singers. Dallas has published ten song folios, and he teamed for thirteen years with the former WLS "Barn Dance" performer Doc Hopkins and for a shorter time with the singer-song writer Tex Owens. Currently, he manages and promotes Sunset Carson and continues to write songs.

He does not sing the bawdy songs, but he knows them. Although Dallas is a religious man and a "metaphysical" minister, his reason for refusing to sing the bawdry is not religious conviction; he decided years ago that he would never make money by singing bawdy songs. However, he has written a few "suggestive" songs under the name Lucky Corrigan.

Dallas "Nevada Slim" Turner is an authentic western man, and it is doubtful that any other cowboy singer knows as many cowboy and western songs both bawdy and "clean" as he does. He has recorded more than two hundred. Although he does alter the lyrics of some traditional songs to suit his own tastes and standards, he does not bowdlerize or expurgate in order to make a song acceptable as have other collectors. In fact, after reading the songs in this collection, he stated that he had better versions of some of the songs but that each singer of traditional songs does them his or her own way—he accepts them as traditional songs.

Nevada Slim uses the slogan "America's Cowboy Folk Singer" along with the description "Radio's Popular Wild West Entertainer"; both are accurate descriptions. His radio shows have been played over many stations around the country, and his material was learned or written in the West—more specifically Nevada and the northwestern states. He sings variants of many of the songs in this collection, but I have only included "Wild Buckaroo," "Peter Pullin' Blues," and variants of "The Castration of the Strawberry Roan" and "Zebra Dun."

II

SONGS ABOUT COWBOYS

W hen applicable, I have included a "Laws" letter and number in the references for each song. G. Malcolm Laws, Jr., has indexed select traditional ballads (folk songs that tell a story) collected in this country in two volumes: *American Balladry from British Broadsides* (1957) and *Native American Balladry* (rev. ed., 1964); he grouped them according to type (War Ballads, Ballads of Cowboys and Pioneers, etc.) and identified them by letter and number. Thus, "Billie Vanero," a cowboy ballad, is "Laws B 6." Additional information about the song along with bibliographical references can be found in the Laws volumes.

Following the text of each song, I have listed field recordings and manuscripts. The entries are abbreviated; complete collection information is found alphabetically in the Bibliography under Unpublished References. Exceptions are abbreviations:

LC-AFS, see: Archive of Folk Culture.

LC-AFC, see: Archive of Folk Culture.

Books and periodical articles are found in the Bibliography under Published References.

"Recordings" refer to commercially pressed phonograph recordings both 78 rpm and long-play discs. The 78s are indicated by recording company and number only; long-play recordings include the title of the album.

I have searched for appropriate photographs that reflect—accurately—the working cowboy's life, and when possible, I placed them with a song closely related in content. However, in the "Other Songs

Cowboys Sing" section, the photos are not necessarily associated with the songs.

In a few songs, my informants remembered only a fragment of a verse. I use a full line of dots to indicate the memory lapses. When a song has no melody line, it means that I received the text only and did not record an informant singing the song.

1.*

"CHARLIE RUTLEDGE"

Original Title: "A Cowboy's Death"
Alternate Titles: "Charlie Rutlage" and "The XIT"

This the first song that Riley Neal sang for me. When asked to sing his favorite song, he replied, "Oh, I don't know as I have any favor-ite; there's one I like—it's 'The XIT,' 'Charlie Rutledge'." He did not indicate from whom or when he learned it, but it was first published a few months before Riley's birth. D. J. O'Malley, a Montana cowboy poet, wrote the poem to be sung to the tune of "The Lake Pontchartrain," and it appeared in the July 11, 1891, issue of the Miles City, Montana *Stock Grower's Journal* under the title "A Cowboy's Death." Apparently, it became moderately popular among cowboys, for it appeared in the 1910 edition of John A. Lomax's *Cowboy Songs and Other Frontier Ballads* with the spelling "Rutlage," which was corrected in the 1938 revision. Ina Sires collected it during the 1920s, but it has not appeared in other printed field collections. Austin E. and Alta S. Fife collected one textual variant, and I found no commercial recordings. However, it is occasionally collected as a recitation, particularly in Montana.

O'Malley's poem inspired Charles Ives, the American composer, to compose a piano score for it. Ives took the poem from the 1910 edition of John A. Lomax's *Cowboy Songs*, and in 1914 or 1915 wrote his voice/ piano version. It is available in Charles Ives, *Seven Songs for Voice and Piano*, Associated Music Publishers, New York. It was not performed enough to become a familiar tune.

Riley's version does not vary significantly from the original O'Malley poem; in fact, it is closer to the original than the Lomax and Sires variants. Also, Riley's version is smoothed into a personal story with less of the poetic style of O'Malley. For the O'Malley story, see John I. White's chapter about him in *Git Along, Little Dogies*.

The XIT was a Texas ranch that owned extensive grazing land in Montana. In 1879, the Texas legislature appropriated 3,050,000 acres of land in the Texas Panhandle to finance a new state capitol building in Austin. A Chicago syndicate won the contract and completed the structure in 1888; they obtained title to the land and organized a ranching enterprise that became the largest *fenced* ranch in the world. At its peak the XIT ranch owned more than 160,000 head of cattle, 1,000 head of horses, employed 150 cowboys, and owned land in Montana for grazing of over 12,000 head of cattle. Between 1904 and 1950, the XIT holdings were systematically sold.

In Montana, the XIT range was in the central eastern region north of Miles City between the Missouri and Yellowstone rivers. It covered two hundred miles east and west and seventy-five miles north and south, and many Texas cowboys worked the Montana range during the summers.

The XIT brand was designed by an old trail driver, Ab Blocker, who was a ranch cowboy. A good brand was and is one that cannot be easily altered, so legend tells that Blocker, thinking about the size of the ranch that lay within ten counties in Texas, devised "Ten in Texas" or XIT. As a brand, it was impossible to alter successfully. For the XIT story, see J. Evetts Haley's *The XIT Ranch of Texas*.

The theme of "Charlie Rutledge" is a cowboy's death on the range, the result of his horse falling and rolling over him.

Note: The abba melody transcribed here is used for stanzas 2–5; stanza 1 takes the form aaba.

D. J. O'Malley, 1896, near Miles City, Montana. (Courtesy John I. White.)

Erwin E. Smith captured this dramatic scene, similar to Charlie Rutledge's accident, on the Turkey Tracks Ranch, Texas, in 1908. The cow horse stepped in a prairie dog hole and threw the cowboy; other cowboys rush to see how serious his injuries are. The horse apparently injured its leg. (The Erwin E. Smith Collection of the Library of Congress on deposit at the Amon Carter Museum, Fort Worth.)

Another jolly cowboy has gone to meet his fate;
We hope he'll find a resting place inside the Golden Gate.
A good man's place is vacant on the range of X I T;
We'll never find another that's liked so well as he.

Kid White was the first, a fellow young and brave;
Now Charlie Rutledge makes the third who's been sent to his
  grave
By a cowhorse falling on him while out a running stock
On the early spring roundup, where death a man doth mock.

So blithely he rode forth on his circle round the hills,
Happy, gay and full of life, and free from earthly ills.
And when they went to cut the herd, to work it he was sent,
Not knowing that his time on earth was very nearly spent.

One X I T it would not go and started back to the herd;
Charlie turned it back again, his cutting horse he spurred.
But when it started back again, to head it Charlie tried,
The creature fell, the horse was thrown, beneath him Charlie
  died.

It was a hard death for a man to meet out on the lone prairie;
His relatives in Dixie his face no more will see.
And when he passes through the Gates with a smile upon his
  face,
Our Father will take his right hand and lead him to the throne
  of grace.

Field Collections and Manuscripts: Fife Folklore Archives, FAC I 126, FAC I 692 (p. 5a).

References: Clark (1932), p. 13, (1937), p. 60; *Hobo News* (n.d.), p. 48; Lingenfelter, Dwyer, and Cohen (1968), pp. 430–31; Lomax (1910 and 1916), pp. 267–68; Lomax and Lomax (1938, 1986), p. 82; O'Malley and White (1934, 1986), p. 9; Rogers (n.d.), p. 8; Rosenberg (1969), p. 16; Sires (1928), pp. 16–17; Tinsley (1981), p. 98; White (1975), pp. 84–85.

2.*

"LITTLE JOE,
THE WRANGLER"

It seemed natural for Riley Neal to sing "Little Joe" as his second song because it is one of the most popular cowboy ballads and I specifically requested songs about cowboys. His comment, laced with a touch of pride was, "That's a pretty good one."

N. Howard "Jack" Thorp wrote "Little Joe" in 1898, some ten years after he made what was probably the first deliberate folk-song collecting trip in the United States (excluding the music of Native Americans); it definitely was the first collecting among cowboys. Thorp told about his travels, collecting, and writing in "Banjo in the Cow Camps," edited by Neil Clark and published in 1940 in the *Atlantic Monthly* and in *Pardner of the Wind*. According to Thorp, he was working as a cowboy trailing a herd of cattle from Chimney Lake, New Mexico to Higgins, Texas, when one night by campfire he wrote "Little Joe," using a pencil stub on a paper bag and the tune of "Little Old Log Cabin in the Lane" for his melody. He sang it to the men who were on the trail drive and later in a saloon in Weed, New Mexico; from those two singings it entered tradition. Riley's version does not vary significantly from Thorp's original words.

Thorp used it in his *Songs of the Cowboys* (1908). In 1910, Lomax included it in his collection, and since then it has appeared in most cowboy songbooks. Variants are also found in field collections throughout the nation.

It is the story of a young Texas stray who left home because of a mean step-mother, became a favorite youngster in a cow camp, and

"Little Joe, the Wrangler" was probably older than this young cowboy from the Three Block Ranch, New Mexico, around 1907. (The Erwin E. Smith Collection of the Library of Congress on deposit at the Amon Carter Museum, Fort Worth.)

died while trying to turn a stampede. The events in the ballad were real. Thus, it is often heard among cowboys that "my dad" or "my grandad knew Little Joe," but his identity died with Jack Thorp. This song also implies a compassion that cowboys had for youngsters who left home because of troubles.

An interesting variant that I have never heard in oral tradition is "Little Joe, the Wrangler's Sister Nell." She appears in the cow camp after having ridden four hundred miles looking for Little Joe; her motivation for finding him is deeper than sibling love, for they are "twins." His friends cannot find strength to tell her; instead she realizes that he is dead when she sees his horse "Chaw." In 1934, this variant was credited to Thorp by Kenneth Clark, who corresponded with Thorp during the 1930s.

Vance Randolph collected "Sister Nell" in Missouri in 1941; Austin E. and Alta S. Fife collected variants, and Edith Fowke (1962) reported collecting a variant in Canada. Her informant said that he "had learned it in the twenties from a Wilf Carter record." However, this is doubtful because Carter's recording career started in approximately 1932–33, and in Don Cleary's *Wilf Carter Discography* there is only on recording of "Sister Nell," which was probably in the 1940s. Because the Clark songbooks were distributed nationwide and were popular, and because no collector mentions collecting it before 1934, I believe that the Clark book was the source for all subsequent singing of "Sister Nell."

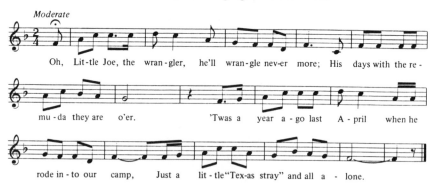

Oh, Little Joe, the wrangler, he'll wrangle never more;
His days with the remuda they are o'er.
'Twas a year ago last April when he rode into our camp
Just a little "Texas stray" and all alone.

He rode into our camp one night as we were sitting around,
On a little old brown pony he called Chaw;
With his brogan shoes and overalls a tougher looking kid
You never in your life before had saw.

His saddle was a Texas kack built many years ago,
And an O.K. spur from one foot lightly hung,
And his "hot roll" in his cotton sack so loosely tied behind,
And a canteen from his saddle horn was swung.

He said he'd had to leave his home, his pa 'ad been married
     twice.
And his new ma whipped him every day or two;
So he saddled up old Chaw one night and "lit a shuck" this
     way,
And now he was trying to paddle his own canoe.

He said if we would give him work he'd do the best he could,
Though he didn't know straight up about a cow;
The boss he cut him out a mount and kindly put him on,
Cause he kind of liked the little chap somehow.

Taught him to wrangle horses and try to know them all
And get them in by daylight, if he could,
How to follow the chuck wagon and always hitch the team,
And to help the "cosinero" rustle wood.

We had driven to the Pecos, the weather being fine,
And camped down on the south side in a bend;
When a norther commenced blowing, we doubled up our
     guard
For it taken all of us to hold them in.

Little Joe, the wrangler, was called out with the rest.
Though the kid had scarcely gotten to the herd,
When the cattle they stampeded; like a hail storm along they
     fled
Then we were all a-riding for the lead.

Through the streaks of lightning I saw a rider in the lead,
It was Little Joe, the wrangler, in the the lead;
He was riding old Blue Rocket with a slicker o'er his head
A-tryin' to check the cattle in their speed.

At last we got them milling and sort of quieted down
So the extra guard could back to the wagon go;
There was one of us a-missin', we knew it at a glance,
'Twas our little Texas tramp, poor wrangling Joe.

Next morning just at daybreak, we found where Rocket fell,
Down in a washout twenty feet below,
And beneath him mashed into a pulp his spur had wrang his
    knell,
Was our little Texas stray, poor wrangling Joe.

Field Collections and Manuscripts: LC-AFS 654 A, 4116; Fife Folklore Archives, FMC I 994 (p. 2), FMC I 994, FAC I 95, FAC I 122, FAC I 194, FAC I 195, FAC I 196, FAC I 250; Todd-Sonkin 29B; Wilgus-Western Kentucky Folklore Archives; Arizona Friends of Folklore, R26; Culwell (1976), p. 158; Gelber (1961), pp. 43–44; Lincoln (1949), pp. 71–72; Scroggins (1976), pp. 177–179.

References: Allen (1933), pp. 65–68; Brumley (1944), no. 71; *Buck Jones Songs of the Western Trails* (1940), p. 29; Clark (1932), pp. 44–45, (1934), p. 19; Edwards (1986), pp. 34–35; Emrich (1972), pp. 496–99; Fife and Fife (1969), pp. 214–16; German (1929 and 1932), n.p.; Hood (1977), pp. 336–37; Larkin (1931), pp. 119–22; Laws (1964), B 5, p. 135; Lingenfelter, Dwyer, and Cohen (1968), pp. 423–25; Lee (1936), pp. 40–41; Lomax (1910 and 1916), pp. 167–71; Lomax and Lomax (1938, 1986), pp. 91–93; McConathy, Beattie, and Morgan (1936), pp. 84–85; *900 Miles* (1965), pp. 74–75; Randolph, 2 (1948, 1980), pp. 234–36; *Reprints from Sing Out!,* 7 (1964), pp. 22–23; Rogers (n.d.), p. 3; Sherwin (1939), pp. 20–21, (1944), pp. 32–34; Sherwin and Klickman (1934), pp. 44–45; Silber (1967), pp. 206–8; *Sing Out!,* 10 (no. 3, 1960), pp. 24–25; Sires (1928), pp. 48–49; Stamps (1936), pp. 20–21; Thorp (1908), 9–10, (1921), pp. 96–98; Thorp and Fife (1966), pp. 25, 28–37; Tinsley (1981), pp. 84–87; Wolfe (n.d.), p. 19.

Recordings: F. E. Abernethy, *Singin' Texas,* E-Heart Press (cassette) EX-4-83; Jules Verne Allen, Victor 21470, on *The Texas Cowboy,* Folk Variety FV 12502, also re-issued by Bear Family BF 15502; Rex Allen, *Sings Boney Kneed Hairy Legged Cowboy Songs,* JMI Records JMI 4003; Cactus Mack and His Saddle Tramps, on *Classic Country-Western,* Radiola 4MR-2; Wilf Carter, *Nuggets of the Golden West,* RCA-Camden CAL 840; Yodeling Slim Clark, *A Living Legend,* Palomino PAL 309; Edward L. Crain, on *The Plains of Alberta,* Historical HLP 8007; Don Edwards, *Songs of the Cowboys,* Sevenshoux (cassette) BTDE 101; Travis Edmonson, *The Liar's Hour,* Latigo (no number); Shug Fisher and the Ranchmen Trio, on Capitol (electrical transcription) G-35; George Gillespie, *Sings "Campfire" Songs of the Old West,* Thorne TR 200-B; Cisco Houston, *Cowboy Ballads,* Folkways FA 2022; Harry Jackson, *The Cowboy,* Folkways FH 5723; Merrick Jarrett, *The Old Chisholm Trail,* Riverside RLP 12–631; Eddie Nesbitt, *Lost Treasures,*

Bluebonnet BL 116; Bunk Pettyjohn, *Bunk and Becky Pettyjohn*, Arizona Friends of Folklore AFF 33-4; The Ranch Boys, Decca 2644 B; Goebel Reeves, on *Songs of the West*, Glendale GL 6020, also *The Texas Drifter*, Country Music History CMH 101, *The Legendary Texas Drifter*, Country Music History CMH 113, Columbia C6424 and C20619, Melotone 12114, Brunswick 629; Tex Ritter, *Blood on the Saddle*, Capitol T1292 and approximately eight additional reissues; Marty Robbins, *More Gunfighter Ballads and Trail Songs*, Columbia Records CS 8272, reissued *In the Wild, Wild West*, Bear Family BFX 15146, also, *All Time Greats*, Columbia GP-15; Lou Schlautman, on *When the Work's All Done This Fall*, Montana Folklife Project MFP 0001; George and Luciy Shawver, *Songs of the West* (cassette, privately produced, #1); Sons of the Pioneers, *Legends of the West*, RCA LPM/LSP 3351; Red Steagall, *For All Our Cowboy Friends*, MCA 680 and *Cowboy Favorites*, Delta DLP 1160; *Arnold Keith Strom of Mooresville, Indiana*, Folk Legacy FSA 18; Nevada Slim Turner, *Songs of the Wild West, 2*, Rural Rhytmn RRNS 163; Roger Wagner Chorale, *Folk Songs of the Frontier*, Capitol P8332; Marc Williams, Brunswick 269.

"Little Joe, the Wrangler's Sister Nell":
    Field Collections and Manuscripts: Fife Folklore Archives, FAC I 123 and FAC I 483.
    References: Clark (1934), pp. 20–21; Cleary (n.d.), n.p.; Fowke (1962), p. 250; Ohrlin (1973), pp. 169–71; Randolph, 2 (1948, 1980), pp. 236–37; Thorp and Fife (1966), pp. 29–30, 32–34.
    Recordings: Wilf Carter, *Old Prairie Melodies*, RCA Camden CAL/CAS 2175; Travis Edmonson, on *Ten Thousand Goddam Cattle*, Katydid KD 10076; Harry Jackson, *The Cowboy*, Folkways FH 5723; Eddie Nesbitt, *Lost Treasures*, Bluebonnet BL 116; George and Luciy Sawver, *Songs of the West* (cassette, privately produced, #1).

3.*

"THE MORMON COWBOY"

Alternate Titles:
"No Balls at All," "No Hips at All," "I'm Ruined Forever," and
"Maids, When You're Young Never Wed an Old Man"

Stories of females who marry impotent males are ageless and numerous. The marriage of a young lady to an older wealthy man is a popular theme, and the percentage of older husbands who cannot perform in the wedding bed is high in song and story. Although impotence is not limited to older men, the older wealthy man's inability to satisfy the young girl has a touch of ironic justice.

One of the most popular American songs about impotence is "No Balls at All." Gershon Legman in *The Horn Book* and in "Bawdy Monologues" (1976) credited William Allen Butler as the writer in 1857 of an anti-woman topical satire, "Nothing to Wear," in which excess in women's clothing was the topic; it was very popular during the Civil War. Some unknown bard parodied it into "No Balls at All," the form in which it has traveled further and has lasted longer in memory.

Ed Cray in *The Erotic Muse* identified it as a member of a family of folk songs with a common theme of the "mismatch in years of marriage partners." He traced the lineage back as far as Robert Burns's "John Anderson, My Jo" in *The Merry Muses of Caledonia*. The version Cray used portrays the dismay of the young bride when:

She reached for his penis; his penis was small.
She reached for his balls; he had no balls at all.

Upon hearing of the girl's plight, her mother told her not to "feel so sad," for there are many young men who will "answer the call." The girl finds pleasure in following her mother's advice, and a baby is born "to the wife of the man who has no balls at all."

Oscar Brand recorded it in his series of bawdy songs and included a bowdlerized variant in his printed collection *Bawdy Songs and Backroom Ballads*. The man with "no balls at all" became a man with "No Hips at All"; only those who knew bawdy versions could understand what was actually missing. Jerry Silverman in *The Panic Is On* included an interesting variant under the title "Maids, When You're Young Never Wed an Old Man"; Peter Kennedy in *Folksongs of Britain and Ireland* included an "anglicized" Scots song, "Never Wed a' Auld Man"; and Peggy Seeger and Ewan MacColl in *Singing Island* indicated that the marriage to an old man theme is more popular in Scotland than in England.

Vance Randolph was the only field collector to find a version similar to Riley Neal's "Mormon Cowboy." However, although Randolph's informant knew the song, he could not, or would not, sing it; instead, he told the story about "Poor Archie" who had "no tool" at all, and a female jury upon hearing about his missing member granted his wife a divorce. She "married a wild cowboy from Oklahoma" who had such a tool that "he's ruint me forever." Randolph's informant heard it in the early 1900s near Berryville, Arkansas.

Riley Neal sang this as the fourth song on the first day on my first visit. In his version "Archie Barber" is only twenty-two (not an old man), and in bed, when his wife wanted some "female sporting," she found that he had "no tool at all" or in slight contradiction—"his hobo would not stand." No matter, the theme is impotence. It is unusual to hear that a jury was totally female; naturally, they were totally unsympathetic with Archie. After getting a divorce, the farmer's daughter married a "Mormon Cowboy" who "knocked her up with a double stroke," and she had a "nine inch hobo, all at her own command." That she found satisfaction from a Mormon cowboy is a reflection of frontier attitudes about Mormons. Because polygamy was a Mormon practice, the Mormon man, who could satisfy so many wives, was considered to be virile and "well hung" with a strong sexual drive. This is the first "ugly" song that Riley sang; to him it was a *real* cowboy song. Indeed, poor Archie Barber could not make the ride; in fact, he could not even get in the saddle.

lived a sin-gle life,   When to his sad mis-for - tune he   got him-self a wife.

A story, a story, a story I'll relate
Concerning Archie Barber and his unlucky state;
He lived till two and twenty, he lived a single life,
When to his sad misfortune he got himself a wife.

He married a farmer's daughter, most beautiful, they said,
Who expected female sporting that night when she went to
    bed;
When she found he had no hobo, she wrang her hands and
    cried;
She threw her arms around him, she pressed him with her
    thighs.

She scratched his shins with her toe nails, pushed him up
    against the wall,
She tried his courage all night long, but he had no tool at all.
She wallowed him, she tumbled him, she rolled him all over
    the bed,
She was so overburdened all with her maidenhead.

Next morning bright and early, this maiden she arose,
Went straightway to her mother's room, her secret to disclose,
Saying, "Mother, you have ruined me by choosing me this man,
I tried his courage all night long, but his hobo wouldn't stand."

"O daughter, daughter, daughter, don't be so quick to accuse,
Don't make it known in public, poor Archie has no tool;
We'll try him before a female jury to see if he's a man,
And if he has no hobo, this bargain will not stand."

Before this female jury, poor Archie he was tried,
And to his sad misfortune, his wife stood by his side,
Saying, "He wallowed me, and he tumbled me, till he made my
    limbs all sore,
And to my sad misfortune, his auger wouldn't bore."

Six weeks or two months later this maiden married again,
She married a Mormon cowboy who understood his game;
He knocked her up with a double stroke, with this you
    understand,
She's got a nine inch hobo now, all at her own command.

Field Collections and Manuscripts: Gordon (Inferno), 3913; Randolph (Mss.), pp. 287–89; LC-AFC (Subject Collection), Bawdy Songs Folder; LC-AFS 2291 A2.

References: Babad (1972), p. 79; Brand (1960), pp. 30–31; Cray (1965), pp. 81–82, (1969), pp. 52–53, 226–27; Getz, 2 (1986), pp. NN 2–3; Hogbotel and ffuckes (1973), p. 13; Hart-*Immortalia* (1971), pp. 30–34; Kennedy (1975), pp. 464, 481; Laycock (1982), pp. 200–1; Legman (1964), p. 377, (1976), p. 103; McGregor (1972), pp. 69–71; Seeger and McColl (1960), pp. 16, 34; Silverman (1966), p. 59, (1982), p. 122.

Recordings: Oscar Brand, *Bawdy Songs and Backroom Ballads, 1*, Audio Fidelity AFLP 1906; *The Unexpurgated Folk Songs of Men*, Raglan R-51.

4.*

"BILLIE VANERO"

Original Title: "The Ride of Paul Venarez"
Alternate Titles: "Billie Venero," "Billy Veniro,"
and "Paul Venerez"

After singing "Billie Vanero," Riley Neal said, "Hell! It's wrote about the Verde Valley and Prescott." Verde Valley is the area some fifty miles northwest of Payson, Arizona, and Camp Verde is the closest community in the valley to Payson. Prescott is approximately forty-five miles further west. Riley was singing with pride about an event close to home, but he was unaware that Vanero was supposedly buried near Payson. Austin E. and Alta S. Fife in *Cowboy and Western Songs* stated that they were told about his burial place near Payson; their informant was Bill Garlinghouse of Globe, Arizona. Keith Cunningham in his liner notes to *Cowboy Songs* (AFF 33-1) stated most of his Arizona informants believe that the ride was made in the White Mountains, east of Payson and the Tonto Basin area, but he made no indication that his informants knew about the Payson burial. Lew Pyle made no comment about Vanero and Payson when he heard Riley sing it; so until the fall of 1985, I was skeptical about the Fifes' source.

On October 5, 1985, I was in Payson for a few hours, and I mentioned "Billie Vanero" to my good friend Raymond Cline, a local rancher who grew up in the Tonto Basin area. I was surprised to learn that Raymond knew "Billie Vanero"; we have been friends since 1960, and he knew that I collect cowboy songs. But he doesn't sing—he recites. My approach to collecting had excluded the tradition of poetry recitation. Raymond recited a few verses and said that the ride occurred between Pleasant Valley and Payson. Pleasant Valley (later changed to Young, Arizona) is approximately twenty-five miles on horseback over rough terrain and trails southeast of Payson, but more than sixty miles by road.

The ride was to warn ranchers about a band of Apache raiders, historically the last major Indian raid in Arizona. On July 17, 1882, a band of White Mountain Apaches, who had been confined by military force in a small reservation near Fort Apache in the Cibuque Creek area, broke out of the reservation, ambushed a detachment of troops, and killed the captain in command. As they traveled northwest across the Tonto Basin toward the Mogollon Rim, they raided ranches and killed a well-liked man, Louie Houdon, at the Sigsbee Ranch. Billie Vanero was in Pleasant Valley when the escape and raids started, and he made his courageous ride to warn the William Burch Ranch in Payson (then known as Green Valley).

Burch was the first person to drive cattle into the Payson area; he drove them down from Utah in 1877 and built his ranch house in what is now "Old Payson." Raymond Cline showed me the small house (adobe with a corrugated tin roof) that was the headquarters of the Burch Ranch. Arizona cowboys commonly use the term *cow ranch* to refer to any ranch that raises cattle.

It is not known if there was a Billie Vanero or if he had a sweetheart at the ranch. But the few families in the area were successfully warned by riders who did make a hard dangerous ride, and it is speculated that the "Vanero" of the song was, indeed, buried in one of the unmarked graves near Pleasant Valley or Payson. The Houdon death occurred east of Payson on Haigler Creek, but "Rocky Run" was retained in the song because Haigler Creek did not rhyme with any words in the poem.

While Raymond Cline told the story, another Payson friend and "old-timer," Richard Taylor, joined our small group and verified Raymond's tale which included a humorous incident. At the Isadore Christopher ranch east of Payson, the Apaches burned two log cabins; during the day before the raid, Christopher had killed a bear and had hung the carcass in or on one of the cabins. The military force in pursuit of the Indians included the legendary scouts Tom Horn and Al Sieber; they along with the troops and other scouts decided that the burned bear carcass was Christopher and gave it a decent, solemn Christian burial. They became the objects of laughter and jokes when Christopher later appeared and identified the body.

Although Billie Vanero may have been a real person, the original character, Paul Venarez, apparently came from the imagination of the Wisconsin poet Eben E. Rexford, who wrote "The Ride of Paul Venarez." The poem appeared in the December 29, 1881, issue of *Youth's Companion* and became a popular recitation. When "Paul" became "Billie,"

The Burch ranch house in 1987, Payson, Arizona, covered with vines. Local legend says that Billie Vanero's ride was to this ranch house. (Photo by Guy Logsdon.)

"Red Plume's Warriors" became "Apache Indians," and a "frontier town" became an "Arizona town" is unknown. However, the appearance of the poem and the Arizona raids were only seven months apart; I assume that the localization and "Billie Vanero" personalization occurred by the mid-eighties and were transmitted by poetry recitation before being set to a melody.

Riley's version is shorter than both the original poem as well as the version first published by Lomax in 1910, but the ride to save Little Bess, the last love letter penned with his blood, and his death remain as the core elements in Riley's narrative. Randolph included three variants in *Ozark Folksongs* (1948) and made the observation that the text of commercial recordings available at that time appeared to have been taken from Lomax.

Billie Vanero heard them say in an Arizona town one day
That a band of Apache Indians were upon the trail of death;
Heard them tell of murder done, three men killed at Rocky
    Run.
"They're in danger at the cow ranch," said Vanero under
    breath.

Cow ranch, forty miles away, was a little place that lay
In a green and shady valley of the mighty wilderness;
Half a score of homes lay there, and in one a maiden fair
Held the heart of Billie Vanero—Billie Vanero's Little Bess.

"Not a soul would dream," he said "of the danger that's ahead;
For my love of Little Bessie, I must see that something's done."

He saddled up his horse of brown, and he left the little town;
And over hills and valleys he galloped on his way.

At the setting of the sun, he drew rein at Rocky Run;
"Here those men met death, my Chapo." Then he started on
    his ride.
Sharp and clear a rifle shot broke the echos of the spot;
"I am wounded," cried Vanero, as he swayed from side to side.

"Where there's life, there's always hope; slowly onward I will
    lope.
I may not reach the cow ranch, but Bessie Lee shall know I
    tried."
From his chaparejos he took with weak hands a little book;
He tore a blank leaf from it, saying, "This shall be my part."

From a branch a twig he broke, then he dipped his pen of oak
In warm blood that was spurting from a wound below his
    heart.
"Beware before it is too late, Apache warriors lie in wait."
Then he tied himself to the saddle and gave his horse the rein.

Just at dusk a horse of brown, wet with sweat came bounding
    down
To the little band at the cow ranch and stopped at Bessie's
    door.
But the cowboy was asleep, and his slumbers were so deep
That poor Bessie could not wake him, if she tried forever
    more.

You may hear this story told, by the young and by the old,
Of the little band at the cow ranch, the night the Apaches
    came.
Of the fierce and bloody fight, how the chief fell in his flight,
Of the panic-stricken warriors, and you'll hear Vanero's name.

They made Vanero's grave on a hill not far away,
And a tombstone was put on it which commended his brave
    ride.
And the heaven and earth between, keep the pretty flowers so
    green,
Which Little Bessie planted ere they laid her by his side.

Field Collections and Manuscripts: Fife Folklore Archives, FMC I 540 (p. 6), FMC I 804, FAC I 163, FAC I 190, FAC I 605 (p. 9), FAC I 606 (p. 7), FAC I 606 (pp. 24–25), FAC I 667 (p. 8), FMC I 983 (p. 7); Wilgus-Western Kentucky Folklore Archives; Arizona Friends of Folklore Archives, R45; Culwell (1976), p. 128; Scroggins (1976), pp.36–38.

References: *American Cowboy Songs* (1936), pp. 28–29; *Back in the Saddle* (1982), pp. 44–45; Botkin (1951), pp. 759–60; Clark (1932), pp. 60–61; Coolidge (1937), pp. (119–22); Fife and Fife (1969), pp. 129–31; Frey (1936), pp. 44–45; German (1929), n.p.; Larkin (1931), pp. 25–29; Laws (1964), B 6, p. 136; Lingenfelter, Dwyer, and Cohen (1968), pp. 262–63; Lomax (1910 and 1916), pp. 299–302; Lomax and Lomax (1938, 1986), pp. 197–200; Ohrlin (1973), pp. 237–39, 280–81; Randolph, 2 (1948, 1980), pp. 222–27; Randolph and Cohen (1982), pp. 184–86; *The Songs You Hear No More* (n.d.), p. 12; Tinsley (1981), pp. 68–71; Wolfe (n.d.), p. 38.

Recordings: Yodeling Slim Clark, *Sings the Ballad of Billy Venero*, Palomino PAL-311; Don Goodman, on *In an Arizona Town*, Arizona Friends of Folklore AFF 33-3; Billy Maxwell, Victor 40148; Harry "Mac" McClintock, Victor 21487 and Montgomery Ward 4344, also on *Hobos and Brakemen*, Country Music History CMH 106; Glenn Ohrlin on *Stone County Singing*, Shoestring Tape SGB 1; Marty Robbins, *In the Wild West*, part 2, Bear Family BFX 15146; Joe and Bennie Rodriguez, on *Cowboy Songs*, Arizona Friends of Folklore AFF 33-1; Luther Royce, on *Folk Songs from Wisconsin*, Archive of Folk Song, Library of Congress L 55; George and Luciy Shawver, *Songs of the West* (cassette, privately produced, #2); Nevada Slim Turner, *Songs of the Wild West*, 1, Rural Rhytmn RRNS-162;

5.*

"COWBOY JACK"

The theme of lost love and death makes this a popular cowboy ballad that was absorbed into the southern hillbilly music tradition. Jack and his sweetheart argue, and he leaves. Later, he decides to return and ask forgiveness. Upon arriving, he finds that she has died, and that as she was dying, she bade her attendants to tell Jack that she still waits for him. "Cowboy Jack" first appeared in Ina Sires's collection *Songs of the Open Range* (1928). In 1932, Kenneth Clark used an almost identical version in *The Cowboy Sings*, and in 1938 John and Alan Lomax included the Clark version in their revised edition of *Cowboy Songs and Other Frontier Ballads*. Early printed texts seem to be from Ina Sires's version collected, according to Jim Bob Tinsley in *He Was Singin' This Song*, in Camp Verde, Arizona. Sires indicated that "Cowboy Jack" was very popular in central Arizona, and that it was a popular dance tune.

While singing at a party during the 1983 convention of the Arizona Cattle Growers held in Payson, I heard one person say that her favorite song—learned from her mother—was "Cowboy Jack." No other guitar-picker knew it, so I helped her sing it. But she had learned it in Arkansas, not Arizona. Because it was a popular song on early phonograph recordings, it is probable that her mother's version came from either a recording or from Mexican border radio station broadcasts.

The earliest known commercial recording of "Cowboy Jack" was made by Peg Moreland for Victor in Atlanta on November 20, 1929. Moreland was an ex-railroad man from Texas who at that time was featured

"A Cowboy's Funeral." Death and burial on the prairie were not limited to cowboys; the sweetheart of Cowboy Jack would have been buried in comparable stark solemnity. See James Cox, *Historical and Biographical Record of the Cattle Industry and the Cattlemen of Texas and Adjacent Territory*, 1895, page 282. (Courtesy of the Denver Public Library, Western History Department.)

as "Tex" Moreland over the WLS (Chicago) "National Barn Dance" and later performed over WFAA (Dallas) for more than twenty years. His repertoire included a few cowboy songs that he probably had learned in Texas or from song books, but generally he recorded sentimental and semipopular country songs of the time. Following Moreland's recording, at least seven other groups recorded "Cowboy Jack" during the 1930s, including Marc Williams "The Crooning Cowboy," the Ranch Boys, the Girls of the Golden West, and the Carter Family.

It is probable that more people heard the Carter Family recording of "Cowboy Jack" than any other individual's or group's. Not only did they record it in 1934, but it was also one of their transcribed songs broadcast between 1938 and 1942 over XERA, Villa Acuna, Mexico. Although the Carter Family's records sold well by 1930s standards, even more people in those years heard their radio shows. According to Dallas Turner, A. P. Carter was drawing royalties for the song in the early 1950s and considered it to be "his song." When Turner told him that he heard it as a young boy, Carter replied, "I don't mean I composed it, but I wrote it down." Others, such as Moreland, had also "written it down," for it was published in sheet music form by a variety of publishers. In 1935, the Calumet Music Company published "Cowboy Jack" as sung by Happy Jack Turner over NBC Radio, an indication that radio, recordings, and sheet music helped spread its popularity.

Nolan "Cowboy Slim" Rinehart was another Mexican border radio personality who joined XERA in approximately 1936 and during the following eleven years was heard over most, if not all, of the border stations. According to his close friend Dallas Turner, Slim often sang "Cowboy Jack" as one of his favorite songs.

All of the variants appeared after Ina Sires's collection; if an earlier variant lies in an archival collection, it has escaped many collectors and researchers. "Cowboy Jack" is a variant of "Your Mother Still Prays for You, Jack"; both songs were popular among southern singers, but "Cowboy Jack" raises the question of origin. Was it written or re-written by a cowboy or by a romanticizer and sentimentalist of the cowboy; was it sung in the South before the cowboys absorbed it, or did the theme capture the sentimental imagination of southern singers? I believe that "Cowboy Jack" is a cowboy song from Arizona. Riley Neal sang his version during the morning of my first visit with him; he knew it before the Sires's collection and phonorecording variants were available.

Riley's version has little structural variation from other texts, with the major difference being that a cowboy named Jim, not Jack, does the singing that makes Jack's mind wander back to his sweetheart.

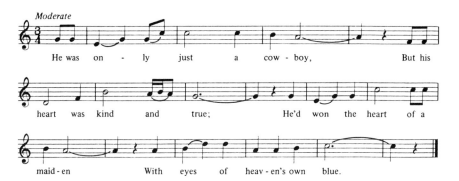

He was only just a cowboy,
But his heart was kind and true;
He'd won the heart of a maiden
With eyes of heaven's own blue.

They'd learned to love each other;
They'd named their wedding day,
When trouble came between them,
And the cowboy rode away.

He joined a band of cowboys,
To forget he tried to learn;
While out on the rolling prairie,
She waited for his return.

"Your sweetheart still waits for you, Jack,
Your sweetheart still waits for you
Way out on the rolling prairie,
Where the skies are always blue."

It was in a lonely cow camp,
Just at the close of day,
Someone said, "Sing a song, Jim,
That will drive all sorrows away."

When Jim commenced singing
Poor Jack's mind wandered back,
For the song told of a brave, true girl,
Who waited at home for Jack.

Poor Jack left camp next morning,
Breathing his sweetheart's name,
"I'll go and beg forgiveness,
For I know that I was to blame."

When he reached the rolling prairie,
He found a new-made mound.
The people kindly told him
They had laid his loved one down.

"In dying she spoke of you, Jack,
In dying she breathed your name.
She bade us with her last breath
To tell you when you came.

"With a heart that's breaking for you, Jack,
Your sweetheart still waits for you,
Way out on the rolling prairie
Where the skies are always blue."

Field Collections and Manuscripts: LC-AFS 899 B1; Fife Folklore Archives, FMC I 983 (p. 3), FMC I 991, FAC I 13, FAC I 109, FAC I 168, FAC I 502; Wilgus-Western Kentucky Folklore Archives, fifteen variants; Arizona Friends of Folklore, R32; Culwell (1976), p. 135; Scroggins (1976), pp. 78–79.

References: Brumley (1970) no. 29; Clark (1932), p. 15, (1937), p. 62, (1940), p. 46; *Cowboy Songs* (1937), p. 12; *Hobo News* (n.d.), p. 18; Laws (1964), B 24, p. 144; Lomax and Lomax (1938, 1986), pp. 230–31; Ohrlin (1973), pp. 10–11, 247–48; Roberts (1974), pp. 115–16; Rogers (n.d.), p. 12; Rosenberg (1969), p. 21; Sherwin (1948), pp. 6–7; Sires (1928), pp. 12–13; Tinsley (1981), pp. 204–7; Turner, folio no. 2 (1950), p. 81; Wolfe (n.d.), p. 6.

Recordings: Callahan Brothers, Columbia 20212; the Carter Family, *The Original Carter Family in Texas-Radio Transcriptions*, Old Homestead OHCS-111, Bluebird 8167, reissued on *'Mid the Green Fields of Virginia*, RCA LPM 2772, and *The Legendary Carter Family* RCA RA 5648; Yodeling Slim Clark, *"Old Chestnuts,"* Palomino PAL 307; Shug Fisher and the Ranchmen Trio, Capitol (electrical transcription) G-93; Girls of the Golden West, Bluebird 5719, reissued on *Girls of the Golden West*, Sonyatone STR 202; Harry Jackson, *The Cowboy*, Folkways FH 5723; Merrick Jarrett, *The Old Chisholm Trail*, Riverside RLP 12–631; Daniel Jeffus, on *Sing Me a Song*, University of Texas Press, Austin (cassette, no number); Billie Maxwell, Aurora 234, Victor 40241; Peg Moreland, Victor 23593, Aurora 417; the Ranch Boys, Decca 2645; George and Luciy Shawver, *Songs of the West* (cassette, privately produced #3); Esmereldy and Dick Thomas, Musicraft 298, reissued on *Esmereldy and Dick Thomas*, Sutton SU 284; Marc Williams, Brunswick 430.

6.

"SCHOOL MA'AM ON THE FLAT"

I found no origin or variant for this cowboy song, but the theme is common in literature, in song, and in life. The cowboy, McClellan, was a ladies' man who lusted after the school teacher; after satisfying his desire, he became conscience-stricken and married her. Married life and responsibilities made him regret courting the school teacher, so every time that he had another urge to go courting, he flogged "John Henry" with his hat.

Riley Neal said that he had forgotten some of the song; therefore, it is possible that a longer and more humorous story once was in tradition.

McClellan was a cowboy of the wild and wooly west;
His horses and his outfit was of the very best;

He was an educated fellow, don't take him for a fool;
One thing about McClellan, he was handy with his tool.

McClellan left the cow camp on one Friday night,
He was going to see the school ma'am at the school house
    painted white;
He'd been courting her for three months now, and thought
    he'd make his try;
Made up his mind this time that he'd have her or he'd die.

He laid her down upon a bench, the best that he could do;
He took his dallies from around his horn and opened her
    hondoo;
He took John Henry in his hand and placed it in her fat;
He stopped the wind from blowing through the school ma'am
    on the flat.

He pulled John Henry out of her, and put it in his pants;
She'd gave him a little diddle that fairly made him dance;
She said he'd have to marry her, now what else could he do?
He surely couldn't turn her down, since she'd gave him that
    good screw.

McClellan now is married and lives on his own spread;
It keeps him toiling day and night to keep them all in bread;
His place is overrun with kids, there are forty dogs and cats;
He wishes to hell he'd never saw the school ma'am on the flat.

He curses the poor school ma'am, which he knows he
    shouldn't do,
For he knew he'd have to marry her if he opened up her flue;
If John Henry gets to raring up, he will flog him with his hat
Before he goes a-courting another school ma'am on the flat.

7

"TEXAS RANGER'S LAMENT"

Alternate Titles:
"The Frontier Ranger" and "The Disheartened Ranger"

J. Evetts Haley in his biography of Charles Goodnight wrote that "two rangers, Tom Pollard and Alec McClosky, composed a bit of doggerel, and sang out the words in camp"; that doggerel was "Texas Ranger's Lament." Haley did not cite any source for the claim of authorship, and his version as described by John A. Lomax in *Cowboy Songs* (1938) was "different and less singable" than the Lomax version. However, the 1938 Lomax version had the same refrain that Haley used, whereas in his 1910 and 1916 editions Lomax used no refrain. Variants in other collections are similar to the earlier Lomax texts.

Haley referred to the song critically as "doggerel" when, in fact, it is an excellent protest ballad—a protest ballad from people who seldom resorted to protest songs. It is a statement protesting the lack of appreciation for Texas Rangers from politicians and citizenry. The Rangers received little financial reward, a limited food supply, and no morale support at all except when they were needed. "The Texas Ranger's Lament" was and is a genuine frontier protest song.

The first printing appeared under the title "The Frontier Ranger" in *Allan's Lone Star Ballads* (1874); there were seven verses with the narrative in the third person and no refrain. Credit for authorship was given to "M. B. Smith, of the Second Texas."

The Texas Rangers were organized in 1835 during the Texas revolt against Mexican authority; they became the official army of the Republic of Texas charged by the Texas congress to protect the Texas frontier from Indian raids. After statehood on December 29, 1845, the Rangers

continued to operate as the law enforcement agency for the state before and after the Civil War. The final line in the song refers to going
"home to the States," which implies that the song was composed before
statehood in 1845. If this is correct, both of the aforementioned claims
to authorship are probably incorrect.

Riley Neal was proud of this song, for he learned it from his father
who had been a Texas Ranger before moving to Arizona. His version is a
mixture between both the Allan and Lomax texts; he knew seven verses.
I have found no recordings of this song.

Come listen to a ranger, you kindhearted stranger,
This song though a sad one, you're welcome to hear;
We've fought the Comanches away from your ranches
And followed them far o'er the Texas frontier.

Your wives and your daughters we have guarded from
    slaughter,
Through conflicts and struggles I shudder to tell;
So fight your own battles and guard your own cattle,
For us Texas Rangers must bid you farewell.

No beans, no potatoes, no beets or tomatoes,
But jerked beef as dry as the sole on your shoes;
All day without drinking, all night without winking,
I'll tell you, kind stranger, this never will do.

Those big alligators, the state legislators,
Are puffing and blowing two-thirds of their time;

But windy orations about rangers and rations
Never put in our pockets one-tenth of a dime.
They do not regard us, they will not reward us,
Though hungry and haggard with holes in our coats;
But the election is coming and then they'll be drumming
And praising our valor to purchase our votes.

Where houses have people and churches have steeples,
Where laws are more equal and ladies are kind;
Where work is regarded and worth is rewarded,
Where pumpkins are plenty and pockets are lined.

We fought the Comanches away from your ranches,
Exposed to the arrows and knifes of the foes;
Though, sir, I may grieve you, the rangers must leave you,
For home to the States I'm determined to go.

References: Allan (1874), p. 92; Haley (1936, 1949), pp. 97–98; Lingenfelter, Dwyer, and Cohen (1968), pp. 268–69; Lomax (1910), pp. 261–62, (1916), pp. 263–64; Lomax and Lomax (1938, 1986), pp. 369–70; Moore (1964), pp. 315–16; Randolph, 2 (1948), pp. 178–79.

8*

"THE CHILD'S PRAYER"

I n this song, the stereotype of the cowboy who hated settlers is expressed, but when the rancher, or owner of the ranch, sees the mother
and child and overhears the child's prayer for her father, he rescinds
his order to kill them. Thus, the cowboy was, indeed, softhearted and
sentimental and a respecter of women and children.

   This song has not appeared in any cowboy collections or songbooks, and Riley Neal did not remember when or where he learned it. It
has the touch of a sentimental song writer.

Moderate, free

Way   out   in   west - ern Tex - as   not so man-y   years a - go,   Where the

ranch-ers hat - ed set - tlers   worse than rat-tle - snakes, you know,   When

one would come in the coun-tr - y   you'd hear a ranch-er say,   "Go

o - ver there,   boys,   tell   them to get a - way.   Tell

them we'll steal their cat - tle,   burn their cab - in in - to coals,   If   they

act   a   lit-tle con - trar - y,   fill them   full   of   bul-let   holes."

Way out in western Texas not so many years ago,
Where the ranchers hated settlers worse than rattlesnakes,
     you know.
When one would come in the country you'd hear a rancher
     say,
"Go over there, boys, tell them to get away;
Tell them we'll steal their cattle, burn their cabin into coals,
If they act a little contrary, fill them full of bullet holes."

There was a man and woman and a lonely little child,
Who built them a cabin out on the prairie wild.
One night when the father to a town far away had gone,
And left his wife and little child to spend the night there alone,
A cowman said to his riders, "We'll go over there tonight,
And we'll fill them full of bullet holes if they try to make a
     fight."

They rode to a lighted window; they saw plainly in there
The mother and her baby of danger all unaware.
Just then the mother ran her fingers through her child's golden
     hair,
"Ain't you sleepy, my little darling? Say your little evening
     prayer."
She knelt down before her mother, laid her head on her knee,
Saying, "God be with my poor daddy, bring him safely back to
     me."

The cowman said to his cowboys, saying, "Boys, we'll ride
     back home,
The father's gone away and the mother's all alone."
Saying, "We could not harm that mother, or that trustful child
     in there,
And if there's a God up in heaven, I'm sure he heard her
     prayer.
And if any of you ever say a word of our coming over here,
You'll find yourself out of a job, get that in your mind real
     clear."

9.*

"JIMMIE TUCKER"

Alternate titles:
"The Old Gism Trail" and "The Old Jizzum Trail"

"The Chisholm Trail" (or "The Old Chisholm Trail") is one of the oldest songs, if not the oldest, with a cowboy theme; it comes from the early trail drive days. It has been included in almost every song book that carries a representation of cowboy songs and has appeared for decades in most elementary school song books. Field collectors such as John A. Lomax have alluded to the vast number of verses that could not be sung in polite society, much less printed. It may be the grandaddy of all bawdy cowboy theme songs, and the number and quality of verses sung depended on the imagination and quality of the cowboy singer. Riley Neal sent five verses to me under the title "Jimmie Tucker" and wrote that it is "ugly" and "filthy—too filthy to write, but I thought you might get a kick out of it."

In all variants, the refrain is repeated after each couplet. The refrain as sung by Riley is almost identical to the Lomax refrain, but Riley sang "yup" instead of "yip":

Come-a ti yi yupi, yupi ya, yupi ya,
Come-a ti yi yupi, yupi ya.

Many non-cowboys remember when they were boys that the refrain —not to be sung around their parents—was:

Come-a tie my root around a tree, 'round a tree,
Come-a tie my root around a tree.

Ed Cray in *The Erotic Muse* credits the following refrain to the version that circulated among high school students and college students in Southern California:

Tie my pecker to my leg
Tie my pecker to my leg.
        or
Gonna tie my pecker to a tree, to a tree,
Gonna tie my pecker to a tree.

Collectors have found many many bawdy verses, and Lomax received verses sent to him, such as:

If I can't get a heifer, I'll take my fist,
I'll wring old Pete, 'til I sprain my wrist.

Now my little tale is told, and I'll tell it to you no more,
And I have a rotten apple up my ass, and you can suck the
        core.

Some are even more graphic, but Lomax, as was necessary at the time, opted to use "cleansed" verses from a variety of informants and weave a series of acceptable verses into the song that is now sung in polite society. No informant ever provided the sequence of verses that Lomax included in his 1910 edition. He greatly influenced this song by his choice and arrangement of verses, for singers have been singing the verses in the Lomax sequence since 1910; collectors and publishers have used the same sequence. One interesting verse that he received, but did not use, may have influenced or may have come from Charles M. Russell's 1898 watercolor paintings, "The Sunshine Series":

Just a little sunshine, and just a little rain,
Just a little happiness [Russell used "pleasure"],
just a little pain.

Robert W. Gordon, founder of the Archive of Folk Song in the Library of Congress and editor of the column "Songs Old Men Have Sung" in *Adventure Magazine*, received verses from around the nation; from Montana by way of Hudson, Massachusetts, he received:

Threw my arms around her and laid her on the grass,
To show her the wiggle of a cow-puncher's [ass].

The hair on her belly was a strawberry brown,
The crabs on her m[ound] were jumpin' up and down.

"The Sunshine Series" by Charles
M. Russell, 1898. (Courtesy of the
Amon Carter Museum, Fort Worth.)

a. "Just a Little Sunshine"

b. "Just a Little Rain"

c. "Just a Little Pleasure"

d. "Just a Little Pain"

In fact, Gordon's informant sent him the finest storytelling sequence of verses that I have seen, but he did not indicate what refrain was sung. Therefore, the reader or singer is free to use a refrain of choice. I have included Gordon's variant as Text B following Riley Neal's verses, and I have inserted, in brackets, the words or letters, such as "ass," that the informant replaced with dashes.

In the Ozarks, Vance Randolph found a variety of singers who knew a verse or two; the longest sequence was four verses, sung by a woman in Southwest City, Missouri, who said that she "learned it from some rodeo cowpokes in Oklahoma":

> Ass in the saddle an' my hand on the horn,
> Best fuckin' cowboy ever was born,
> Come a ti ri bug a jig a bug a roo,
> Come a ti ri jig a bug a roo.

> Playin' with my peter on the old Gism Trail,
> Come to Kansas City for to get a piece o' tail.

> Prettiest little gal that ever I saw,
> She lived on the rim of Wiggle-Ass Draw.

> I'll run that gal to the top of the hill,
> I'll fuck her in the ass, God damn I will.

In 1976, a few months after I had published an article about cowboy songs, I received a letter from John E. Caswell, professor of history at California State College at Stanislaus, in which he related a story by Philip Ashton Rollins, the author of the cowboy classic, *The Cowboy*. Rollins shared this experience with a group of graduate students at Princeton in either 1937 or 1938. His father had a cattle spread in Texas near the Chisholm Trail, and herders on their way up and down the Trail would stop by to visit and refresh themselves. Rollins's father set out a ledger in which the traveling cowboys would record their verses of "The Chisholm Trail"; Rollins told the students, "There were 1042 verses in the book, of which 1040 weren't fit to print." He inherited the ranch and later sold it, taking the ledger with him. During his sojourns, he loaned it to an assistant professor of history, and when a preacher called at the teacher's home, he saw the ledger and looked in it. The preacher was "aghast," and threw the book into a nearby stove to be consumed by the flames. "Thereafter," Rollins concluded, "I have had no use for Assistant Professors of History or Preachers."

In April 1987, I received a letter from Elton Miles, professor of English at Sul Ross State University in Alpine, Texas, in which he stated that he had heard the song called "The Old Jizzum Trail," "because it was slick with the leavings of masturbating cowboys up and down the line." He sent sixteen verses learned from an Oklahoma soldier in 1946 as they traveled from Fort Smith to Dallas by bus: "We both were still in uniform and had just been released from the army." The Oklahoman said that ten of his verses can be sung to the tune "Talking About You." However, six verses, including the following, are sung only to "The Old Chisholm Trail":

Saddled old Bald and I throwed him in the grass,
And the son-of-a-bitch throwed me right flat on my ass.

Saddled old Bald and I throwed him in the herd,
And the son-of-a-bitch throwed me on a flat cow-turd.

I'm an old cow-hand, and I'm gonna quit;
I never had a nickle and I don't give a shit.

In 1961, Austin E. Fife collected a variant from a twenty-two-year-old student at Utah State University, Logan. The student told Fife that he learned a few bawdy songs from a sheepherder in Idaho, but this version of "The Old Chisholm Trail" is identical to the version in *Shitty Songs of Sigma Nu*. Although I have no evidence to support my opinion that Fife's informant learned it from the songbook or from a similar fraternity songbook, it is possible that the fraternity variant came from that student. Each variant has eleven verses with the sequence of action based on offering the girl a penny, a nickle, a dime, and on and on until she consents to sex for $5. The cowboy gets a venereal disease, and the doctor tells him:

You can put away your holster, you can put away your gun,
Your barrel's been breached and your shootin' is done.
Come a tie my root around a tree, around a tree,
Come a tie my root around a tree.

Because sex with animals has long been a popular source of jokes and stories, that activity appears in some verses of "Jimmie Tucker." In the early 1960s, Lew Pyle sang only one verse for me:

Woke up one mornin' on the old Chisholm Trail,
With my hobo in my hand and a heifer by the tail.

This verse and "The Old Chisholm Trail" have an impressive lineage. Gershon Legman in "Bawdy Monologues and Rhymed Recitations" (1976) stated that " 'I Woke Up This Morning with a Hard On' has lived as a folksong at least since 1640, when it appeared in *Bishop Percy's Folio Manuscript* as 'A Dainty Duck'; later entitled 'A Knave Is a Knave' and 'A Guy Is a Guy.' Another strain of this same song became the cowboy favorite, 'The Old Chisholm Trail'." Lew Pyle's verse fits the 1640 pattern. Riley Neal's verses can be adapted to many different lyrical tunes; in fact, they appear to be the result of singers who were trying to see who could out do the others in dirty song competition.

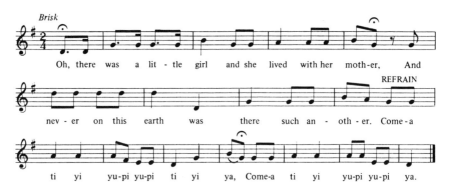

Oh, there was a lit-tle girl and she lived with her moth-er, And nev-er on this earth was there such an-oth-er. Come-a ti yi yu-pi yu-pi ti yi ya, Come-a ti yi yu-pi yu-pi ya.

Text A

Oh, there was a little girl and she lived with her mother,
And never on this earth was there such another.
Come-a ti yi yupi yupi ti yi ya,
Come-a ti yi yupi, yupi ya.

She had scales on her cock, like a damned old sucker,
And her tits hung down like two tin buckets.

There was a little man, and his name was Jimmie Tucker,
And he swore, by God, that he's a-gonna fuck 'er.

He got her in the shithouse up against the wall,
And the first damned job, he stuck in balls and all.

He took her in the kitchen and thought he'd get some more,
And the damned bitch farted—blowed a hole through the floor.

Text B, Gordon Manuscript (3781), Montana

Looking for a job, and I went broke flat.
Got a job riding on the Double O Flat

Signs pinned up on the bunk-house door,
"Punchers allowed at a quarter after four."

"Round up and saddle up some old pitching hoss,
If you can't ride him, you're fired by the boss."

As I come a-riding 'cross the Double OO range,
I was thinking of my sweetheart that I left on the ranch.

I rode out with the old man's daughter,
Guess I said a few words what I hadn't oughter.

I told her that I'd love her like I loved my life,
I asked her how she'd like to a cowpuncher's wife.

'Said she'd like it fine, but I better see her dad,
For he got the dough, and it might make him mad.

I went to the old man, as all lovers oughter,
I says, "Old Man, I'm in love with your daughter."

He grins and he points to the Double O roan,
That's piled every puncher that ever rode alone.

Says, "If you can ride that hoss, and not pull leather,
You and my daughter can throw your things together."

Went to the hoss, and slammed on my saddle,
Best damn rider that ever punched cattle.

All the punchers yelled, as all punchers oughter,
For they knew I was riding for the Old Man's daughter.

Jumped in the saddle and gave a little yell,
What's going to happen is damned hard to tell.

Spurred him on the shoulder, and hit him with my quirt,
Gave four jumps, and rolled me in the dirt.

Went to the Old Man to have a little chat,
Hit him in the face with my old felt hat.

Went to the girl, and offered her a quarter,
Says she, "Go to Hell! I'm a cow-puncher's daughter!"

Offered her a dollar, and she took it in her hand,
Punched me in the belly, says, "Well, I'll be damned!"

Threw my arms around her and laid her on the grass,
To show her the wiggle of a cow-puncher's [ass].

The hair on her belly was a strawberry brown,
The crabs on her m[ound] were jumping up and down.

Took my old jockey to the watering trough,
Washed him and I scrubbed him till his head fell off.

In about nine days, when I looked for to see,
Cancers on my p[ecker] were big as a pea.

She found it out, and called me a kid,
Told me to remember her, and by God, I did!

Wrote her a letter, don't think I lied,
Said, "I'm leaving Texas fast as I can ride.

Know a little Injun, damn' pretty squaw,
Guess I'll go and see her, fore I leave for Arkansas.

Going to leave Texas, going to head for home,
All on account of the Double O roan.

Sheep man a-stealing of the Double O grass,
Boss says, "Shoot him, but not in the [ass]."

So we pulled out our guns and we got him on the fly,
Crawled in the weeds, and I guess he's going to die.

Chased a bunch of hosses thru the G[od] d[amn] sheep,
The scatterment they made, made the sheep men weep.

Camped over night at the A bar B's,
Got so damn' cold, I thought I would freeze.

Raining hard and muddy as Hell,
Trailing thru the gumbo sure is Hell!

Hit Belle Fourche, and went on a spree,
Sheriff come a running, and he picked on me.

Locked me up in his lousy old jail.
Boss said he'd be damned if he went my bail.

Just because I worked for him wa'n't no sign
That a cow-poke's boss had got to pay his fine.

Met a girl and thought I'd seen her before,
Tried her, and I found she was a G[od] d[amn] whore.

Went to make a date as a cowpuncher oughter,
Found out the girl was that damn sheriff's daughter.

Sheriff on my trail, left town on the run,
If he catches up, have to use my gun.

Left Belle Fourche, and left her on the lope,
To keep my neck from wearing out a scratchy old rope.

Going to leave Montana, and marry my squaw,
Going to settle down in Arkansas.

Bawdy variants only:

Field Collections and Manuscripts: Lomax (Mss.), folder 2E397; Randolph (Mss.), pp. 169–73; Gordon (Inferno, Mss.), 3781; Fife Folklore Archives, FAC I 838; Caswell to Logsdon, July 27, 1976; Miles to Logsdon, April 2, 1987; Larson (Eastern Idaho), n.p.; Larson (Countryside), n.p.; Legman (TS VF), n.p; "Immortalia" (1927), pp. 25–26; *Shitty Songs of Sigma Nu* (n.d.), n.p.

References: Babad (1972), p. 131; Cray (1969), pp. 62–63; Getz, 2 (1986), pp. KK 3–4, TT 14–15; Hart-*Immortalia* (1971), pp. 96–99; *Immortalia* (1960), pp. 38–40; Laycock (1982), pp. 260–62; Legman (1976), p. 88; McGregor (1972), pp. 34–37.

Recordings: Oscar Brand, *Bawdy Western Songs*, Audio Fidelity AFLP 1920.

10.*

"THE CROOKED TRAIL TO HOLBROOK"

This is the first song that Riley Neal sang on my return trip to interview him in August 1970. Little is known about the song other than that John A. Lomax collected it by 1907. Only three printed collections have included it, and G. Malcolm Laws, Jr., considered it to be a "native ballad of doubtful currency in tradition." However, it is an Arizona song that is still sung in the state, and it is a statement about the difficulties encountered in driving cattle northward from below Globe to the railtown of Holbrook.

The Atlantic and Pacific Railroad laid track westward through Arizona Territory in 1881, and in 1882 Holbrook emerged as a cattle and railroad town—a hard, rough shipping center comparable to other cow towns in the West. To drive cattle to Holbrook involved climbing the Mogollon Rim (a sudden 1800-foot rise in elevation) and crossing a dry plateau. Jim Bob Tinsley wrote a very fine account of "The Crooked Trail to Holbrook" in *He Was Singin' This Song*. The Lomax version in each edition came from one of his best "mail" informants, Mrs. M. B. Wrights of Fort Thomas, Arizona, and Thorp received his copy, by mail, from a friend in Arizona.

Slim Critchlow, singer of cowboy songs, learned his version from a sheepherder in Idaho and believed it was a "forgotten" Arizona song. Indeed, his is the only traditional recording I have found. Daniel Kingman used "The Crooked Trail to Holbrook" as the title for his 1985 string quartet (recorded by Horse Sense and the Camellia Symphony on *The Hills of Mexico*, Real Time Cassette K or C 340).

Trail driving on the Matador Ranch, Texas, 1910. Even though this trail drive did not occur in Arizona, the dust there would have been as bad, and singing would have been equally difficult. (The Erwin E. Smith Collection of the Library of Congress on deposit at the Amon Carter Museum, Fort Worth.)

Moderate

Come all you hunk - y punch-ers that fol - low the bron - co steer, I'll

sing to you a verse or two your spir - its for to cheer. It's

all a - bout a jour - ney, a trip I did un - der - go On that

crook - ed trail to Hol - brook, in Ar - i - zo - na, oh.

Come all you hunky punchers that follow the bronco steer,
I'll sing to you a verse or two your spirits for to cheer.
It's all about a journey, a trip I did undergo
On that crooked trail to Holbrook, in Arizona, oh.

It was on the seventeenth of February when our herd started
    out,
It would make your heart shudder to hear them bawl and
    shout;
As wild as any buffalo that ever rode the Platte,
Those were dogies we were driving, and every one was fat.

We crossed the Mescal Mountains on the way to Gilson Flats,
And when we got to Gilson Flats, Lord, how the wind did blow!
It blew so hard, it blew so fierce, we knew not where to go,
But our spirits never failed us, and onward we did go.

That night we had a stampede; Christ, how the cattle run!
We made it to our horses; I tell you, I tell you we had no fun;
Over the catclaw brush and prickly pear we quickly made our
    way,
We thought of our long journey and the girls we'd left one day.

It's along by Sombrero we slowly punched along,
While each and every cowboy would sing a merry song,
To cheer his comrades onward, as onward we did go,
On that crooked trail to Holbrook, in Arizona, oh.

We crossed the Mogollon Mountains where the tall pines do
  grow,
Grass grows in abundance and sparkling streams do flow;
Our packs were always turning; our journey it was slow
On that crooked trail to Holbrook, in Arizona, oh.

We finally got to Holbrook, a little gale did blow,
It blew up sand and pebblestones—it didn't blow them slow.
We had to drink the water from that muddy little stream,
And swallowed a peck of dirt when we tried to eat a bean.

But the cattle now are shipped and we are homeward bound
With a lot of tired horses as ever could be found.
Across the reservation no danger did we fear,
But thought of wives and sweethearts and the ones we love so
  dear.
Now we are back in Globe City, all our friends to share,
Here's to every puncher who follows the bronco steer.

Field Collections and Manuscripts: Fife Folklore Archives, FAC I 605 (p. 10), FAC I 606 (p. 8), FAC I 667 (p. 9); Utz (1938), pp. 88–89.
  References: Laws (1964), dB 30, p. 259; Lomax (1910 and 1916), pp. 121–23; Lomax and Lomax (1938, 1986), pp. 27–28; Thorp (1921), pp. 53–54; Tinsley (1981), pp. 54–59.
  Recordings: Slim Critchlow, *"The Crooked Trail to Holbrook,"* Arhoolie 5007.

11.*

"RED LIGHT SALOON"

L ew Pyle sang this song at least three different times during four to five years of encouragement from me. Eventually, he allowed me to record it, so his limited melody line is preserved. It is one of those songs that *seems* to be popular and widespread in tradition, but I have found only a few variants. One cowboy variant is in the Wilgus-Western Kentucky Folklore Archives, collected in 1957 as the "Red Eye Saloon." And in the Archive of Folk Culture, Library of Congress, there is a lumberjack variant collected in Wisconsin in 1940.

Oscar Brand used a lumberjack version in *Bawdy Songs and Backroom Ballads*, and Jerry Silverman in *The Panic Is On* and *The Dirty Song Book* used a similar version. Ed Cray in *The Erotic Muse* mentioned Brand's version as a member of the family of songs sung to the tune of "Villikins and His Dinah" ("Sweet Betsy from Pike"); however, Cray did not supply a text. Even with limited texts in collections, I believe that "The Red Light Saloon" enjoyed popularity among different occupations.

I asked Riley Neal if he knew it, and he said that he learned it when he was a "kid." He had heard cowboys sing it, but had forgotten the words. Lew said, "I heard different ones sing it around 1900 or before. I think I did hear it along in the '90s." The setting is in Rawlins, Wyoming, and the price for pleasure with the lady was much higher, $5, than most other women of the West; she must have had unusual beauty and talents.

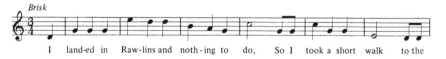

Brisk

I land-ed in Raw-lins and noth-ing to do, So I took a short walk to the

Cowboys drinking at a bar (a popular cowboy pastime) in Old Tascosa, Texas, 1908. (The Erwin E. Smith Collection of the Library of Congress on deposit at the Amon Carter Museum, Fort Worth.)

Red Light Sa - loon.   I o - pened the door, stepped up to the

bar, Says a danc - ing young beau - ty, "Will you have a ci - gar?"

I landed in Rawlins and nothing to do,
So I took a short walk to the Red Light Saloon.
I opened the door, stepped up to the bar,
Says a dancing young beauty, "Will you have a cigar?"

I took the cigar and sat down in a chair,
'Twas not very long till she crept around there.
She stepped up a-smilin'; sat down on my knee,
"You are a gay fellow, and this I can see.

"You are a cowpuncher, and this I do know,
Your muscles are hard from your head to your toe."
She twisted my mustache, she smoothed down my hair;
My "ellick" grew hard; it did, I declare.

I got up from the chair, the cigar I threw down,
Says I to this fair one, "Let's go have a round."
She got up a-smilin', led the way up the stair,
The stairs they were covered with those draperies most rare.

Her room, she led the way to,
She pulled down the curtains, and at it we flew.
I pulled out my hobo, and I gave her a shove,
Such glorious feelings from the Power above.

She lay there contented, looked up with a smile,
Said, "Up you young cowboy, you've got me with child."
She's a dancing young beauty; she's a rose in full bloom,
And she fucks for five dollars in the Red Light Saloon.

Field Collections and Manuscripts: LC-AFC 4167 B; Wilgus-Western Kentucky Folklore Archives.
References: Brand (1960), pp. 50–51; Cray (1969), p. 177; Silverman (1966), p. 95 and (1982), p. 139.
Recordings: Oscar Brand, *American Drinking Songs*, Riverside RLP 12-630.

12.

"OLD ZEBRA DUN"

Original Titles: "Educated Fellow"
and "Zebra Dun"
Alternate Title: "Z Bar Dun"

This song has been the source of much controversy, not about its origin or tradition, but about the markings of the horse. Margaret Larkin in *Singing Cowboy* wrote that the song referred to "a dun colored horse bearing the Z Bar brand." Since then the controversy has been wrangled by song collectors and cowboy singers. For those who knew little about horses and their colors, there was no such animal as a zebra dun; yet horsemen knew that the color and markings did and do exist.

Dr. Ben K. Green compiled the only thorough study of hide and hair color pigmentation and markings of horses in *The Color of Horses*. He wrote that early-day cowboys considered the dun, buckskin, and grulla colored horses to be the toughest. He decided to test the belief, and after months of riding and working seven horses of those colors, they "stayed sound in spite of hard riding." Green's belief is that the colors belong to "native, western" bred horses in which an instinctive sense of "self-preservation and survival" is a part of their nature.

Horses with a dark hide and an abundance of pigment are classified as having "intense colors"; the dun falls within this classification. Green states that "dun is a color that has always been found among horses in a wild state"; the dun has "black points, black mane and tail and often times has black zebra-like stripes above its knee and hock." The dun also has a "dark stripe over the shoulder," as well as a "black stripe down the spine from the mane to the tail." A zebra dun has more intense stripes.

There is little doubt that many ranches in the West used a brand configuration of a Z and a bar. Therefore, either to put the controversy to rest or to start another one: the horse in the song was, indeed, a zebra dun with a Z Bar brand on it. The controversy reminds me of a horse breeder, west of Oklahoma City, who in the early 1970s attempted to breed a zebra to a donkey hoping to come up with a new breed to be known as the "Striped Ass."

"Zebra Dun," also known as "Educated Fellow," is among the oldest and best of the cowboy ballads. It tells about the prankster characteristic found in cow camps; the "dude" astonishes and irritates the cowboys with his worldly knowledge and big words, so when he asks to borrow a horse, they give him Zebra Dun. The description of the wild pitching and fighting by "Old Dunny" is contrasted by the confidence and ease with which the dude makes the ride. The dude turns out to be a better rider than the pranksters.

A variation of the song is sung by Marty Robbins, the legendary country-western singer whose roots were in Arizona. He was described by a newswriter as a "cowboy in a continental suit" (western clothes designed in Europe), so Robbins adapted the line to the story of "Zebra Dun." The setting was changed to the rodeo arena in his song "The Cowboy in the Continental Suit," and the ending was the traditional admonition—don't judge a man by his appearance.

In 1986, Dallas Turner sent yet another version of "Zebra Dun" to me. It is sung to the tune, "Battle Hymn of the Republic"; the protagonist is a New Mexico mortician who is a Yale graduate, riding a burro and headed for Wyoming. The action is traditional, with the added feature of the stranger, in anger, whipping everyone in camp and trading the burro for the "Zebra Dun." Turner wrote that he learned it from an old cowboy in Del Rio, Texas, and that he revised the meter and made it rhyme. With the permission of Dallas Turner, I have included it as an interesting, unique "Zebra Dun."

The origin of "Zebra Dun" is not known, but it first appeared in Thorp's *Songs of the Cowboys* (1908) as the "Educated Feller," and in his 1921 edition Thorp stated that he first heard it sung by Randolph Reynolds of Carrizozo Flats, New Mexico, in 1890. The 1908 variant is not as complete as the one he used in 1921, which obviously Thorp took from Lomax. In fact, it is identical to the Lomax variant, with the exception of deleting the third and fourth lines of Lomax's last verse and moving the two final lines of Lomax's into the quatrain in order to make a complete verse.

"Breaking a bucking bronco, Wyoming." (Prints and Photographs Division, Library of Congress.)

"Zebra Dun" is a widely collected and printed song with moderate variation. Most variants refer to the dude's talk about the Spanish-American War and Admiral Dewey, but Riley Neal's version has an unusual update—he used the Japanese and Tojo in World War II. Lew Pyle was the only person whom I have heard sing it as the "Z Bar Dun," but Nevada Slim Turner used the "Z Bar Dun" title on his Rural Rhytmn recording (RRNS-163). Bill Long of Roff, Oklahoma, still sings the more commonly known variant. The following variant is Riley Neal's version.

Text A

We camp out upon the plains on the head of the Cimarron,
Along came a dudish fellow and stopped to augur some.
Such an educated fellow we'd seldom ever heard,
He astonished all the natives with his jaw-breaking words.

We asked if he'd been to breakfast; he said he hadn't had a
    sniff;
We opened up the chuck box and bade him help himself.
He took a plate of beefsteak, some biscuits and some beans,
Sat down and began to talk about the foreign kings and
    queens.

He told about the Japanese and the fighting on the seas,
With guns as big as beefsteers and ramrods as big as trees;
He told about old Tojo, the fighting son of a gun;
He said he was the bravest man that ever drew a gun.

He said he'd lost his job down near old Santa Fe,
He was traveling across the plains to catch the 7-D.
He never told his troubles, his trouble with the boss;
He said he'd like to borrow a fresh fat saddle hoss.

"Oh, you can have a hoss just as fresh as you please,"
And it tickled all the cowboys till they laughed down in their
    sleeves.
Shorty grabbed a lasso, and he roped old Zebra Dun,
Turned him over to the stranger to see the coming fun.

Old Dunny was an outlaw, had been for quite a while,
He could paw all the white out of the moon and jump for over
    a mile.
Old Dunny was an outlaw, but he didn't let it show,
Till the stranger had him saddled and was ready for to go.

When the stranger mounted Dunny, old Dunny left the earth,
He went straight up for all that he was worth;
The stranger sat upon him and curled his black mustache,
Just like a summer boarder a-waitin' for his hash.

Old Dunny bucked and bawled, he had those wall-eyed fits,
His hind feet perpendicular, his forefeet in the bits.
He spurred him in the shoulders, he whipped him as he
    whirled,
Just to show those flunky cowboys he was a wolf of the world.

When the stranger had dismounted and stood upon the
    ground,
He was recognized a thoroughbred and not a dude from town.
"If you can whirl a lasso like you rode old Zebra Dun,
You're the man I've been looking for ever since the year of
    one."

"Oh! I can whirl a lasso and not do it very slow;
I can catch nine out of ten for any old kind of dough."
And when the herd stampeded he was Johnnie on the spot,
He could mill a thousand longhorns as easy as you could turn
    a pot.

Come all you flunky cowboys, I've learned since I've been born
That all the dudish fellows are not plum greenhorns.

Text B (contributed by Dallas "Nevada Slim" Turner;
sung to the tune of "Battle Hymn of the Republic"):

We were camped down in the valley, not too far from Cimarron,
When the dogs all got to barkin', just before the crack of dawn.
Tex rolled out and lit the lantern, and we quickly heard him
    hiss;
"I think I've met the devil! Come, and get a load of this!"

On a burro sat a stranger, and he didn't look too "sound,"
For he was so durn long legged that his big feet touched the
    ground.
He was wearin' peg top britches, and a funny high silk hat,
His eyes shone in the darkness, like the boss's pussy cat.

You could tell he was a feller not accustomed to the trail,
With his 'gators and his leggin's and his fancy swaller tail.
Then he said, "I'm a mortician, I'm a graduate of Yale,
I'm Rev'rend Doctor Alexander Rexford Milton Hale."

Shorty said, "Pard, are yuh hungry? Come, get down and have
    a bite,
I brought out a jug of whiskey, just to whet his appetite.
So he drank up all our whiskey, and he polished off the beans
Then started tellin' stories 'bout the foreign kings and queens.

This old boy was educated, all his thoughts just came in herds,
And he drove the punchers crazy with his durn jawbreakin'
    words.
He soon had ol' Shorty yawnin', and the rest of us were bored.
This was an undertaker who refused to be ignored.

Well, he started spoutin' scriptures, spoke of pirates on the
    seas.
Of the "skeeters" big as buzzards, and the monkeys in the
    trees.
Of his good friend Gen'ral Custer, and the battles he had won,
Then told us Harry Tracy was much faster with a gun.

He had just closed up his practice at the little town of Hobbs.
But he'd heard up in Wyomin' there were undertakin' jobs.
Then he said, "My jack is weary, there are sev'ral hills to cross.
I want to trade my burro for a gentle riding hawse."

Well, I heard ol' Lefty snicker, and the first to speak was Sam.
And he says, "I've got a pony, he's as gentle as a lamb.
I will trade him for your burro; he's a perfect, gentle horse.
Before you take my offer, you can try him out, of course."

Well, ol' ZEBRA DUN THE OUTLAW was a bronc that wouldn't bust,
Fifty hands had tried to ride him, ev'ry last one bit the dust.
That ol' jumper and sunfisher pawed the white out of the
  moon.
And now this undertaker would start dancin' to his tune.

But the dude said, "Just a minute! We are going by the book,
You said you would trade your pony, you can't wriggle off the
  hook.
You have swapped him for my burro, you will never get him
  back.
I've got myself a pony, and you've got yourself a jack."

So we roped and saddled Dunny, then the greenhorn climbed
  aboard.
When the outlaw started buckin', how the flunky punchers
  roared.
The mortician dropped the lingo that we all had thought so
  strange.
He now used ev'ry cuss word that the folks use on the range.

We could see clear down to Vegas, 'neath ol' Dunny every
  jump,
But the greenhorn's in the saddle, stickin' like a camel's hump.
He now rolls himself a "quirley," and he's curlin' his mustache,
Just like a winter boarder who's a waitin' for his hash.

He thumps Dunny on the shoulders, calls ol' Sam a dirty name,
He's a-yellin', "All you so and so's, you said this hawse was
  tame!
Well, I'll ride him! I'm his owner! But I'm takin' care of you.
You boys now have a burro! You can go to Timbucktoo!"

He came off the Dun a cussin', and a-swingin' left and right,
And he beat up all the punchers; that mortician, he could fight.
Then the boss said, "You're a top hand! I could use you on the
  drive."

The greenhorn said, "No, thank you! I prefer to stay alive."
The mortician got the burro, and he tied him to the fence,
Then he rode away on Dunny, and we haven't seen him since.
When Sam's burro starts to brayin' at the settin' of the sun,
We think about the tenderfoot who rode ol' Zebra Dun.

Field Collections and Manuscripts: LC-AFS 2616 Al, 4140 A2; Fife Folklore Archives, FAC I 80, FAC I 90, FAC I 143, FAC I 217, FAC I 218, FAC I 238, FAC I 430, FAC I 508, FAC I 549 (p. 5), FAC I 711; Gordon (Mss.), 577; Todd-Sonkin 53 A2; Culwell (1976), p. 189; Owens (1941), pp. 114–16; Plumb (1965), pp. 132–33; Scroggins (1976), pp. 266–68.

References: Allen (1933), pp. 159–61; *American Cowboy Songs* (1936), pp. 46–47; Barnes (1925), pp. 125–28; Cannon (1985), pp. 8–10; Clark (1932), pp. 68–69; Coolidge (1912), pp. 508–10; Edwards (1986), pp. 16–17; Felton (1951), pp. 28–33; Fife and Fife (1969), pp. 194–95; Frey (1936), pp. 62–63; German (1929 and 1932), n.p.; Gray (1925), pp. 98–101; B. Green (1974), pp. 2–3, 60–61; Hood (1977), pp. 390–91; Larkin (1931), pp. 35–38; Laws (1964), B 18, p. 141; Lee (1936), pp. 32–33; Lingenfelter, Dwyer, and Cohen (1968), pp. 402–3; Lomax (1910 and 1916), pp. 154–57; Lomax and Lomax (1938, 1986), pp. 78–81; McConathy, Beattie, and Morgan (1936), pp. 82–83; *900 Miles* (1965), pp. 86–87; Ohrlin (1973), pp. 54–57, 257–58; Randolph, 2 (1948, 1980), pp. 244–45; Sherwin (1934), pp. 54–56; Silber (1967), pp. 262–64; Thorp (1908), pp. 27–29, (1921), pp. 171–74; Thorp and Fife (1966), pp. 135–47; Tinsley (1981), pp. 134–38; *Treasure Chest of Cowboy Songs* (1935), p. 45; White (1934), n.p., (1975), pp. 148–52; Wolfe (n.d.), p. 47.

Recordings: Jules Verne Allen, Victor 40022, Montgomery Ward 4464, reissued on *Authentic Cowboys and Their Western Folksongs*, RCA LPV-522; Don Edwards, *Songs of the Cowboys*, Sevenshoux Records (cassette) BTDE 101; Tex Fletcher, Decca 5302 and Melotone C45010; Cisco Houston, *Cisco Sings*, Folkways FA 2346; Harry Jackson, *The Cowboy*, Folkways FH 5723; Frank Luther, Decca 1428; Glenn Ohrlin, *Cowboy Songs*, Philo 1017; Ray Reed, *Sings Traditional Frontier and Cowboy Songs*, Folkways FD 5329; Frances Roberts, on *Cowboy Songs*, Arizona Friends of Folklore AFF 33-1; Larry Schutte, on *Favorite Cowboy Recitations*, Cowboy Poetry Gathering, 1985 (cassette, no number); George and Luciy Shawver, *Songs of the West*, (cassette, privately produced, #1); Carl T. Sprague, *Cowboy Songs from Texas*, Bear Family BF 15006; Ken Trowbridge, on *When the Work's All Done This Fall*, Montana Folklife Project MFP 0001; Nevada Slim Turner, *Songs of the Wild West, 2*, Rural Rhytmn RRNS-163; J. M. Waddell, on *Cowboy Songs, Ballads, and Cattle Calls from Texas*, Archive of Folk Song, Library of Congress L 28.

"The Cowboy in the Continental Suit":

Recordings: Chris LeDoux, *Songs of Living Free*, American Cowboy Songs NR 5835; Marty Robbins, Columbia 4-43049, reissued on *Marty Robbins*, Time-Life Records TLCW-8, and on *In the Wild West*, part 5, Bear Family BFX 15213, also Headliner KH 32286.

13.*

"THE CASTRATION OF THE STRAWBERRY ROAN"

Original title:
"The Emasculation of the Strawberry Roan"

On November 10, 1982, the cowboy poet, humorist, and philosopher, Baxter Black spent the evening with me in Tulsa; while visiting about my interest in bawdy cowboy songs, he offered to sing the "Castration," which I recorded. Although I had heard of it, I had never heard anyone sing it. A few weeks later, while singing at a cattlemen's Christmas Eve party in Phoenix, Arizona, I handed my guitar to one of the hosts, and he sang "The Castration of the Strawberry Roan." Within two months, I heard the song twice.

The host told me that following his discharge from World War II military service, he was in Los Angeles. Wanting a recording of the original "Strawberry Roan," he went to a large record store. When he asked if they had the record, the clerk glanced around to see if anyone was watching, reached under the counter, and handed him a record in a brown wrapper. Assuming it to be what he wanted, he paid for it, only to find out later that it was the Sons of the Pioneers' recording of "The Castration of the Strawberry Roan." The host learned his version from that recording; Baxter Black learned his from on old bachelor cowboy, Albert Stone, of the Alder Creek Ranch at Denio, Nevada.

Trying to find a copy of the Sons of the Pioneers' record, I wrote to Ken Griffis in Los Angeles, a well-known authority on Sons of the Pioneers personnel and history. He replied that although he had heard about it, he had never seen or heard the recording. Then I wrote to the Country Music Foundation in Nashville. According to Charlie Seemann,

Deputy Director for Collections and Research and a folklorist who is an interested in cowboy songs, their collection contains two recordings, neither identified as being the Sons, even though they are. The flip side of one is Tex Ritter under the name of Eurasmus B. Black singing "The Juice of the Forbidden Fruit," which was written by Curley Fletcher. The flip side of the other record is the recitation, "The Baseball Game," by an unidentified artist listed as Claude Balls. My interest in learning more about the song and recording increased.

The original song "The Strawberry Roan" was written in 1914 by Curley Fletcher; it was printed in the Globe *Arizona Record* on December 16, 1915, under the title "The Outlaw Bronco." Two years later Fletcher included it, with revisions to the original poem, under the title "The Strawberry Roan" in his first collection of poems, *Rhymes of the Roundup*. It did not take long for some unknown singer to set the words to music, and it soon became a cowboy favorite. The first printing of a field-collected text was in 1925 after Freda Kirchwey, a journalist and editor, heard a cowboy named Charlie sing it in the Green River Valley country of Wyoming.

John I. White has written an excellent account about Fletcher and his song in *Git Along, Little Dogies*. Hal Cannon in his preface to the reprint of Fletcher's *Songs of the Sage* tells the story of Fletcher's creative and often traumatic life as recalled by Fletcher's relatives. Harlan Daniel compiled an extensive biblio-discography for "The Strawberry Roan" in Glenn Ohrlin's *The Hell-Bound Train*.

The song did not have a chorus as originally written. In 1931, two Hollywood songwriters, Fred Howard and Nat Vincent ("The Happy Chappies"), published a sheet music version that included a chorus and other alterations they had written. Fletcher had asked them to help promote the song, but was furious over their tampering with it. In May 1986, I learned more of the story when I visited with Dallas Turner.

Turner, who was acquainted with Fletcher, told me that Fletcher was highly offended and angered by the unauthorized addition of a "bridge" (musicians' term for a chorus) by Howard and Vincent; he hated the "bridge" (see John I. White's account and also Nat Vincent's recollection in Dorothy Horstman's *Sing Your Heart Out, Country Boy*). Years later, when Fletcher heard Turner sing the Howard-Vincent version over the radio, he sent Turner a mimeographed copy of "the way it should be sung" with the demand that Turner never again mention Howard and Vincent in connection with the song. In order to get even with them,

Many rodeo bucking horses were named "The Strawberry Roan" after the song became popular; rodeo cowboy Bud McDaniels on Strawberry Roan at the Free State Fair, Muskogee, Oklahoma, late 1930s. (Photo by R. R. Doubleday, National Cowboy Hall of Fame Collection, Oklahoma City.)

Fletcher wrote the bawdy version, including a chorus. However, he probably had already written some bawdy verses and another variant.

Dallas Turner had learned a different bawdy version (Text B) from his mother, who was a friend of Fletcher, long before he knew the "Castration" words. He stated that in the early 1930s when Fletcher traveled and made personal appearances with the Arizona Wranglers, they always introduced him as the "greatest cowboy song writer," and cowboys would always "yell for the dirty version." It was not the well-known "Castration" song, which Turner did not hear until the 1940s when a friend told him about the Sons of the Pioneers' record.

Turner recalled that on the flip side of that original record Carson Robison (not identified on the label) sang "Those Hardy Sons-a-Bitches":

> They use their pricks for walking sticks,
> Those hardy sons-a-bitches.

Turner related that on one radio show he mentioned the bawdy songs written by Fletcher, and Fletcher heard him. Fletcher called Turner and "chewed" him out for emphasizing the bawdy songs. He wanted credit for writing excellent cowboy songs that were not vulgar. And Fletcher's daughter, Bevreley Haller, told me that she did not know that her father wrote bawdy songs until long after she was married; she emphasized that her father was always a "gentleman" around the family and ladies.

Before my visit with Dallas Turner, I received from Charlie Seemann a copy of *Original Record Finder* (no. 146) compiled by Lou Curtiss, owner of Rare Records in San Diego. One of the annotated records was "The Castration" by the Sons of the Pioneers, featuring the B-western singing cowboy star Dick Foran as the lead singer.

Curtiss directed me to Mervin Grigsby in Yuma, Arizona, and on July 10, 1985, I called Grigsby. He told the following story about that recording. Grigsby performed with the Sons during the late 1930s and the late 1940s and was a close friend of Bob Nolan, a founding member of the group and outstanding songwriter. His "Sons Collection" includes "everything they ever did and some that they didn't." In 1942, the Sons signed a contract with the Dr. Pepper corporation for a series of fifteen-minute radio transcriptions (Mutual Radio Network), the "10-2-4 Ranch." Dick Foran appeared as the star and range boss, with the Sons as his crew of cowboys. In 1943, they were asked to appear before the Dr. Pepper's annual stockholders' and board of directors' meeting held in

New York City and were requested to sing "The Strawberry Roan," the favorite song of the company's president. The Sons did not know the words because they did not sing many traditional cowboy songs at that time. At their rehearsal in New York City, "someone" came up with the words of the "Castration." Later in the week, they went to a studio and recorded it, using the words from the manuscript that had been given to them. The original and complete record includes Pat Brady saying at the end, "Whoa, you son-of-a-bitch," followed by Hugh Farr saying, "Oh! Horse shit!"

The two records that I have heard do not have this ending. Lou Curtiss said that he knows of at least seven different records that use the song and that pirating of this type of record is common. I have received information that one record label was named "High Society." Since starting this song trek, I have heard other cowboys sing the "Castration"; it is alive and well among working cowboy singers. For example, Keith Cunningham, professor of English and Folklore at Northern Arizona University in Flagstaff, collected the "Castration" as a recitation in Winnemucca, Nevada, on October 12, 1979. A copy of the interview can be found in the Arizona Friends of Folklore Archives at Northern Arizona University and the American Folklife Center, Library of Congress.

The non-bawdy version has been sung by cowboy and non-cowboy singers throughout the world and has been recorded commercially numerous times. It is sung with and without the chorus; but the Howard-Vincent version is probably more familiar to most listeners because it was featured in two motion pictures that used the song title as the film title—starring Ken Maynard in 1933 and Gene Autry in 1948. In 1972, Austin E. Fife compiled the extensive and amazing travels of this song in the article "The Strawberry Roan and His Progeny," including a "Castration" variant as collected by Vance Randolph; the "Roan" has inspired more imitators and parodists than any other song that I know of. In fact, Fletcher used the "Roan" structure for additional songs such as "The Ridge-Running Roan" and "Flyin' U Twister." Fife also reproduced a text sung in Pennsylvania Dutch as collected and transcribed by J. Barre Toelken. I heard Toelken sing this variant in Logan, Utah, in June 1987, and I think Curley Fletcher would have enjoyed it.

In the mid-1980s, Stephen Makara, a Fletcher devotee in La Mesa, New Mexico, complied a lengthy study of Fletcher and "The Strawberry Roan" and deposited a copy in the Archive of Folk Culture, Library of Congress. A few years later in 1987, Jim Bramlett—cowboy artist, sculptor, and biographer—included Curley Fletcher in his biography of the cowboy artist Will James. Bramlett published a booklet, *The Original Strawberry Roan*, to accompany his sculpture of Will James riding the Strawberry Roan. The legendary horse is living in song, literature, and art.

Additional "Strawberry Roan" parodies continue to be written. C. W. "Bill" Getz in *The Wild Blue Yonder*, 2 (1986), includes two Air Force parodies. One is bawdy, "Bumming Around Town," and could be sung in relation to any war, any time, or any town; it is included as Text C. The other, "Tchepone," is a Vietnam War parody and is not bawdy.

The "Strawberry Roan" is a classic riding song in which the braggart cowboy is thrown after suffering the wildest ride he ever experienced. The "Castration" expresses the frustration of the cowboys over an untamable and unridable wild horse; the best method to quell his wildness and to get even with him is castration. In tribute to the "Roan's" spirit, instead of being castrated, he bites off the testicles of the owner. Gershon Legman stated in *The Horn Book* that the "Castration" is "almost unbearably long and detailed."

Red roan horses have a chestnut-colored hair base intermingled with white hair; they usually are solid-colored, including the mane and tail. A strawberry roan is a red roan that has a decidedly *red* base color.

Moderate, easy

1st Verse

I was lay-in' round town in a house of ill fame, Laid up with a rough, tough hu-stl - in' dame, When a hop-head-ed pimp with his nose full of coke Beat me out-ta that

2nd Verse

wo-man and left me stone broke. When up steps a fel-ler and he says, "Say, my lad, You an-y damn good rid-in' hors - es that's bad?"

(half spoken)

I says, "You damn right! That's one thing I can do, I'm a sec-ond-rate pimp, but a good buck-a-roo."

CHORUS

Oh! the Straw-ber-ry Roan, how man-y colts has he thrown? He's got gon-or-rhe-a, the can-kers, and syph, He's stric-tured with clap but his cock is still stiff, Oh! that ren-e-gade Straw-ber-ry Roan.

Text A (Baxter Black version)

I was layin' round town in a house of ill fame,
Laid up with a rough, tough hustlin' dame,
When a hop-headed pimp with his nose full of coke
Beat me outta that woman and left me stone broke.

When up steps a feller and he says, "Say, my lad,
You any damn good ridin' horses that's bad?"
I says, "You damn right! That's one thing I can do,
I'm a second-rate pimp, but a good buckaroo.

"Bring on your bad horses 'cause I never saw one
That had me a guessin' or bothered me none."
He said, "Guess again, there's one horse that I own,
You might have heard of him, the Strawberry Roan."

I says, "I guess we've all heard of that ball bearin' stud,
He's got epizootic, the glanders, and crud,
He's the worst fuckin' outlaw that ever been foaled,
He hadn't been rode, and he's twenty years old."

CHORUS:
> Oh! the Strawberry Roan, how many colts has he thrown?
> He's got gonorrhea, the cankers, and syph,
> He's strictured with clap but his cock is still stiff,
> Oh! that renegade Strawberry Roan.

The upshot of it was that I found myself hired
To snap out some colts that that breed stud had sired;
They was knot-headed cayuses just like their dad,
Most of 'em roan, and all of 'em bad.

From mornin' till night how those bastards did fight,
Till my ass drug my tracks out way before night,
With my balls in my boots and my mouth full of shit,
I's plum tuckered out and all ready to quit.

When up steps the boss and he says, "That's enough,
Them strawberry roan colts is just too damn tough;
I'm plum sick and tired seein' you take them falls,
Rope that man-killin' stud and we'll carve out his balls."

CHORUS:
> Oh! the Strawberry Roan, we went out to unbend his bone;
> I built a big loop and went in the corral,
> Roped his front feet, and he farted and fell,
> And we flattened ol' Strawberry Roan.

The boss held his head, and I hog tied his legs,
Got out my jackknife and went for his eggs;
When I carved on his bag, he let out a squall,
And squealed like a pig when I whittled one ball.

But all I could locate was one of his nuts,
The other was hidden somewhere in his guts;
So I rolled up my sleeves and all over blood
I fished for the seed in the guts of that stud.

I thought I had found it, I felt something pass,
But it was only a turd on the way to his ass;
Just then I heard one of them blood-curdlin' squalls,
And I looked and the roan had the boss by the balls.

I tromped on his head, but it wasn't no use,
He was just like a bull dog, he wouldn't turn loose;

So I untied his legs, and he got to his feet,
But the boss's voice changed, and I knew we was beat.

CHORUS:
> Oh! the Strawberry Roan, I advise you to leave him alone,
> He's a knot-headed cayuse with only one ball,
> And the boss he's a eunuch with no balls at all,
> Lay off of the Strawberry Roan.

Text B (contributed by Dallas "Nevada Slim" Turner)

No job and no money, I'm shit out of luck,
And I'm stranded in Elko, a drunkard to fuck.
Down at the Commercial I runs into Mitch,
And he sez to me, "Fletch, you old sunuvabitch.

"Well, what ya been doin'? Pard, how have ya been?
It's shore good to see you in these parts again.
Lay off uv that redeye, get rid of that whore,
And I'll take you on at the old Forty-Four."

So I sez, "Mitch, you bastard, ya just made a deal,
I'm busted, I'm hungry, could do with a meal."
We jumps in the buckboard, and we're headed south,
The bull shit is flowin' from Frank Mitchell's mouth.

He sez, "Fletch, I'll tell you, in case ya ain't heard,
I bought a damned outlaw, a frog walkin' turd.
I call him Strawberry, hell, Fletch, he's a roan,
And you'll wish to Christ you had left him alone."

We got to the ranch, and I takes out my gear,
I heads for the bunkhouse, I'm nursin' a beer.
I'm still kind o' wobbly, I still got the shakes;
I shit like a wild cat, my damned belly aches.

I slips off my Levis, my Stetson I doff,
I flops on a bunk and starts sleepin' it off.
I gotta be ready, tomorrow's the day,
I'll ride that Strawberry who's feedin' on hay.

I rolls out at sun up, I've still got the shits,
I fills up on coffee to sharpen my wits.
And then we all saunters down to the corral,
And there stands Strawberry, he's purty as hell.

He lets out a nicker and tosses his head,
There's blood in his eyes and that blood's turnin' red.
I sez, "You damned outlaw, just wait till I'm through,
'Cause I'm gonna kick all the shit out of you."

I takes my reata, I makes me a loop,
Old Strawberry's ready, he lets out a poop.
I walks right up to him, he offers no sass,
But reached down and bit out a piece of my ass.

The hands were all laffin' and doin' a dance,
I'm hurtin' and jumpin' and shittin' my pants.
They throws on my Hamley and I climbs aboard,
And he starts into buckin' like a Model T Ford.

Well, talk about buckin', he lets out a fart,
And it seems to ol' Fletch that the world's come apart.
He goes to sunfishin' and takes to the air,
A-doin' his damndest to leave me up there.

He's buckin' and bawlin' and playin' no pranks,
My Garcia gut-hooks are fuckin' his flanks.
When all of a sudden he lands on all four,
That bastard's as useless as tits on a boar.

He starts his frog walkin', and sure as you're born,
I'm crackin' my balls on that damned saddle horn.
I loses both stirrups, my Stetson, my rein,
And I makes a grab for that shitass's mane.

The corral was all muddy and slicker than glass,
I lands on a rock and I busted my ass.
Old Strawberry's chargin', he's mean, yes sir-ee,
That bastard's a-kickin' the shit out of me.

Now I'm here to tell you that bastard could kick,
I sez, "Motherfucker, I'll slice off your prick."
I takes my old jackknife and I made a stab,
But Strawberry's wiser 'cause he made a grab.

I lays in the mud, its the end of the trail,
Old Strawberry turns and he lifts up his tail,
For I was the loser, went down in disgrace,
And now that it's over, he shits in my face.

Text C, "Bumming Around Town"

I was bumming around town, not spending a dime,
So steps in a whorehouse, to have a good time.
Up steps an old bitch, who says I suppose,
That your a good cunt-man, by the cut of your clothes.

I'm a young airman a'building my fame.
Do you happen to have any old whore to tame?
Yes, I am one that you cannot fuck;
At throwing good riders, I've had lots of luck.
So I lays an old ten spot right down on the line,
And she steps in the bedroom and pulls down the blind.

She lay on the bed with a horrible groan
The hair on her ass was strawberry roan;
She commenced her wild movement, and I made my pass,
And landed my donneker right square in her ass.
Now, I'm telling you boys that old gal could step,
And I was an airman a'building my rep.
With a hell of a lunge and a god-awful cry,
She left me a'sitting way up in the sky.

I turned over twice 'ere I came back to earth,
And I lay there a'cussing the day of her birth;
Now I'm telling you boys, there's no pilot alive,
That can ride that old bitch when she makes that high dive.

Field Collections and Manuscripts: Randolph (Mss.), pp. 549–51; Turner to McCulloh, n.d.; Griffis to Logsdon, December 11, 1983; Seemann to Logsdon, November 29, 1984; Curtiss to Logsdon, April 1985; Grigsby-Logsdon, interview, July 10, 1985; Turner-Logsdon, interview May 8, 1986; Cunningham to Logsdon, November 11, 1986; Makara, LC-AFC (Subject File), "Strawberry Roan."

References: Curtiss (n.d.), no. 320 (auction catalog); Fife (1972), pp. 149–65; Fletcher and Cannon (1986), pp. v–xiii; Getz, 2 (1986), pp. BB 21, TT 2–3; Horstman (1975), p. 301; Kirchway (1925), pp. 21–25 (original song); Legman (1964), p. 404; White (1975), pp. 137–47.

Recordings: Val Geissler (cassette privately produced, no title, Hamilton, Montana); Glenn Ohrlin, *Just Something My Uncle Told Me*, Rounder 0141.

14.*

"THE FLYIN' U TWISTER"

Alternate Titles:
"The Bad Brahma Bull," "The Bull Rider Song,"
"The Big Brahma Bull," "The Flyin' U Bull,"
and "Old Flyin' U"

This is the first rodeo song that I ever heard, back in the late 1950s. At that time I paid little attention because it obviously was a rodeo version of "The Strawberry Roan." I was interested only in what I thought to be the "old" cowboy songs. It was only years later, after I began to conceptualize the true development of cowboy singing, that I returned for Bill Long's version.

Bill rode bulls on weekends in small shows in Oklahoma and he did not attempt to follow the rodeo as a professional. And he did not learn this song from other bull riders. Instead, as a young man during the 1930s, he received the words as written out by his niece. Because he knew the tune, it was easy to learn the words, but from whom she obtained the words is not known.

Other variants are numerous on commercial recordings. Austin E. Fife in 1972 used a slightly longer variant in his study about the "progeny" of "The Strawberry Roan." It is another poem written by Curley Fletcher that appeared in print in 1942 in *WWVA World's Original Jamboree Famous Songs* folio; sheet music was available the same year. According to John I. White, Fletcher wrote it in 1933, and sent him a copy that year. It is one of the early songs about rodeos and bull riding, and also a good example of a song that quickly entered oral tradition. Bill Long's variant differs from the original; it does not have the line: "But the brand on his hip was a big Flyin' U". Fletcher emphasized the ironic experience of being thrown by an animal from the cowboy's home ranch.

Saying good-bye to a bad bull at the Payson, Arizona, Annual Rodeo, 1962. (Photo by Guy Logsdon)

It is probable that the Flying U brand is used by ranchers in different states, but rodeo stock that carry the brand belong to one of the oldest rodeo stock contracting companies in the nation, the Flying U Rodeo Company, Inc. The company was formed in 1929 to provide rodeo stock—bulls, horses, and calves—for rodeos; today Flying U promotes, finances, and stages rodeos for individuals and organizations that want a rodeo in their community. The Flying U company's largest ranch for raising rodeo stock is near Marysville, California; Ed Rutherford, an Imperial Valley cattleman is the president of the Flying U. The company occasionally uses the lines by Fletcher in advertisments to promote their company.

I was a-bustin' out broncos for the old Flyin' U
At forty a month and not much to do,
When the boss comes around and says, "My lad,
You look pretty good a-bustin' broncos that's bad.

"At a-straddlin' the rough ones, you're not so slow,
And ya might do some good at the big rodeo;
Ya see, I don't have any more horses to break,
But I'll buy you a ticket and get you a stake."

"So sack up your saddle and be on your way,
You look like to me you'll be a champion some day;
So go down and choose 'em, and when you are through
Just tell 'em what you learned from the old Flyin' U.

"Stay off of the liquor and don't get too full
To think you can ride the old Brahmer bull;
He's mean as they make 'em, and don't you forget
He's hurt a lot of twisters and never been set."

Well, I sack up my riggin', and I start a-raisin' dust
A-huntin' that show with that big bull ta bust;
I enters that contest, I pays 'em that fee,
And I tells 'em to look at the "champion," that's me.

"Well, bring on your bad ones, you never had one
That could set me to guessin' or bother me none;
I'll bet you this bankroll and outfit beside
You've not got nothin' that I cannot ride."

Well, they look me all over and say, "Guess he's full,
Let's give him a seat on the big Brahmer bull."
I says, "Good enough; I ain't here to brag,
But I've come a long ways just to gentle that stag.

"You claim he's a bad one; although he may be,
He looks like a sucklin' or weaner to me."
Well, I looked that bull over and to my surprise
He was a foot and a half between his two eyes.

He's got big high horns that looks pretty bad,
He weighs a good ton and that whole ton is mad;
Right over his wethers he packs a big hump
So I takes a deep seat right back of that lump.

"Allright, I've got 'em, just jerk that gate wide,
I'll be back in a minute, I'll bring you his hide."
I jabs in my spurs and he bows like a moose,
He leaps that chute and then he cuts loose.

I got a deep seat and a-sittin' there tight
When he jumps to the left and then to the right;
At a-sellin' his belly he couldn't be beat,
He's a-showin' the grandstand the soles of this feet.

He's snappin' the buttons right off of my clothes;
He's a-buckin' and a-bawlin' an' blowin' his nose.
He dips so low, my boots fill with dirt;
He's makin' a whip outa the tail of my shirt.

It's just nip-and-tuck, you can't tell who'll win,
He's a-diggin' those horns right into my chin;
Well, he starts inta spinnin' and a-weavin' behind,
My head goes to snappin' and I sorta go blind.

Well, then he high-dives and turns handsprings,
And I takes to the air just like I had wings;
Way up I turn over and below I can see
He's a-pawin' that dirt and a-waitin' for me.

I pictures a grave and a big slab a' wood
Readin', "Here lies a twister who thought he was good."
I hits on the ground and I let out a yelp,
I'm plumb tired, stricken, and howlin' for help.

I get to my feet and I've got enough sense
To outrun that bull to that hole in the fence;
I dives through that hole and I wants you to know
I'm not a-goin' back to no Wild West show.

At a-ridin' bad Brahmers you bet I'm all through,
I'm a-high-tailin' back to the old Flyin' U.

Field Collections and Manuscripts: Fife Folklore Archives, FAC I 673, FAC I 416, FAC I 204, FAC I 402.

References: Fife (1972), pp. 152–154; Fife and Fife (1969), p. 189; Tinsley (1981), pp. 162–66; White (1975), p. 146; *WWVA Radio Jamboree Famous Songs* (1942), pp. 76–77.

Recordings: Dave Branch, on *Cowboy Songs*, Arizona Friends of Folklore, AFF 33-1; Yodeling Slim Clark, *Happens Again with Famous Old Balads (sic) and Yodels*, Palomino PAL-310; Charles Huff, Crystal 162; Hermes Nye, *Texas Folk Songs*, Folkways FA 2128; Tex Ritter, Capitol CA-8141, Capitol 1058 and 20068, reissued on *Best of Tex Ritter*, Capitol T-1292, on *An American Legend*, Capitol SKC 11241, and on *High Noon*, Pickwick JS 6138 (also on approximately fifteen additional Tex Ritter reissues); George and Luciy Shawver, *Songs of the West* (cassette, privately produced, #2); Nevada Slim Turner, *Sings Songs of the Wild West*, 1, Rural Rhythm RRNS-162.

15

"WILD BUCKAROO"

While I have not collected this song myself, I have included it here because the bawdy version is still known among cowboys. Curley Fletcher included it (the non-bawdy version) in his 1931 *Songs of the Sage* as a four-verse—eight lines per verse—poem with a two-line rhyme sequence, *aa bb cc dd;* thus, any two lines can be moved within the song without altering the brags. The song is "brag talk," i.e., boasting about abilities, prowess, and actions that usually transforms reality into fantasy.

Glenn Ohrlin recorded his version on his *Wild Buckaroo* LP, issued by Rounder Records in 1983. In his notes, he states that he first learned it in the early 1940s as a recitation and later learned the tune from Slim Critchlow's, Arhoolie LP, *"The Crooked Trail to Holbrook"*; Ohrlin credits Dallas Turner with supplying him with the bawdy version. On *Wild Buckaroo*, Ohrlin hums the bawdy words, while on the record *Just Something My Uncle Told Me*, he sings the "un-hummed" version.

Dallas Turner sent his version, with comments, to a few collectors, including Judith McCulloh; my copy came from her files, and later Turner sent me one also. On October 12, 1983, he wrote that "Curley W. Fletcher wrote much bawdy material . . . I met Curley many times," and he named four mutual friends of his, Curley's, and Glenn Ohrlin's who knew all of Fletcher's bawdry. Unfortunately, the four men are now dead. Perhaps they passed Fletcher's songs on to other cowboys. About the song, Slim wrote:

A wild buckaroo in the photographer's studio in Cheyenne, Wyoming, 1880s.
(Photo by C. D. Kirkland; courtesy of the Denver Public Library, Western History
Department.)

I first heard this song in 1936. I was only 8 or 9 years old at the time. I had just learned the old Belle Starr ballad, "BUCKING BRONCO." My mama sang a bawdy version to that number. Asher Hanks—an ex-convict who had just got out of prison—got a job workin' on the ol' Quarter Circle Nine. He taught Mama a lot of songs he had learned while doing a stretch for cattle rustling. This was one of them. Mama liked it so much that she even came up with a cowgirl version. I can't remember the words to her version. Just a few years ago—up home in Elko—I heard a drunk cowboy sing this song at a rodeo. He had added some verses of his own.

Curley Fletcher included the non-bawdy version in *Songs of the Sage*, and when, the scholar, Norm Cohen read my first draft of this collection, he wrote that his copy of *Songs of the Sage* does not correspond with mine; my copy has more of the vernacular and the pagination for "Wild Buckaroo" is different. He sent a photocopy of the title page and copyright page along with the "Wild Buckaroo." The Cohen copy was $1.00, mine was $2.00; the Cohen copy gives credit to Guy M. Welch for the sketches, mine does not. Other differences came to light in late 1986, when Hal Cannon of the Western Folklife Center in Salt Lake City arranged to have a reprint of *Songs of the Sage* published; he used a copy identical to Cohen's. When I compared it to mine, I found that the reprint title and copyright pages are new, so I could make no comparisons to them, but the Contents pages show a complete rearrangement of the poems. Three poems in the reprint are not in my copy, which has a poem, "The Cowboy's Prayer," that is not in the reprint. My copy has a photograph of Loyal Underwood, a member of the Arizona Wranglers, that is not in the reprint, and my copy has photographs of rodeo scenes not found in the reprint.

The price difference indicates that I own a second or subsequent printing, and the photograph of Underwood indicates that Fletcher was or had been traveling with the Arizona Rangers at the time of the printing. The rodeo photos took the place of poems in order to keep the format seventy-five pages. My copy contains more of the vernacular, so possibly, as Fletcher's audience grew, he thought the vernacular would sell better. Neither text included musical scores.

To add to textual confusion, Fletcher made additional changes to the song in his *Ballads of the Badlands*, a folio published in 1932. All of his books were published by Frontier Publishing Company, which was Curley Fletcher and his brother. He used the publishing name instead of his own in his privately printed books.

In the song folio, the melody line for "Wild Buckaroo" differs very little from the melody sung by Critchlow and Ohrlin, and the Critchlow text is almost identical to the version in *Ballads of the Badlands*. This leads me to believe that Critchlow had a copy of the song folio or learned the song from the Arizona Wranglers or Fletcher. We will probably never know who set it to music; Fletcher composed some tunes or adapted existing melodies. And friends in Hollywood composed tunes for him. To my knowledge, the bawdy variant circulated only orally until Dallas Turner typed a copy and shared it with friends (Text B).

The Fifes included the song in *Cowboy and Western Songs* in the category of "Cowboy Boasters." Indeed, all variants, including the bawdy one, are in the tradition of the cowboy brag. I offer the polite-society version (Text A) first, as found in *Ballads of the Badlands*. The melody line is Fletcher's. The bawdy variant (Text B) came to me from Dallas Turner.

The line "rode for old Trassus down in old Mexico" refers to Don Luis Terrazus, who owned the greatest ranch of all time. His property ran 235 miles starting at Ciudad Juarez southward to the city of Chihuahua; in the 1880s, he owned 6.2 million acres and more than four hundred thousand head of cattle.

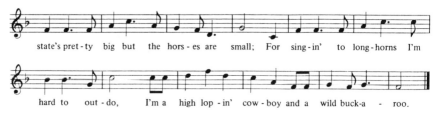

state's pret-ty big but the hors-es are small; For sing-in' to long-horns I'm

hard to out-do, I'm a high lop-in' cow-boy and a wild buck-a - roo.

Text A

I've been ridin' for cattle most all of my life;
I ain't got no fam'ly and I ain't got no wife;
I ain't got no kith and I ain't got no kin;
I never did finish and I never did begin.
I've rode down in Texas where cowboys are tall;
The state's pretty big but the horses are small;
For singin' to longhorns I'm hard to out-do,
I'm a high lopin' cowboy and a wild buckaroo.

I have rode in Montana and in Idaho.
I've rode for old Trassus down old Mexico,
I've rode cross the desert with water far between
And crossed old Death Valley without a canteen.
I've roped mountain lion and she grizzly bear,
I've used choy-a cactus for combin' my hair;
At ropin' wild grizzles I'm hard to out-do,
I'm a high lopin' cowboy and a wild buckaroo.

Oh, I talk lots of Spanish and I talk Piute,
I pack a long knife and a pistol to boot;
I've got no senorita and I've got no squaw,
I've got no sweetheart nor no mother-in-law.
I've never been tied up to no apron strings,
I ain't no red devil but ain't got no wings;
For singin' to the ladies I'm hard to out-do,
I'm a high lopin' cowboy and a wild buckaroo.

Oh, I don't like the whiskey but do like my beer,
I don't care for mutton but do like my steer;
I'll leave you alone if you just let me be,
But don't never think you can jump on to me.
I'll fight anybody who'll go to the mat,
He'll think he's in a sack with a wild panther cat;

For rough and tough mixin' I'm hard to out-do,
I'm a high lopin' cowboy and a wild buckaroo.

Text B

I've been bustin' broncos since I was a squirt,
When I ain't bronc stompin' I'm braidin' a quirt.
But there's one thing better I know how to do;
I'm a cunt crazy cowboy and a Wild Buckaroo.
I work for John Taylor up north at Lovelock,
Where gals judge a man by the size of his cock.
When it comes to fuckin' I'm hard to out-do;
I'm a cunt crazy cowboy and a Wild Buckaroo.

Out here in Nevada the fellers stand tall,
You won't find a cowboy whose pecker is small.
Come all ye wild virgins, I'll teach you to screw;
I'm a cunt crazy cowboy and a Wild Buckaroo.
One evenin' in Bishop, I walked up the street,
And I was damn fed up with beatin' my meat.
I met a fair maiden, her name it was Lou,
And she said, "You must be that damned Wild Buckaroo."

We stopped at a pool hall and got pretty tight,
She said, "You can fuck me the rest of the night.
I came here from Frisco from Pine Avenue;
And my cunt needs the prick of the Wild Buckaroo."
So I lays her down by the side of the road,
.I poured the prick to her, I shot off my load.
She screamed, "You jack rabbit! You shot off, you're thru;
You can go fuck yourself now you Wild Buckaroo."

Field Collections and Manuscripts: Turner to Logsdon, October 12, 1983;
Cohen to Logsdon, June 4, 1985.

References: Fletcher (1931), pp. 32–33 [Cohen copy, pp. 68–69], (1932), pp.
30–31, (1986), pp. 68–69; Fife and Fife (1969), p. 106; Rogers (n.d.), p. 7.

Recordings: Slim Critchlow, *"The Crooked Trail to Holbrook,"* Arhoolie
5007; Glenn Ohrlin, *The Wild Buckaroo*, Rounder 9158, and on *Just Something
My Uncle Told Me*, Rounder 0141 (bawdy variant).

16.

"THE OPEN BOOK"

Alternate title: "The Open Ledger"

The tradition of cowboy poetry recitation and poetry writing, until recently, has taken a back seat to cowboy singing. A singing cowboy has a romantic flair that a poetry-reciting cowboy does not enjoy. Yet, both forms of expression were equally popular for recreational pastime. In fact, the singing ability and vocal quality of many working cowboys make it difficult to distinguish between song and recitation. And the songs were usually introduced as poems, as indicated many times throughout this collection.

The Cowboy Poetry Gathering held each year since 1985 in Elko, Nevada, has enhanced the image of the cowboy poet and reciter in the eyes of the general public. It was during the 1985 Gathering when I collected the "classic" cowboy poem "The Open Book" from an excellent cowboy reciter. On February 2, 1985, I was visiting with Sonny and Alice Hancock, ranchers from Lakeview, Oregon; Sonny grew up near Williams, Arizona, and cowboyed in a few other states before moving to Oregon. I asked him if he knew "The Open Book," and with pride he said, "Yes." It was not possible to record it then, but he promised to recite it later in the day. I recorded Sonny Hancock's version of the song, although he indicated that he had forgotten a few lines. At the 1986 Gathering, Hancock brought a typescript that he had worked on during the fall, including the twelve lines he had not remembered in 1985. It is the version that I use as Text A.

Through the years I have been asked if I had heard "The Open Book"; my answer was, "No," until I heard Glenn Ohrlin's version on *Just Some-*

thing My Uncle Told Me. When Glenn and I visit, it is always in a setting in which recitation is impossible, but, at least, I inquired about "The Open Book" during two visits. Glenn said that he had learned his version from Johnny Baker, a rodeo performer, song writer, and singer, and that he knows the complete poem, which is much longer than his recorded version.

"The Open Book" is another poem written by Curley Fletcher. It is a scathing, but humorous, attack against cowboys; few western states and cowboy types are spared, and it reflects the cowboy's ability to laugh at himself, his friends, and his occupation. Also, it verbalizes criticism for those who do not like cowboys; it is a poem for cowboys and non-cowboys. For polite society, Fletcher wrote a "clean" version.

Curley Fletcher was a creative and productive man. He wrote not only poems and songs, but also magazine articles and short stories, and he edited and produced magazines and annuals. (Hal Cannon in the 1986 reprint of *Songs of the Sage* discusses Fletcher's career in detail.) In 1946, Fletcher edited and produced *Silverado, Nevada's Annual Souvenir Magazine*; he wrote every item in it using such pseudonyms as Dewlap Wattles, Bourbon Bill, Curt Crabb, Breezy Summers, and many more. He scattered a few of his poems throughout *Silverado*, including the non-bawdy "The Open Book" (Text B).

Text A

You've been tamped full of shit about cowboys;
they are known as a romantic band—
Bold knights of the saddle, who round up wild cattle,
and roll cigarettes with one hand.
Now according to movie and story,
he's a sheik in a ten gallon hat.
All he knows of romance is the crotch of his pants,
what the hell do you think about that?
So it's high time somebody debunked him;
he's so plumb full of crap, and, besides,
A bullshittin' bastard who's always half-plastered
is no hero just 'cause he rides.

Now I've harvested wool in Wyoming
and rawhide in New Mexico.
I've worn a bandana in Sheepshit, Montana,
and raped squaws over in Idaho.

Curley Fletcher, ca. early 1930s. (Courtesy John I. White.)

So me, I'm plumb soured on cowpunchers;
in fact, I ride sour long ago.
The clap ridden slats in their ten gallon hats
ain't worth a damn that I know.

But each range breeds its own brand of bastard
and boozefighter, bugger or bum;
Every half-assed vaquero who wears a sombrero
is marked by the range he is from.
Some come from the Canadian Rockies,
some drift from the southwestern plains.
It surely beats hell, but it's easy to tell
where each learned to tighten his reins.

Take for instance the Panhandle hairpin,
widely known by the moniker "Tex";
He's a son-of-a-bitch with a bad trigger itch
and a big Bowie knife complex.
Why at heart he's an unpaid policeman,
and he'll brag of tough spots he's been in.
But his powder is damp, and his gun hand will cramp
when he draws near a cotton gin.

Take the clip-cock from California,
he's been christened "The Native Son."
A half-baked vaquero who has no dinero,
but no worse than the general run.
He's a cross between a greaser and gringo,
produced by the whore from the mine,
A renegade breed that's gone plumb to seed,
since the gold rush of forty-nine.

There's boosters from Oklahoma,
and bastards from Arkansas,
But they're just cotton pickers and tinhorn dice lickers
with not too much in their craw.
There's the pistol prick out in Nebraska,
he's known as the corn sucker class.
From the cootie that crawls on his crab ridden balls
to the piles that blister his ass.

Count the cocksman from Colorado,
where Pike's Peak ponders and broods.

A miner and mucker, the phony cock-sucker,
and his racket is wranglin' dudes.
He sponsors a double-rigged saddle;
his gifts are the gifts of the gab;
With a rope made of grass and teeth in his ass,
the best he can get is the tab.

Take the "never sweat" from Nevada,
he's known as the "Son of the Sage."
A tinhorn card hustler and discard cunt rustler,
a throw back to some ancient age.
He sponsors a center-fire saddle,
and his brains have a chronic limp.
Just a contrary fart and a cow thief at heart,
and actually just a lunch bucket pimp.

Now we can't overlook Arizona;
he's a son of the old Sacatone.
An ornery critter and a famous bullshitter,
about the sorriest seed ever sown.
He's bothered by Mexican heartburn
with protruding piles and gut;
A red hot tamale is right down his alley,
'tis a diet his ass hole can't cut.

There's that whistle-prick out there in Utah;
he was sired by old Brigham Young,
The sap sucking swizzler and cunt cheating chiseler,
of the barrel he's only the bung.
Often called the crying Jack Mormon,
his penchant is guzzling booze.
He's got a round ass and can't ride nor lass',
and he'd give a sad jackass the blues.

There's a flute blower out in Dakota,
just a liar, and, what's more,
A psalm singing sooner, a guitar picking crooner
and as worthless as tits on a boar.
His tongue is diseased with diarrhea,
the half-breed gut eating tramp.
He knows more of plows than he savies of cows,
and was born with his ass in a cramp.

That greaser from down in Chihuahua,
he claims he's a cowpuncher, too.
He curses the gringo in that Mexican lingo,
but that's about all he can do.
He sponsors a rawhide riata,
and he straddles a silver trimmed rig;
Just a counterfeit chump, the result of a hump,
twixt a Spaniard, a Yaqui, and a Jig.

There's a herd in the Hollywood movies;
you can find them at Sunset and Gower.
And brother to brother they bullshit each other,
and just bellyache by the hour.
'Course they're just a mixed bunch of bastards
of that there is damn little doubt.
And each sorry hand wears the mark of the brand
of the country that had him run out.

All in all, they're considered half-witted
and the curse of the wide open west.
Whether Canada twister or Oregon mister,
they're just sons of bitches at best.
No, there isn't much difference in cowboys,
whether hemorrhoid, stool or hard turd;
Spring, summer, and fall, I've rode with them all
and maintain they're a plumb sorry herd.

Now I might be a gullible gunsel, but at that,
why, I ain't too damn dumb;
If a she-sheep don't cross with her herder or boss,
where in hell are them cowpunchers from?
So not that I've opened the ledger
on cowpunchers as they be,
Some frijole chomper or half-assed bronc stomper
will kick all the shit out of me.

Now, just so you won't die of wonder,
why a "Native Son" is what I am,
And what I've tried hard to say in an indirect way
is that cowpunchers ain't worth a damn.
As for those I've neglected to mention,
why, it's not that I can't find the rhyme;

But between me and you, I've got work to do
and those bastards just ain't worth my time.

Text B (by Curley Fletcher)

We've been tamped full of tales about cowboys,
They're known as a romantic band,
Bold knights of the saddle, who round up wild cattle,
And roll cigarettes with one hand.
Well, it's high time that someone debunked 'em—
Let the air from their counterfeit hides—
Every boastful galoot with a spur on his boot,
Is no hero just 'cause he rides.

Hell, I've known all kinds of cowpunchers,
Throughout fifty long years in the west,
Whether Canada twister, or Oregon mister,
They all looked like bums at their best.
I have harvested wool in Wyoming,
And some rawhide in New Mexico;
I've worn a bandana in sheepstunk Montana,
And I've dug spuds in old Idaho.

They wear those ten-gallon sombreros,
And they think they're God's gift to the range,
But they take up more slack than a dumb lumberjack,
And then talk you out of your change.
You can bet that I savvy the hairpins,
I know 'em for what they *ain't* worth,
They're as dumb as sheep come, out west where they're from,
An' should have been strangled at birth.

Some hail from out east of the Rockies,
Some ride from the southwestern plains,
But its easy to tell, by the brag and the smell,
Where each learned to tighten his reins.
As a group they're a bunch of bunch quitters,
With less brains than God gave a goose,
They're caught short of thinking and cry when they're drinking,
But they all like the forbidden juice.

Take, for instance, the Panhandle hairpin,
Widely known by the monaker, "Tex,"

He's a famous lie floater and boastful gun toter,
With a big bowie knife complex.
He will brag of the big plains in Texas,
Or of getting men out on a limb;
But his powder is damp and his gun hand will cramp
If someone screams "cotton" at him.

There's that prune gloming Californian,
He's known as the nice Native Son;
A half baked vaquero, who has no dinero,
But no worse than the general run.
He thinks that he's clever and handsome,
This product from orchard and mine;
But he's only a weed from that pioneer breed,
In the gold rush of old Forty-nine.

Take the lame-brain from cold Colorado,
Where high Pike's Peak ponders and broods;
A miner, a mucker, this hungry stump sucker,
His racket is waiting on dudes.
He sponsors a double rigged saddle,
And he thinks he's a wolf gone plumb wild,
But he's a chump, who is easy to dump,
With the sense of a two year old child.

'Course, we can't overlook Arizona,
He's the son of the dry Sacatone;
Of all nature's blunders, he's one of the wonders—
The sorriest seed ever sown.
He's a sucker for Mexican cooking,
Chili beans with cigarette butts;
A red hot tamali is right down his alley,
That's why he ain't got any guts.

And then there's the rodeo cowboy,
By far he's the pick of the lot;
He makes his best ride, and then fills his fool hide
Full of whiskey that someone else bought.

(Contributed by Sonny Hancock; not in Fletcher's text.)

Now there's boosters from poor Oklahoma,
And there's brokers from old Arkansaw;
But they're cotton pickers and tinhorn dice slickers,
With none too much sand in the craw.

They travel in herds like cayuses,
They're cocky and flip with the lip,
But they know more of plows than they do about cows,
Out there on their Cherokee Strip.

There's a so-called cowhand in Utah,
Who thinks he's the salt from Salt Lake;
He's only small change from that locoweed range,
With less brains than to make his head ache.
He thinks he's a wonderful twister,
This boob with the jack-mormon brand,
But he's nutty more than a peach orchard boar,
In fact, he's a plumb sorry hand.

Take that gunsel from out in Dakota,
Who claims he can "sure stand the gaff,"
Though raised on the prairies, he only knows dairies,
And was caught stealing milk from a calf.
He'll tell how his folks scalped the Indians,
The Cheyennes, the Crows and the Siouxs;
But this calf robbing lad and his sod busting dad
Spend most of their time fighting booze.

There's the cholo from down in Chihuahua,
He claims he's a cowpuncher, too;
He curses the gringo in Mexican lingo,
But that's about all he can do.
He sponsors a rawhide riata,
And he straddles a silver trimmed rig;
This locoed vaquero, with spangled sombrero,
Has locoweed under his wig.

Take this tinhorn right here in Nevada,
He maintains he's the Son of the Sage;
Like the tree climbing crew you see in a zoo,
He'd feel right at home in a cage.
But he likes to smoke, drink and gamble,
And for that reason, he's always broke,
So his aim is to tame some thrice divorced dame,
Who has plenty of cash in her poke.

There's a mixed herd in Hollywood's movies,
They all hang around Sunset and Gower,

And brother to brother, they beef with each other,
While they bellyache, hour after hour.
Some hail from New York or New Jersey;
Some are young, some are bearded and gray,
But each sorry hand wears the earmark and brand,
Of the range where he first learned to bray.

Yes, I've known every kind of cowpuncher,
Through winter, spring, summer and fall;
Gaucho and greaser, and gringo bronc squeezer,
I've mingled and mixed with them all.
I may be a cranky old codger,
But I know that I wouldn't exchange,
A razorback hog nor a sheepherder's dog,
For the best so-called knight of the range.

Course, there's some who are better than others,
But they're few, and they're damned hard to find;
Take them all, man to man, they're a bad boastful clan,
Like four deuces, they're all of a kind.
As for those I've neglected to mention,
It's not that I can't find the rhyme,
But, between me and you, I've got work to do,
And those chumps are not worth the time.

But now that I've opened the ledger
On the romantic braggarts who ride,
Some frijole chomper or locoed bronc stomper,
Will be after my scalp or my hide.
So I'll just have to let you all wonder,
If I'm a cowpuncher and dumb—
Well, guess for a spell, 'cause I don't dare tell
Which country and range I am from. . . .

References: Cannon (1986), pp. v–xiii; Fletcher (1946), pp. 10–11.
Recordings: Glenn Ohrlin, on *Just Something My Uncle Told Me*, Rounder
0141 (bawdy version).

17.

"THE SKEWBALD BLACK"

Original Title: "The 'D2' Horse Wrangler"
Alternate Titles: "The Tenderfoot," "The Horse Wrangler,"
"Bronco Buster," and "Cowboy's Life"

This D. J. O'Malley ["R. J. Stovall"] ballad first appeared in the Miles City, Montana, *Stock Growers Journal* on February 3, 1894. It was to be sung to the tune of "The Day I Played Base Ball." The original version identified a hotel in Miles City, as well as the D2 brand in the title, but by the time John A. Lomax collected his variant for inclusion in the 1910 edition of *Cowboy Songs and Frontier Ballads*, the "D-2" had been dropped from the title and the specific hotel had been changed to the "Plaza." However, Jack Thorp had already collected and used it as "The Tenderfoot" in his 1908 edition of *Songs of the Cowboys*.

In his 1921 edition, Thorp used a different and more complete text. He gave credit to Yank Hitson of Denver for its composition in 1899, writing that "I got the song from old Battle Axe [Hitson], whom lots of old punchers remember, at Phoenix, Arizona, 1899." In Thorp's personal copy of the 1916 edition of the Lomax collection, he made corrections or changes that he used in his 1921 edition, but he made no additional comment about his source. In contrast, by 1938 John A. Lomax had learned of O'Malley's claim of authorship, and gave him proper credit.

Two verses were used by Eugene Manlove Rhodes, the New Mexican cowboy-novelist, in 1920 when the *Saturday Evening Post* serialized his 1921 novel, *Stepsons of Light*. In that book, a sixteen-year-old cowboy, Bob Gifford, sings verses two and four in Riley Neal's version used here. The Rhodes verses are similar to the original O'Malley poem, but enough differences exist to indicate that Rhodes learned the song from other cowboys. They also vary from the Thorp and Lomax verses.

"Making a Tenderfoot Dance," probably in Montana or Wyoming. (Prints and Photographs Division, Library of Congress.)

Variants are close to the original O'Malley text and tell of the tender-foot's attempt to become a cowboy. He was given the lowly position of horse wrangler and found even it to be beyond his ability. The final blow came when he was given—in a standard cowboy prank—"an old gray hack" to ride. The innocent-looking, worn-out horse was an outlaw that quickly threw the tenderfoot. Riley Neal's version changes the narrative closer to the practical joke story; he goes straight to the horse ride and identifies the horse as the "Skew-Ball Black." By either eliminating or forgetting three of the seven verses, he makes the song move quickly toward the tenderfoot's decision to walk back to town instead of trying to ride another horse that might be lent to him. Lew Pyle remembered only a few verses and sang them for me in 1966. For the O'Malley story, along with this song, see John I. White's *Git Along, Little Dogies*.

A skewbald horse is marked with spots and patches of white; thus a black horse with white markings about the head is a skewbald black.

I thought one spring, just for fun, / I'd see how cow-punch-ing was done, So just as the round-up had be-gun I tack-led the cat-tle king. Says he, "My fore-man is in town, He's at the Pla-za, and his name is Brown. If you'll see him, he'll take you down." Says I, "That's just the thing."

I thought one spring, just for fun,
I'd see how cowpunching was done,
So just as the roundup had begun
I tackled the cattle king.
Says he, "My foreman is in town,
He's at the Plaza, and his name is Brown.
If you'll see him, he'll take you down."
Says I, "That's just the thing."

We started out for the ranch next day,
Brown augered me most all the way.

He said cowpunching was nothing but play,
It was no work at all;
Said all you had to do was ride,
Only drifting with the tide,
The son-of-a-bitch, oh, how he lied!
And I believed it all.

They roped me out a skewbald black
With two big setfasts on his back,
I padded him up with a barley sack—
I used my bedding all.
When I got on, he quit the ground,
He went into the air and he whirled around,
He busted my ass when I hit the ground,
And he gave me a hell of a fall.

They picked me up and packed me in,
They rolled me out with a rolling pin.
"Oh! that's the way they all begin,
Your're doing well," said Brown.
"And tomorrow, if you don't die,
I'll give you another horse to try."
"Oh, why can't I walk?" says I.
Says Brown, "Yes, back to town."

Field Collections and Manuscripts: Gordon (Mss.), 982 and 1137; Fife Folklore Archives, FAC I 507, FAC I 555; Culwell (1976), p. 180; Scroggins (1976), pp. 234–36.

References: Allen (1933), pp. 89–90; *American Cowboy Songs* (1936), pp. 44–45; Brand (1961), pp. 176–77; Cannon (1985), pp. 28–29; Clark (1932), p. 58; Coolidge (1937), pp. 126–27; Davis (1935), p. 52; Fife and Fife (1969), pp. 197–98; Fowke (1962), p. 253; Frey (1936), pp. 60–61; German (1929 and 1932), n.p.; Glassmacher (1934), pp. 13–15; Klickman and Sherman (1933), pp. 38–39; Laws (1964), B 27, p. 145; Lingenfelter, Dwyer, and Cohen (1968), pp. 338–39; Lomax (1910 and 1916), pp. 136–38; Lomax and Lomax (1938, 1986), pp. 119–22; *Nebraska Folklore: Cowboy Songs*, pamphlet 1 (1937), pp. 1–3; Ohrlin (1973), pp. 45–47, 255–56; O'Malley and White (1934, 1986), pp. 11–12; Pound (1922, 1972), pp. 176–78; Rhodes (1921, 1969), pp. 36, 41; Sandburg (1927), pp. 274–75; Sires (1928), pp. 2–3; Thorp (1908), pp. 13–14, (1921), pp. 146–48; Thorp and Fife (1966), pp. 44–57; *Treasure Chest of Cowboy Songs* (1935), pp. 28–29; Turner (1977), pp. 24–25; White (1929), pp. 46–48, (1934), n.p., (1975), pp. 87–91; Will (1913), p. 185.

Recordings: Bill Bender, Varsity 5148; Oscar Brand, *Pie in the Sky*, Tradition 1022; Slim Critchlow, *"The Crooked Trail to Holbrook"*, Arhoolie 5007; Glenn Ohrlin, *Cowboy Songs*, Philo 1017; Frances Roberts, on *Cowboy Songs*, 2, Arizona Friends of Folklore AFF 33-2; Roger Welsch, *Sweet Nebraska Land*, Folkways FH 5337.

18.*

"THE OLD BLACK STEER"

Alternate Titles: "Windy Bill,""The Steer Roper,"
and "Driftin' Down the Draw"

Riley Neal never did get to sing this to me, but he sent the words in January 1969. Under the title "Windy Bill" it first appeared in Thorp's *Songs of the Cowboys* (1908); Lomax did not include it until 1916, and in Thorp's copy of that Lomax edition he wrote "from my book" and made numerous word corrections. However, the verse structure and basic story remained the same. In Thorp's 1921 edition he wrote, "Sung first to me by John Collier, Cornudas Mountain, New Mexico, July, 1899." The earliest tune appeared in Ina Sires's *Songs of the Open Range* (1928).

G. Malcolm Laws, Jr., (1964) categorized "Windy Bill" as a "native ballad of doubtful currency in tradition"—an unfortunate conclusion because the ballad is alive and well. It has appeared in most cowboy song collections, most recently in Glenn Ohrlin's *The Hell-Bound Train: A Cowboy Songbook* (1973). Ohrlin wrote that "Windy Bill" was a favorite among his cowboy friends; he learned his version in 1944 from "Powder River" Jack Lee in Arizona.

Riley Neal's version of the song has only five verses; he did not use the fifth verse in the Thorp and Lomax variants. Ohrlin also included only five verses, but left out still a different verse. Nevertheless, the story remains intact in both variants: a young Texas cowboy who makes a brag has to eat his words.

The song concerns a contrast between Texas and California roping styles, and Ohrlin believes that the conflict occurred in Arizona where the two styles met. A "dally" is a half-hitch knot wrapped around the saddle horn. The Texas style of roping is to rope the steer with the rope

Roping an "outlaw" steer to doctor it, O R Ranch, Arizona, 1909. The cowboys are dally men as indicated by the length of the coiled rope held and ready to be loosened if necessary. (The Erwin E. Smith Collection of the Library of Congress on deposit at the Amon Carter Museum, Fort Worth.)

tied hard and fast to the saddle horn, and then jerk the steer to the ground. The California style is to rope the steer, wrap one dally around the saddle horn, and leave the rope loose enough to work the running steer into a position to be jerked down. There is enough rope to slide around the saddle horn if necessary, or even to release the steer if need be. A large, powerful steer can jerk a horse and roper down or can jerk the saddle off when the Texas style of roping is used. Windy Bill lost his saddle, and with cowboy humor, the California dally style was proved superior to the Texas style. A typical cowboy rough prank is to teach a lesson through a little pain combined with much humor. The melody line comes from Glenn Ohrlin's *The Hell-Bound Train.*

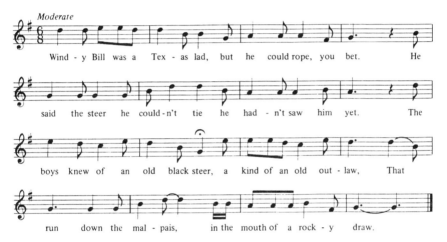

Wind - y Bill was a Tex - as lad, but he could rope, you bet. He
said the steer he could - n't tie he had - n't saw him yet. The
boys knew of an old black steer, a kind of an old out - law, That
run down the mal - pais, in the mouth of a rock - y draw.

Windy Bill was a Texas lad, but he could rope, you bet.
He said the steer he couldn't tie he hadn't saw him yet.
The boys knew of an old black steer, a kind of an old outlaw,
That run down the malpais, in the mouth of a rocky draw.

With his chaps and taps and overalls and his boots and spurs
    to boot,
His Sam Stack tree and his old maguey, he knew he could tie
    the brute.
So he saddled up his old gray horse, and said with a loud, "Ha!
    Ha!"
He thought he could tie any old black steer that run down in a
    draw.

Windy found the old black steer in the mouth of the rocky
    draw.

When Windy first rode up to him, he started to bawl and paw.
When Windy took his maguey down, he suspicioned
    something raw;
He curled his tail up over his back and went drifting down the
    draw.

The old gray horse flew after him, for he'd been a-eatin' corn;
And Windy piled his old maguey right around old Blackie's
    horns.
When he hit the end of the old maguey his clinches broke like
    straw,
And his Sam Stack tree and his old maguey went drifting down
    the draw.

Come all you flunkie cowpunchers, I've learned since I've been
    born,
Whenever you go to rope a steer don't tie it to the horn.
But take your dally welters according to California law,
You won't see your old Texas tree go drifting down the draw.

Field Collections and Manuscripts: Fife Folklore Archives, FAC I 53, FAC I 235, FAC I 222; Owens (1941), pp. 101–2; Scroggins (1976), pp. 262–63.

References: Allen (1933), pp. 140–42; *American Cowboy Songs* (1936), pp. 58–59; Cannon (1985), pp. 26–27; Clark (1934), pp. 50–51; Felton (1951), pp. 54–57; Fife and Fife (1969), pp. 204–5; Frey (1936), pp. 74–75; German (1929 and 1932), n.p.; Glassmacher (1934), pp. 74–75; Larkin (1931), pp. 57–60; Laws (1964), dB 41, p. 260; Lingenfelter, Dwyer, and Cohen (1968), pp. 354–55; Lomax (1916), pp. 381–82; Lomax and Lomax (1938, 1986), pp. 113–15; Ohrlin (1973), pp. 12–15, 248; Sherwin (1944), pp. 20–21; Sires (1928), pp. 28–29; Thorp (1908), pp. 11–12, (1921), pp. 168–70; Thorp and Fife (1966), pp. 38–43; *Treasure Chest of Cowboy Songs* (1935), pp. 46–47.

Recordings: Rex Allen, *Boney Kneed Hairy Legged Cowboy Songs*, JMI Records JMI 4003; Slim Critchlow, *"The Crooked Trail to Holbrook,"* 007; J. D. Farley, "Bill Was a Texas Lad," reissued on *Authentic Cowboys and Their Folksongs*, RCA LPV-522; Harry Jackson, *The Cowboy*, Folkways FH 5723; Jack and Kitty Lee, Bluebird 5298, Electradisk 2169, Sunrise 3379; Glenn Ohrlin, *The Hell-Bound Train*, Campus Folksong Club, University of Illinois, CFC 301 and *The Wild Buckaroo*, Rounder 0158; Nevada Slim Turner, *Songs of the Wild West*, 1 Rural Rhythm RRNS-162.

19.*

"THE SOUGHRTY PEAKS"

Original Title: "Sierry Petes"
Alternate Titles: "Tying the Knots in the Devil's Tail,"
"Sierra Peaks," and "Rusty Jiggs and Sandy Sam"

Written by a highly respected and greatly loved genuine cowboy, this is truly an Arizona song. Gail I. Gardner was born in Prescott, Arizona, in 1892, and with the exception of a few years of education in the East—including four years at Dartmouth—Arizona has always been his home. Most of his adult years were spent as a cowboy-rancher in the Prescott area, as well as the postmaster of Prescott from 1936–57.

Camped out with a friend in the Sierra Prieta ("Sierry Petes") Mountains west of Prescott, Gardner and his friend rode to town for a little diversion. During their return to civilization, one of the men mentioned "that the devil got cowboys for doing what we had been doing"; the remark inspired one of the most popular of all cowboy songs. Gardner wrote the verse in 1917 while on a train to Washington, D.C., where he joined the military service. He returned to Prescott in late 1918, where he shared his "Sierry Petes" with family and friends—it was his friend Bill Simon who set it to music. It did not take long for the song to spread throughout Arizona and the West. The earliest printed version appeared in George B. German's *Cowboy Campfire Ballads* (1929).

John I. White heard Gardner sing it in the summer of 1924 near Prescott, and through the years maintained a friendship with the cowboy poet. As a result, the best coverage of Gardner's life and story is found in White's *Git Along, Little Dogies*. However, Gardner saw other singers publish his song as their own; one of the offenders was "Powder River" Jack Lee, who in 1933 published it with a few word changes but with no commentary in his book *West of Powder River*. In 1936, he included it in

Gail I. Gardner, 1984, Prescott, Arizona. (Photo courtesy of Jay Dusard)

his song folio *Powder River Jack and Kitty Lee's Cowboy Song Book* and claimed to be the author. This was followed by a collection of poetry, *The Stampede and Other Tales of the Far West* (circa 1941), in which Lee stated, "I wrote this as a poem but later made a song of the story. . . ."

To put it mildly, Gardner was unhappy about the misuse of his song and told his side of the story in the folk song magazine *Sing Out!* (August–September 1967). He and Curley Fletcher, who also was angry with Lee for claiming "Strawberry Roan" as his own (actually Lee gave credit to Frank Chamberlin), confronted Lee about his claim of authorship. But because Powder River Jack was nearly destitute, they merely "cussed" him and made him admit that he didn't write the songs. (For a variant account and additional information about Gardner's story see Marshall Trimble's *Arizona Adventure*, 1982, pp. 150–54.)

One cowboy singer is adamant, however, in his belief that Lee wrote "Tying Knots in the Devil's Tail." Dallas "Nevada Slim" Turner said that at the age of six he learned the song from a phonograph record of Lee singing it. After meeting Powder River Jack and Kitty Lee that summer at the Pendleton Round-up, Turner became Lee's fan and defender, even though he recognized that Powder River Jack had a propensity for elaborate embellishment. Turner supports his position with his memory of visiting with old-timer cowboys who told him that they either heard or knew the song around the turn of the century. Moreover, in 1962 Edith Fowke reported that an informant in Alberta, Canada, claimed that he had learned "Tying Knots in the Devil's Tail" before World War I. It is generally accepted and documented however, that Gail Gardner did, indeed, write the poem that became the song. In 1935, Gardner published a small collection of his poetry under the title *Orejana Bull for Cowboys Only* with "Sierry Petes" as the lead song—it was finally copyrighted under his name. In 1976, the collection was reprinted for the fifth time and contained an additional poem, a photo, and personal information not found in earlier printings. In 1987, the Sharlot Hall Museum in Prescott, Arizona, published a new edition edited by Warren Miller. This "seventh edition" contains additional biographical information, and previously unpublished photographs of Gardner, along with musical transcriptions. One of the finest compliments paid to Gardner was written by J. Frank Dobie on his personal copy of the second printing (1950), "The real thing in spirit and language. . . ."

Riley Neal's version lacked one verse of the original, and it varies in some terminology, but it indicates how well oral tradition and folk memory can transmit a tightly written narrative. Gardner added no poetic fat that needed to be trimmed out by the folk process. Riley had no idea that the song was set in Arizona; to him, it was the "Soughrty Peaks." This is one of the songs that Riley did not sing for me, but not long after my first visit he sent these verses. The text is reproduced exactly as Riley wrote it out. The melody line comes from Glenn Ohrlin's *The Hell-Bound Train.*

Away up north in the Soughrty Peaks,
Where the yellow pines grow tall,
Sandy Bob and Rusty Jigs,
Had a roundup camp last fall.

They took their ponies and a runnin' iron
And maybe a dog or two,
And allowed they'd brand any long-eared calf,
That came within their view.

And any old dogie that flopped long ears,
Didn't bush up day by day,
Got his old ears whittled and his old hide scorched
In the most artistic way.

One very fine day Sandy Bob
Threw his seago down,
"I'm tired of riding day by day,
And I allow we're a-goin to town."

They saddled their ponies and struck a lope,
Not being a very long ride
'Twas the good old days when an old cowboy
Could wet up his old inside.

They started in at the Kentucky Bar,
At the head of Whiskey Row,
They ended up at the Depot House,
Some seventy drinks below.

Then they got their horses and started out,
Carrying a pretty good load,
When who should they meet but the Devil himself
Come a prancing down the road.

"Hi there, you ornery cowboy bums,
You better be a-huntin' your holes;
I've come all the way from Hell's Rim Rock
Just to gather in cowboys' souls.

"No, you don't," said Sandy Bob,
For he was a-feeling tight;
"You'll gather in no cowboy souls,
Without you put up a hell of a fight."

He taken down his old seago,
And he threw it strong and true;
He roped the Devil right around the horns,
And he took his dallies, too.

Rusty Jigs, riata man,
Catgut coiled nice and neat,
He took it down and built a loop,
And he roped the Devil's hind feet.

They stretched him out and they tied him down,
While their irons was a-gettin' hot;
They swallow forked and cropped his ears,
Then they burned him up a lot.

They pruned his horns with a dehorning saw,
Tied knots in his tail for a joke;
Then they went off and left him there,
Tied up to a black jack oak.

If you're ever up in the Soughrty Peaks,
And you hear a terrible wail;
You'll know it's the Devil bellowing around,
With the knots tied in his tail.

Field Collections and Manuscripts: Turner to McCulloh, September 20, 1974; Turner-Logsdon interview, May 8, 1986; LC-AFS, 9145 B2; Fife Folklore Archives, FAC I 29, FAC I 115, FAC I 139, FAC I 203, FAC I 264, FAC I 270, FAC I 485, FAC I 605 (p. 13), FAC I 606 (p. 10), FAC I (609), FAC I 611, FAC I 643, FAC I 667 (p. 11), FAC I 540; Culwell (1976), pp. 176, 184; Scroggins (1976), pp. 246–47.

References: Edwards (1986), pp. 50–52; Fife and Fife (1969) pp. 201–3; Fowke (1962), p. 253; Gardner (1935), pp. 6, 9–10, (1967), pp. 7–9, (1987), pp. xiii, 1–2; German (1929 and 1932), n.p.; Larkin (1931), pp. 65–68; Laws (1964), B 17, p. 141; Lee (1933), pp. 167–69, (1936), pp. 12–13, (c. 1941), pp. 149–51; K. Lee (1976), pp. 43–45; Lingenfelter, Dwyer, and Cohen (1968), pp. 358–59; A. Lomax (1960), pp. 365, 388–89; Lomax and Lomax (1934), pp. 406–9; *900 Miles* (1965), pp. 68–69; Ohrlin (1973), pp. 69–72, 259–60; Silber (1967), pp. 283–85; Tinsley (1981), pp. 158–61; Trimble (1982), pp. 150–54; White (1975), pp. 117–25.

Recordings: Rex Allen, *Boney Kneed Hairy Legged Cowboy Songs*, JMI Records JMI 4003; Bob Archer, *The Dean of Cowboy Singers*, Columbia CS 9032; Earsel Bloxham, on *When the Work's All Done This Fall*, Montana Folklife Project MFP 0001; Wilf Carter, *Calgary Horseman's Hall of Fame*, RCA CAL/CAS-943; Cartwright Brothers, on *When I Was a Cowboy*, Morning Star 45008; Yodeling Slim Clark, *A Living Legend*, Palomino PAL 309; Travis Edmonson, on *Ten Thousand Goddam Cattle*, Katydid KD-19976 and *Liar's Hour*, Latigo (no number); Gail Gardner, on *Cowboy Songs*, Arizona Friends of Folklore AFF 33-1 and *Songs of Local History and Events*, Music Division, Library of Congress LBC 12; George Gillespie, "Campfire" *Songs of the Old West*, Thorne TR 200; Sam Hinton, *Singing Across the Land*, Decca DL 8108; Cisco Houston, Disc 608, *Cowboys Songs*, Folkways FA 2022, and *Traditional Songs of the Old West*, Stinson SLP 37; Harry Jackson, *The Cowboy*, Folkways FH 5723; Peter LaFarge, *Songs of the Cowboys*, Folkways FA 2533; Jack and Kitty Lee, Victor 23527, Montgomery Ward 4462, reissued on *Authentic Cowboys and Their Western Folksongs*, RCA LPV-522; Rosalie Sorrels, *Folksongs of Idaho and Utah*, Folkways FH 5343; Red Steagall, *Cowboy Favorites*, Delta DLP 1160; Nevada Slim Turner, *Songs of the Wild West*, 3, Rural Rhythm RRNS 164.

20*

"THEY'RE DOWN AND THEY'RE DOWN"

Alternate Titles:
"Arizona Boys and Girls," "Texas Boys,"
and "Cheyenne Boys"

This is a cowboy adaptation of a widespread satire on the manners of frontier people. It has appeared in a localized, or in this case applied to an occupation, form in different collections.

Riley Neal's version is similar to the one John A. Lomax used in 1910 with the title "Arizona Boys and Girls," in which the refrain "And they're down, down, and they're down" is heard. But Jack Thorp, in his copy of Lomax's book, marked through the refrain, and in his 1921 edition used no refrain. In Missouri, there was no refrain, and the song was about "Texas Boys." In Nebraska, the fourth line of each verse was repeated, and it was called the "Cheyenne Boys." Each state apparently had its own derogatory version about another state, but the cowboy version made no mention of states. Instead, someone, at an unknown time, gave it the title "Arizona Boys and Girls" even though Arizona is not mentioned in the text.

Norm Cohen in the 1982 abridged edition of Randolph's *Ozark Folksongs* (and in a letter to me) quoted a similar opening verse to sheet music published in 1841 under the title "Free Nigger." The songs are indeed related. No author/composer credits were included on the sheet music, which may indicate that it was taken from oral tradition. Because it was sung in eastern theaters during the 1840s, it is possible that the western versions were parodies of "Free Nigger."

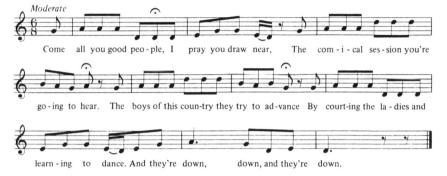

Come all you good people, I pray you draw near,
The comical session you're going to hear.
The boys of this country they try to advance
By courting the ladies and learning to dance.
And they're down, down, and they're down.

They go to the dances, their whiskey they'll take,
And out in the dark their bottles they'll break.
You'll hear one say, "There's another round here,
So come on, boys, we'll all have a share."
And they're down, down, and they're down.

They'll go in the dance hall, their spurs on their heels,
They'll get them a partner to dance the first reel.
It's "How do I look in my new brown suit,
And my pants stuffed down in my high heeled boots?"
And they're down, down, and they're down.

I think it's quite time that we left off these lads
For here are some girls that's nearly as bad.
They fluff and they flounce, they lace and they flair,
In front of the mirror like an owl they will glare.
And they're down, down, and they're down.

They go to the church house, their snuff box in hand,
They'll give it a tap to make it look grand.
And perhaps there is another or two
They'll pass it around and it's "Madam, won't you"
And they're down, down, and they're down.

You can tell a good girl where ever they're found;
No primping, no lacing, no creations bound,

Just a long tailed bonnet tied under their chin,
They're just the ones to catch all the young men.
And they're down, down, and they're down.

Field Collections and Manuscripts: Scroggins (1976), pp. 28–29.

References: Belden (1940), pp. 426–28; Cox (1925), p. 253; Lomax (1910 and 1916), pp. 211–13; Lomax and Lomax (1938, 1986), pp. 256–258; Pound (1922, 1972), pp. 175–76; Randolph, 3 (1949, 1980), pp. 12–14; Randolph and Cohen (1982), pp. 277–278; Thorp (1921), pp. 1–2.

Recordings: F. E. Abernethy, "Texas Boys," *Singin' Texas*, E-Heart Press, Cassette EH-4-83; Cousin Emmy, Brunswick OE 9258; Merrick Jarrett, *The Old Chisholm Trail*, Riverside 12-631.

21.*

"THE BUCKSKIN SHIRT"

Alternate Titles:
"The Roving Gambler," "The Gambling Man,"
and "Rambling Gambling Man"

In Riley Neal's variant of "The Roving Gambler," the hero is a cowboy not a gambler, and the setting is Dallas. For seven verses the story follows the "Gambler" structure and action, but verses eight, nine, and ten are from the family of songs that begin "I would not marry a —————" or "A ————— for me"—any occupation completes the statement. The final verse is from the "Gambler," but instead of going to prison, the cowboy marries "the pretty little girl"—a situation working cowboys saw as analogous to prison. The story starts from a male perspective, as do "Gambler" variants, but it moves to a female perspective similar to most "A ————— for me" variants.

Because both song types have similar characteristics, it is possible that one is a variant of the other. However, Norm Cohen in *Long Steel Rail* refers to "A Railroader for Me" as a courting song that is sung about soldier boys, farmer boys, and other occupations and is not convinced that songs of this type are variants of the "Gambler" type, or vice-versa. Although there are similar verses within each type, the structure and point of view vary.

The "Roving Gambler" song family tells the story of a rambling, roving, or traveling man who lands in a town, meets, and romances one or more girls. A girl tells her mother she loves and will marry him in spite of the mother's objections. The final verse tells of happy marriage or deception; the "Roving Gambler" often leaves the girl, kills a "cheating" gambler, and is imprisoned. But the "Gambler" lineage is impressive; the English version is usually "The Roving Journeyman," and in Ireland, it is "The Rambling Irishman." The song's subject travels to Australia and Canada as well as the United States, where he became the gambler.

The three "I would not marry . . ." verses have no impact on this variant; their absence would not be missed. Riley's tune, with the exception of the first phrase, is the standard country-western melody used by many recording artists. In fact, as a teen-ager I learned the version sung by the western swing star, Hank Thompson, and because the chord progression was the standard and simple I-IV-V (*D–G–A*) structure, it was the first song I learned to play on the guitar. G. Malcolm Laws, Jr., in *Native American Balladry* (1964) states that the "Gambler" variants are legion, and practically every state has had a variant recorded. This cowboy variant appears to be unique.

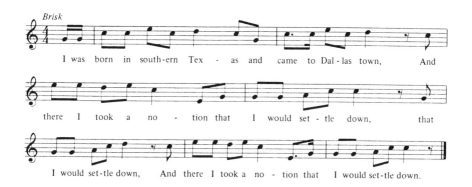

I was born in southern Texas and came to Dallas town,
And there I took a notion that I would settle down, that I would
  settle down,
And there I took a notion that I would settle down.

The years that I had been there was one and two and three,
When I fell in love with a pretty little girl and her in love with
  me, and her in love with me,
When I fell in love with a pretty little girl and her in love with
  me.

I asked her to marry me and with me run away,
She said, "I'll ask my mother and see what she would say, and
  see what she would say."
She said, "I'll ask my mother and see what she would say."

She got her in the parlor and cooled me with her fan,
And whispered low in her mother's ear, "I love that cow man, I
     love that cow man."
And whispered low in her mother's ear, "I love that cow man."

"He asked me to marry him and with him run away,
I told him that I'd ask you and see what you would say, and see
     what you would say,
I told him that I'd ask you and see what you would say."

"Oh! Daughter, dearest daughter, how could you treat me so,
To leave your dear old mother and with the cowboy go, and
     with the cowboy go,
To leave your dear old mother and with the cowboy go?"

"Oh! Mother, dearest mother, 'tis true I love you well,
But the love I have for the wild cowboy is more than tongue
     can tell, is more than tongue can tell,
But the love I have for the wild cowboy is more than tongue
     can tell.

"I would not marry a farmer who toils in the dirt,
I'd rather marry the wild cowboy who wears a buckskin shirt,
     who wears a buckskin shirt,
I'd rather marry the wild cowboy who wears a buckskin shirt.

"I would not marry a merchant who handles all his wealth,
I'd rather marry the wild cowboy who wears a pistol and a
     belt, who wears a pistol and a belt,
I'd rather marry the wild cowboy who wears a pistol and a
     belt.

"I would not marry a banker who handles his silver and gold,
I'd rather marry the wild cowboy who rides through the heat
     and the cold, who rides through the heat and the cold,
I'd rather marry the wild cowboy who rides through the heat
     and the cold."

And now that we are married and live on the lone prairie,
A happier little couple you seldom ever see, you seldom ever
     see,
A happier little couple you seldom ever see.

Field Collections and Manuscripts: LC-AFC 2833 B2, 455 A, 60 B1, 827 B2,
1594 A1, 859 B2, 2638 A1, 826 B1, 1522 B, 835 A3, 1818 B2, 1610 A1; Fife Folklore

Archives, FAC I 404, FAC I 447; Culwell (1976), pp. 143, 174; Gelber (1963), pp. 67–68.

References: Brand (1961), p. 183; Cohen (1981), pp. 461–65; Fowke (1981), pp. 86–88; Hood (1977), p. 235; Kennedy (1975), pp. 781, 800–1; Laws (1964), H 4, pp. 231–32; *900 Miles* (1965), pp. 64–65; *Reprints from Sing Out!* (1964) pp. 18–19; Rosenberg (1969), p. 109.

Recordings: Elton Britt, *The Best of Britt*, RCA LPM-2669; Crockett's Kentucky Mountaineers, Paramount 3302; Vernon Dalhart, Edison 51584, Romero 330, and Paramount 3018; Logan English, *Gambling Songs*, Riverside 12-643; Woody Guthrie and Cisco Houston, *Cowboy Songs*, Stinson SLP 32; Kelly Harrell, *The Complete Kelly Harrell*, Bear Family BF 15508; Cisco Houston, *Cisco Sings*, Folkways FA 2346; Burl Ives, *The Wayfaring Stranger*, Columbia CL 628 and *Return of the Wayfaring Stranger*, Columbia CL-5068; Alan Lomax, *Texas Folksongs*, Tradition TLP 1029; John Jacob Niles, *Sings Folk and Gambling Songs*, Camden CAL 219; Carson Robison, *The Immortal Carson Robison*, Glendale GL 6009; Hank Thompson, *Songs for Rounders*, Capitol ST 1246 and *Hank Thompson*, Hilltop JS 6057; Welby Toomey, Gennett 6005; Nevada Slim Turner, *Songs of the Wild West*, 4, Rural Rhythm RRNS-165.

22.*

"ROOT, HOG, OR DIE"

David Ewen, in *American Popular Songs From the Revolutionary War to the Present*, attributes the words and the tune of this song to Richard J. McGowan in 1856. It quickly became a blackface minstrel favorite, and because the tune was easily remembered, lyric writers have often used it, a practice that has continued into the twentieth century.

In 1858, "Root, Hog, or Die" appeared in *Charley Fox's Ethiopian Songster*, "the only authorized edition of Banjo Songs, Duetts, Trios, and C. Composed and Sung by C. H. Fox," as compiled by E. Byron Christy. In 1859, *Beadle's Dime Song Book: A Collection of New and Popular, Comic and Sentimental Songs* carried four different versions. The *Arkansas Traveller's Songster* of 1864 included another variant, and the list of songsters goes on and on—almost to suggest that one was incomplete if it did not include at least one variant of "Root, Hog, or Die." But they were all "clean" songs. G. Malcolm Laws, Jr., classified it as a cowboy and pioneer song (B 21). The text I collected is much different from other texts, similar only by title. I found only one other bawdy variant; it is in the Lomax papers at the University of Texas, Austin.

Riley Neal's version is a genuine cowboy song about Arizona. The ranch area could easily be around Payson or Camp Verde or farther into the Mogollon Rim country; but the ranch is unimportant, for the cowboy's trouble starts in Phoenix. There he meets a friendly young lady who gives him a dose of a disease that made him lose the head of his "root, hog, or die," or in polite company—his penis.

The "hot springs" referred to may well have been the Verde Hot

Springs between Payson and Camp Verde, where hot baths were taken as a cure or relief for a variety of ailments by both Indians and whites. However, there were hot springs in Southern Arizona, as well.

Riley commented, "I just remembered this filthy old song, but I thought that as long as you had the rest of them, you may as well have it, too. I learned it from a young cowpuncher named Martin Marcoot, who was around Payson for a year or two along in the early 1920s. He was raised around Tucson, I think. He played the guitar and sang; he was quite an entertainer."

Moderate

I was born in In - di - an - a,   a   state   you all know well,   But I

moved to Ar - i - zo - na,   that coun-try hot as hell;   I   had a no-tion in my head, cow-

punch-ing I would try,   Nev-er think-ing what I'd do a-bout   my   root, hog,   or die.

I was born in Indiana, a state you all know well,
But I moved to Arizona, that country hot as hell;
I had a notion in my head, cowpunching I would try,
Never thinking what I'd do about my root, hog, or die.

I got a job upon a ranch, one hundred miles away,
Up north from old Phoenix, and there I had to stay,
Until the next spring came around, and then we had to go
And drive those steers to market, on a journey long and slow.

When we got to Phoenix, and the cattle were all sold,
The cowboys spread out over town to buy themselves some
    clothes;
We got our shaves and baths, and then struck out to try
To see if we could find release for our root, hog, or die.

I met a fair young maiden; her glances were so sly
That I thought I'd make a try for my root, hog, or die;
She Said, "Go get some lemons and some good old rock and
    rye,
And then I'll see what I can do for your root, hog, or die."

We went up to her room, and my prick it quickly rose,
Before I got it in the bitch, I shot it all over her clothes;
I took her in my arms, "Now, baby, don't you cry,
I'll get another hard on, and we'll root, hog, or die."

About nine days from this date, my prick began to swell;
If cursing would have sent the bitch, she would have surely
    been in Hell;
When I went to piss, my asshole was on fire,
And I had a dozen shankers on my root, hog, or die.

I went to see a doctor, saying, "Doctor, I am sick."
The first damn thing he said to me was, "Let me see your
    prick."
He pulled it out and twisted it, my God, he made me cry.
He says, "You've got a case of root, hog, or die!"

He gave to me some medicine, the stuff it stunk like hell,
He says, "If you'll only take it, it will surely make you well."
    .   .   .   .
    .   .   .   .

For six long weeks I taken it—the bastard how he lied!
That's how I lost the head off my root, hog, or die:
Come all you young punchers and listen to me,
Don't be so quick to stick your prick in everything you see.

For if you do you'll surely rue, and you will be like I,
You'll have to go to the hot springs with your root, hog, or die;
The way had been long and weary, that's why I was so quick to
    try;
That's why I lost the head off my root, hog, or die.

Field Collections and Manuscripts: Lomax (Mss.), Folder 2E397 (bawdy variant).

References: For references and information about non-cowboy and non-bawdy variants, see *The Arkansas Traveler's Songster* (1864), p. 46; *Beadle's Dime Song Book* (1859), pp. 38–41; Christy (1858), pp. 32–33; Ewen (1966), p. 331; Laws (1964), B 21, p. 143; Lingenfelter, Dwyer, and Cohen (1968), pp. 58–59; Silber (1967), pp. 142–44.

III

OTHER SONGS
COWBOYS SING

23*

"THE WHOREHOUSE BELLS
WERE RINGING"

This is the eighth song that Riley Neal sang during the morning of my first visit in 1968. It appears to be a bawdy version of the 1893 sentimental song "The Fatal Wedding." The music was composed by Gussie L. Davis, the first successful black Tin Pan Alley composer; three years later he composed the music and wrote the words to "In the Baggage Coach Ahead," which became his most popular song, as well as a folk and country music standard. "The Fatal Wedding," with words by H. W. Windom, quickly became a favorite in minstrel shows and vaudeville. The melody uses phrases from Mendelssohn's "Wedding March," and the story is a classic example of sentimental tragedy. The lyrics describe a wedding scene in which the bride and groom are confronted by another wife, who carries the groom's baby. As she shows the baby to the preacher to prove her story, the baby dies. The parents of the bride take her and the outcast wife away and swear to care for the outcast "through life." The husband commits suicide:

No wedding feast was spread that night, two graves were made
   next day,
One for the little baby, and in one the father lay.

This was an excellent song for a cynical humorist to transform into a bawdy song.

There are other songs patterned after "The Fatal Wedding" that could have been the inspiration for "The Whorehouse Bells Were Ringing" such as "Those Wedding Bells Shall Not Ring Out" and "The Church

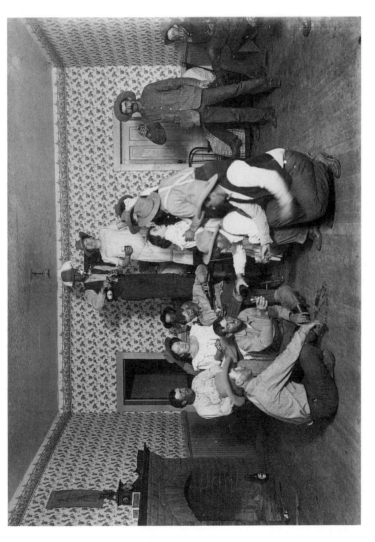

Cowboys having a beer party in a "house" with three, possibly four, ladies in attendance (ca. 1907). The cowboys appear to be relaxing after a hard day in the saddle; the cowboy in the forefront has not removed his spurs. (The Erwin E. Smith Collection of the Library of Congress on deposit at the Amon Carter Museum, Fort Worth.)

Bells Are Ringing for Mary," but "The Whorehouse Bells Were Ringing" melody is closer to "The Fatal Wedding" than it is to the other songs. In his collection *Southern Folk Ballads*, William K. McNeil provides additional information about Davis and Windom.

Vance Randolph collected "The Fatal Wedding" and a fragment (the first verse only) of "The Whorehouse Bells Were Ringing." The fragment came from a man in Eureka Springs, Arkansas, who told Randolph that he had learned it in Moberly, Missouri, in 1912:

> The whore-house bells were ringing,
> A man stood in the door,
> He'd fucked all night the night before,
> And was back to fuck some more.

This is the only variant that I found. Riley's comment about the song, after singing it, may be the most appropriate: "That one was just plumb nasty."

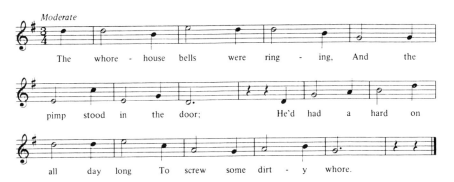

The whorehouse bells were ringing,
And the pimp stood in the door;
He'd had a hard on all day long
To screw some dirty whore.

At last his choice being made,
They went upstairs and pulled off their clothes;
He asked her if she'd suck him off,
And blow it through her nose.

"Oh, no! Oh, no!" the old bitch cried,
Her head was full of snuff,
"I'd like to suck your juicy cock,
But blowing is too tough.

"But I know a game we both can play,
You'll like it when we are through;
I will suck your juicy prick,
While you lick out my flue."

The whorehouse bells were ringing,
While this pair's upstairs in bed,
Trying to get their guns off first
Into each other's head.

Field Collections and Manuscripts: Randolph (Mss.) pp. 573–74.

"The Fatal Wedding":
    References: McNeil (1987), pp. 110–12; Randolph, 4 (1948, 1980), pp. 277–79; Spaeth (1927), pp. 172–74.
    Recordings: Ernest V. Stoneman, Edison 52026.

24.*

"LORENA"

No collection of cowboy songs has included "Lorena," for most singers and collectors associate it with the Civil War, not with cowboys. Indeed, it was popular not only with Confederate troops as is usually stressed, but among Union troops as well. It often is written that "Lorena" did not gain popularity until the soldiers adapted it to their longing for their sweethearts and homes; in fact, the song became an instant success following its publication in 1857. "Lorena" was a national sweetheart before the outbreak of warfare.

The poet, H. D. L. Webster, and the composer, J. P. Webster, who collaborated to write "Lorena" were not related. In 1848, the poet, Henry De Lafayette Webster, was a twenty-four-year-old Universalist church minister in Zanesville, Ohio. There he met nineteen-year-old Martha Ellen Blocksom, who was living in Zanesville with her sister and brother-in-law. A steady courtship developed between Henry and "Ella," and, apparently, after a year of friendship, they reached an understanding. But Ella's sister, wanting a better future for Ella than a small-town minister could provide, made them stop their courtship. Although both were shattered, they abided by the sister's decision, and Henry soon left Zanesville. He spent his life as an itinerant minister. Both he and Ella eventually married other mates and enjoyed successful, happy lives.

Joseph Philbrick Webster was a musician who, through natural talent combined with musical study under the direction of such teachers as Lowell Mason and George James Webb, had directed his efforts toward composition. He developed wanderlust, traveled as a piano salesman,

Roundup wagon and crew leaving the + L Ranch headquarters, Prairie Cattle Company, Ltd., New Mexico, circa 1893. It is probable that some of these cowboys were friends of N. Howard, "Jack" Thorp. (Courtesy of the Museum of New Mexico, Santa Fe.)

music teacher, and composer, and eventually settled in Madison, Indiana. There he and Henry Webster became friends.

In 1856, Joseph went to Henry with a new melody that he knew had potential; he needed an appropriate sentimental poem that would fit the music. Henry Webster, who still loved the girl in Zanesville, wrote his poem, but he made alterations to the setting in order to save her from embarrassment—a poetic consideration that did not work. When "Lorena," not "Ella," was published in 1857, Zanesville friends knew the true identity of "Lorena." (For the complete story, see Ernest K. Emurian's *The Sweetheart of the Civil War*.)

"Lorena" was the consistent sentimental favorite during the last half of the nineteenth century but a sequel—the girl's reply, "Paul Vane" (1863)—did not have its popular appeal. However, Joseph P. Webster collaborated with another friend to publish the timeless song, "In the Sweet By and By."

The popularity of "Lorena" among the Civil War soldiers may have been the reason for its popularity among the cowboys, but more likely it was the cowboys' lonely lives that made them respond to the loneliness of the lost love expressed in the song. Whatever the reason, "Lorena" was widely sung among cowboys. John A. Lomax wrote that the cowboy "had his favorites among the popular airs of his time. . . . such songs as 'Darling, I Am Growing Old' and 'Lorena.'" In 1908, Sharlot M. Hall wrote about Arizona cowboys and their work:

> A puncher turned impatiently: "Say, some of you that *can* sing, tune up. I've heard Lorena put them steers to sleep all I can stand. I'll bet Lorena's bedded down more cattle an' milled more stampedes than any song that ever struck the range."

> "Don't you all be makin' of Lorena none," said the trail boss. "Me an' Tex, we walked on foot clean from Virginny to the Rio Grande, an' that old song sounded mighty good when we heard some other old Grayback singin' it . . . (p. 216).

Will C. Barnes, the early Arizona cowboy, forest ranger, and writer, told about other Arizona cowboys and "Lorena." He knew a cowboy who had one leg that was six inches shorter than the other and because of the problems with his gait and his horses, he was known as "Fall-Back Joe." Joe was not the best of singers, but he always started with "Lorena":—"I can see and hear Joe right now, sitting on a bed roll by the fire, making a perfect wreck of Lorena, musically and poetically. . . . Once in the

Bucket of Blood Saloon in Holbrook, Arizona, the boys were celebrating the departure of the last trainload of Hash Knife steers for the season. In the height of the revelry someone called upon Fall-Back Joe to sing Lorena. The whole bunch was in just the maudlin, sentimental condition that would cause the most hardboiled fire-eating cow-puncher to shed tears as large as Mexican beans over a sentimental song . . ." (p. 122).

This is a good example of how sentimental songs were absorbed into folk culture. In fact, tears came to Riley Neal's eyes when he sang the older sad songs. Riley remembered only four verses of "Lorena": verses one, two, five, and six as originally published, and they were almost identical to the original wording.

The years creep slowly by, Lorena,
The snow is on the grass again;
The sun's low down the sky, Lorena,
The frost gleams where the flowers have been.
But the heart throbs on as warmly now
As when the summer days are nigh;
Oh, the sun can never dip so low
A-down affection's cloudless sky.

A hundred months have passed, Lorena,
Since last I held that hand in mine,
And felt that pulse beat fast, Lorena,

Through mine beat faster far than thine;
A hundred months, 'twas flowery May
When up the sunny slope we climbed
To watch the dying of the day,
And hear the distance church bells chimed.

Yes, these were words of thine, Lorena,
They burn within my memory yet.
They touched some tender cords, Lorena,
Which thrill and tremble with regret.
'Twas not thy woman's heart that spoke—
Thy heart was always true to me—
A duty stern and pressing broke
The tie which linked my soul with thee.

It matters little now, Lorena,
The past is in the eternal past;
Our heads will soon lie low, Lorena,
Life's tide is ebbing out so fast.
There is a future, oh, thank God!
Of life it is so small a part!
'Tis dust to dust beneath the sod;
But there, up there, 'tis heart to heart!

Field Collections and Manuscripts: LC-AFS 1792 B2, 3351 A1; Fife Folklore Archives, FAC I 353, FAC I 706.

References: Barnes (1925); Belden (1940), p. 222; de Charms (1966), p. 141; Dolph (1942), pp. 335–37; Emurian (1962), pp. 20–25; Ewen (1966), pp. 232–33; Hall (1908); Hubbard (1961), pp. 130–32; Jackson (1976), pp. 121–25, 274–75; Lomax and Lomax (1938), p. xvii; Moore (1964), pp. 367–68; Pound (1922, 1972), p. xxiii; Randolph, 4 (1948, 1980), pp. 257–58; Rosenberg (1969), p. 75; Silber (1960), pp. 115, 119, 134–36.

Recordings: Johnny Cash, Columbia B-2155, on *Country Music in the Modern Era*, New World Records NW 207; Thomas Pyle, on *The Confederacy*, Columbia DL 220.

25.*

"MY LULA GAL"

Alternate Titles:
"My Lula Gal," "Lula," "My Lulu," "Bang Away, My Lulu,"
"Bang, Bang Lulu," "She Is a Lulu," and many more

"**L**ula" or "Lulu" has traveled thousands, maybe millions, of miles through many decades from camp to camp and from generation to generation. She has been good, and she has been bad. Whatever her origin, she still lives in song, if not in cow camps, than at least in fraternity houses.

Credit for the first printed mention of Lula among the cowboys belongs to Owen Wister, who had the hero in *The Virginian* (1902) sing one verse (the same as Riley Neal's first verse). Wister wrote that the other seventy-eight verses were unprintable—an early indication that not all cowboy songs were pure and romantic. Fortunately, Wister did not expurgate or bowdlerize Lula and print fifteen or so verses that would have given Lula's virginity back to her.

In his article published in the *Saturday Evening Post* in 1925, Will C. Barnes wrote that: "One of the most celebrated of all range songs is known as My Lula Gal. This lady's amours, escapades, flirtations and general cussedness are told in hundreds of verses, mostly the work of local poets and with considerable local color. George Pattullo, the well-known story writer, once said he had heard about two hundred verses so far in his young life, and only half a dozen could be sung in polite society" (p. 128). Following Barnes's enticing comment were three verses that could and did escape the censor's scissors.

Robert W. Gordon received at least five variants during the 1920s; Randolph collected six in the Ozarks; Carl Sandburg knew the song; Kenneth Larson collected it in Idaho; and Gershon Legman probably

Cowboys and two young wranglers take time for lunch at their campsite in New Mexico (circa 1890). The lady sitting under the tree is probably the photographer's wife, not "My Lula Gal." (Courtesy of the Museum of New Mexico, Santa Fe.)

has found more variants than anyone else. A cleansed variant was included in the Brown-North Carolina collection; and John W. Thomason, Jr., in *Fix Bayonets!* (1926) tells that a "brazen-throated gunnery sergeant" led a U. S. Marine platoon in singing "Bang Away, Lula" while they were stationed in France during World War I (p. 68). However, even though "Lula" was well known among soldiers of many nations, Edward Arthur Dolph in *Sound Off!* emphasizes that "she was a myth, an ideal," who possessed such beauty and sex appeal that her admirers would have delighted in being any intimate object in her life. The feelings and thoughts expressed by soldiers were so intimate that Dolph would include only the opening verse; he was confident that a million men would understand. No longer do veterans and military personnel have to "understand," for Anthony Hopkins in *Songs from the Front and Rear* (1979) and C. W. "Bill" Getz in *The Wild Blue Yonder* (1986) include the uncensored Lula known and loved by servicemen.

The variants continue and continue. Richard Reuss collected a most interesting variation in setting and used it in his 1965 thesis about songs collected among American college students. He found that "Lulu" had become an acquaintance of many fraternity brothers and was found at football games and other collegiate activities. "Lulu" also was and is known in other countries as well.

John A. Lomax did not include "Lulu" in his 1910 edition of *Cowboy Songs and Other Frontier Ballads*, yet it is difficult to believe that he had not heard of her. In the 1938 edition, "Lula" or "Lulu" appeared as a woman who could readily kill her baby but had no obvious sexual bad habits.

The following variant as sung by Riley Neal contains verses related to, or that can be adapted to, a variety of folk songs, which is true of all "Lulu" variants. The first verse could easily be southern black music; "my Lulu gal" could be "my yeller gal" or any other gal. The ninth verse in which Lula makes enough "water" to "wash away a four mule team" is found in "The Ram of Darby" or "The Darby Ram," which is an ancient bawdy song that encourages the singer's ability to exaggerate. The ram's urine, or blood in polite society, exceeds Lula's and can "run twenty-four mile." (For the bawdy version and explication of "The Darby Ram," see Ed Cray, *The Erotic Muse*, pp. 17, 180–81.)

The seventh verse of "Lulu" is related to "Ten Broeck and Mollie" ("Ten Brook and Mollie"), which was composed in 1878 following the famous race that matched the Kentucky thoroughbred, Ten Broeck, against a California mare, Miss Mollie McCarthy. (For the analysis of this song see D. K. Wilgus, " 'Ten Broeck and Mollie': A Race and a Ballad," *Kentucky Folklore Record*, vol. 2, 1956, pp. 77–89.) The phrase "a-shitin' and a-flyin' " is a bawdy variant of "old Ten-Brooks a-flyin'."

The final verse is the same as found in the southern mountain song "Roll in My Sweet Baby's Arms," which is a standard bluegrass number recorded by the Monroe Brothers, Flatt and Scruggs, and many, many more.

The verses reflect Lulu's travels as well as the practice of adapting verses from one song to another. In *The Erotic Muse*, Cray includes a greater diversity of travel and song lineage than I have shown.

Riley said, "I remember hearing that all my life. Some Texan would sing it."

If you monkey with my Lula gal,
I'll tell you what I'll do,
I'll carve around your heart with a razor,
And I'll shoot you with a shotgun, too,
And I'll shoot you with a shotgun, too.

My Lula went to Sunday School,
To learn her A B C's.
She got stuck on the preacher,
And she wouldn't go home with me,
And she wouldn't go home with me.

My Lula went to the circus
The animals for to see;
She got stuck on Jumbo
Because she saw him pee,
Because she saw him pee.

My Lula went to the circus
The animals for to see;
Old Jumbo got a hard on,
And he wouldn't let Lula be,
And he wouldn't let Lula be.

My Lula had a baby,
It was born on Christmas day;
She washed its ass in a wine glass
And named it Henry Clay,
And named it Henry Clay.

My Lula was raised in the country,
She didn't know the law;
They fined her five dollars and fifteen cents
For banging her father-in-law,
For banging her father-in-law.

Got a message from my Lula gal,
It stated that she was dyin';
I jumped a-straddle of the telegraph wire,
And just went a-shitin' and a-flyin',
And just went a-shitin' and a-flyin'.

My Lula went a-fishin',
She was a-fishin' on a rock;
The wing blowed up her petticoat,
And I saw my Lula's cock,
And I saw my Lula's cock.

Did you ever see my Lula make water,
She can throw a beautiful stream;
She can throw it a mile and a quarter,
And wash away a four mule team,
And wash away a four mule team.

My Lula had a baby,
She had it in the grass;
The way she came to have it was
From the wiggling of a cowboy's ass,
From the wiggling of a cowboy's ass.

My Lula's a-goin' to leave me,
I won't know what to do;

I'll wake up in the morning
And I won't have nothin' to screw,
And I won't have nothin' to screw.

I will not work on the railroad,
I will not work on the farm;
I'll lay around town till the sun goes down
And sleep in my Lula's arms,
And sleep in my Lula's arms.

Bawdy variants:

Field Collections and Manuscripts: LC-AFS 4225 A1, 1768 A1; Gordon (Inferno, Mss.) 448, 1109, 3007, 3144, 3912; Randolph (Mss.), pp. 347–51; Larson (Countryside), n.p.; Legman (in Larson's "The Folklore Trade"), n.p; *Shitty Songs of Sigma Nu* (n.d.), n.p; Reuss (1965), pp. 264–68; Scroggins (1976), p. 185.

References: Cray, 1968, pp. 54–56, 157–60; Getz, 2 (1986), pp. BB 9–10; Hopkins (1979), p. 159; *Immortalia* (1927), p. 67, (1960), p. 103; Silverman (1982), pp. 20–21.

Recordings: Oscar Brand, *Bawdy Sea Chanties*, Audio Fidelity AFLP 1884.

Non-bawdy variants:

Field Collections and Manuscripts: LC-AFS 3946 A1 and A3.

References: Barnes (1925); Brown, 2 (1952), pp. 222–23; Dolph (1942); Lomax and Lomax (1934), pp. 182–84, (1938, 1986), pp. 263–64; Sandburg (1927), pp. 378–79; Thomason (1926); White (1975), p. 35; Wister (1902), p. 96.

Recordings: Frank Marvin, Brunswick 320; The Bang Boys, Vocalion 03372; Wilf Carter, Bluebird B-8924, Montgomery Ward 8464, Victor 28046, *Walls of Memory*, RCA Camden CASX-2490; New Lost City Ramblers, *Earth Is Earth*, Folkways 869.

26*

"BORING FOR OIL"

This song may be the oldest bawdy oil occupation song in tradition. In fact, according to Archie Green, renowned scholar of labor lore and folk song, it is the oldest petroleum song of any kind in living tradition. This variant comes from Riley Neal.

Oil City was at the junction of Oil Creek and the Allegheny River in Pennsylvania. Originally known as Cornplanter, the small community became the hub of the petroleum industry shortly after Edwin L. Drake drilled his discovery well a few miles north of Titusville in August 1859. A few years later the petroleum industry grew in importance and moved westward as new fields were discovered. However, refined petroleum was not accepted overnight as a new cheap source of illumination; there were skeptics. The skeptics and the optimistic speculators became the target of topical songwriters of the day. How many "petroleum" songs were written I do not know, but there were many such as "I've Struck Ile," composed in 1865. Again, it is possible that "Boring for Oil" is the bawdy version of an early petroleum industry song, but because no thorough study of the songs of the petroleum industry has been made, it is impossible to determine its exact origin.

Vance Randolph collected three verses from a man who said that he had learned it in Pearl Starr's (Belle Starr's daughter) whorehouse in Fort Smith, Arkansas, around 1910. Randolph collected another variant that had no mention of Oil City and included the venereal disease theme.

In 1985, Professor Doug Wickson of the University of Missouri-Rolla wrote to me with information about Jack Conroy, Randolph's "Boring for Oil" informant. When I called Conroy on July 10, 1985, he related that he was born in 1898 (at the time of our conversation he was eighty-six years old) and was reared in a coal mining camp near Moberly, Missouri. Around 1910, Conroy heard an Irish miner sing the song, "He spoke with a broad Irish accent, probably an immigrant." Conroy did not know where the miner might have learned it, and he did not learn any other bawdy songs from the Irishman or other miners. He continued our conversation with information (told with justifiable pride) about his years as editor of the literary journal *The Anvil*; he claims to be the first editor to publish any of Tennessee Williams's works, as well as the work of others who later gained literary acclaim.

Robert W. Gordon received a three-verse variant from R. M. David of California in 1924. Two variants, one from Michigan in 1938 and the other from Wisconsin in 1940, were recorded and deposited in the Archive of Folk Culture in the Library of Congress. One variant is in the Fife Folklore Archives, and Edith Fowke collected another variant in Ontario, Canada—it is a five-verse version set in Calgary. Riley's version is the most complete of all the variants. He sent the words to me and wrote, "I had not thought of this one for many years, but as I sat here at the table this morning, it suddenly came back to me. I learned it from an old prospector; his name was John Fuller. I don't know when he came—he came here when I was a kid—in my 'teens, anyway. He had a mine over on Spring Creek below Diamond Butte (northeast of Payson). He went crazy finally, and they took him to the asylum—he died in the asylum. I think he was from Tennessee or one of them places back there. Why, he couldn't even read or write."

In the fall of 1983, I sent my collection to Glenn Ohrlin, who replied, "happy to find 'Boring for Oil.' I heard it once. Wallace Brooks sang it back of the chutes one night at the Houston rodeo in 1948. He sang it 'Drilling for Oil.' Wallace was the younger brother of Louis Brooks, all-around champion in '43 and '44." so cowboys, other than Riley, knew and sang "Boring for Oil."

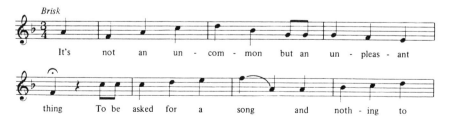

sing; So I'll sing you an old one, if an old one will

do, This world, it's been search-ing for some-thing that's new.

It's not an uncommon but an unpleasant thing
To be asked for a song and nothing to sing;
So I'll sing you an old one, if an old one will do,
This world, it's been searching for something that's new.

I went to Oil City, a place of renown,
To view the oil wells, I looked all around,
Around and around prospecting the soil,
In search of someplace to go boring for oil.

As I was out searching for oil wells one day,
I met a fair damsel and to her did say,
"It's all for a fortune I'm willing to toil
If you'll show me some place to go boring for oil."

"I know of one place, sir," she said with a smile,
"Which I've guarded and protected since I was a child;
I've always been taught, sir, this place not to spoil,
And if you bore there, sir, you're sure to get oil."

She lifted her garments in fear they might soil,
And showed me the place to go boring for oil;
My feelings did tremble, my blood it did boil
As I pulled out my auger to go boring for oil.

I hadn't bored more than six inches I know,
And the oil from my auger so freely did flow;
"My character you've ruined, my garments did soil,
You've bursted the bedrock while boring for oil."

Field Collections and Manuscripts: LC-AFS 2267 A2, 4961 B1; Gordon (Davids, Mss.), 5; Randolph (Mss.), pp. 29–32; Conroy-Logsdon interview, July 10, 1985; Wickson to Logsdon, November 23, 1984; Green to Logsdon, September 17, 1984; Ohrlin to Logsdon, October 4, 1983.
   References: Fowke (1966), pp. 53–54.

27.*

"THE BANKS OF MY NATIVE AUSTRALIA"

Alternate Titles:
"The Maids of Australia" and "The Bush of Australia"

D uring a few years both before and after the turn of the century, cowboys from the United States traveled to South America, South Africa, New Zealand, and Australia to seek work. Some of them, Will Rogers is the best known, worked for wild west shows that toured the world. They took cowboy traditions with them and brought foreign traditions back home. "The Banks of My Native Australia" is probably one such import, but because Australian cowboys came to this country to work in the cattle states, it is also possible that the song immigrated with them.

Lew Pyle sang it to me in 1962 and said that he had learned it many years earlier from a young cowboy, Jamie Holder. In 1968, when Riley Neal sang it, he said that Guy Solomon had brought the song to Payson and that Holder had learned it from Solomon. In fact, the identity of the cowboy or cowboys who brought it back to this country has long since been lost.

At least four men in Arizona knew it by the 1920s, and I found two variants collected in the United States. One is in the Gordon Collection in the Library of Congress and is not as complete as Riley's. The other is in the Lomax papers and is almost as long as Riley's. I found no mention of the song in the printed collections of Australian bawdy songs that were available to me, but it has been included in at least four British collections.

Peggy Seeger and Ewan MacColl in *The Singing Island* reported "The Maids of Australia" to be a "great favorite among country singers in

Cowboys branding a steer during a roundup in Utah, around 1900. (Prints and Photographs Division, Library of Congress.)

Norfolk" (England) and that it had not been reported in Australia. Peter Kennedy (*Folksongs of Britain and Ireland*) collected a variant in Norfolk in 1953, and he cited discussions and controversy about the theme of miscegenation in the English variants. I have difficulty in reading "miscegenation" into Riley Neal's variant; at least his performance and discussion did not imply any awareness of intercourse with a "native."

In the Kennedy variant the action takes place by the "Hawkesborough Banks." The Hawkesborough is a river that flows into the Pacific Ocean approximately twenty-five miles north of New South Wales. Other Norfolk variants state "Oxborough banks" and "Oxberry banks"; the Arizona variant is "Oxbury Branch." This variation of pronunciation opens the possibility that the cowboy variant came by way of England.

The length of verses varies in Riley's version; in the longer verses the basic two-line melody is repeated. The ballad belongs in the "As I walked out" or "As I went walking" family.

As I walked out on the Oxbury Branch,
Where the maids of Australia play their wild pranks,
The forest so wide and the trees were so green,
[I] stood gazing around at this beautiful scene;
On the banks of my native Australia,
Where the maidens grow handsome and free.

As I turned around a maiden there stood,
As naked as Venice [Venus] just sprung from the wood,
Saying, "I came here to bathe, I came here to swim,
I came here to wash off my delicate skin,
In the stream of my native Australia,
Where the maidens grow handsome and free.

"I came here to play, to splash, and to wade,
And I'm sure you'll not harm an innocent maid,
On the banks of my native Australia,
Where the maidens grow handsome and free."

In the water she plunged without fear or doubt,
In a moment her delicate limbs she spread out;
The hair on her snatch being curly and black,
"Watch me, young man, while I swim on my back,
In the streams of my native Australia,
Where the maidens grow handsome and free."

She swam and she swam till she came to the brink.
"Your assistance, kind sir, or I fear I will sink,
In the streams of my native Australia,
Where the maidens grow handsome and free."

Like lightening I flew, caught hold of her hand,
She carelessly slipped and fell back on the sand,
And I entered the bush of Australia,
Where the maidens grow handsome and free.

In about nine months, as the year rolled around,
This maiden she brought forth a very fine son;
The father was sought but could not be found,
'Twas then she remembered her slip on the sand,
In the streams of my native Australia,
Where the maidens grow handsome and free.

Field Collections and Manuscripts: Gordon (Inferno, Mss.), 2010; Lomax (Mss.), folder 2E409.
 References: Kennedy (1975), pp. 412–413, 433; McCarthy (1972), pp. 70–71; Palmer (1980), pp. 239–240, 251; Seeger and MacColl (1960), pp. 14, 22.
 Recordings: *Folk Songs of Britain*, 2, Caedmon TC 143 and Topic 12 T 158.

28.*

"ALL NIGHT LONG"

Alternate Titles:
"Three Old Whores," "Four Old Whores," "Five Women in
Canada," "Three Whores from Canada," "Four Old Whores
of Mexico," "Three Whores of Winnipeg," "Three Old Maids
from Boston," and many more

As the alternate titles suggest, the bragging episodes number between
three and five, and the home of the "old whores" is Canada, Mexico,
or cities in the United States. The women drink either brandy or cherry
wine (in Baltimore it's beer) while they brag or, more correctly, lie about
the size of their sex organs, a practice usually associated with men, not
women.

Gershon Legman has collected numerous variants and researched
its origins and in *The Horn Book* referred to the song as a transformation
of "A Talk of Ten Wives on Their Husbands' Ware," which was first written in manuscript form in 1460. Robert Burns's version had the wives
trying to decide if "their husbands' penises" were "sinew or bone." Cray
in *The Erotic Muse* provides additional comparative texts in the development of this song that some scholars consider to be the oldest surviving
erotic song in the English language.

Visitors who make a trip into the "snatch" vary in occupation; in
Riley Neal's version that follows, two cowboys ride in and stay for four
months.

Moderate, free

Three   old whores in   Mex - i - co   a - drink - ing cher - ry   wine,   The

first one said, "I'll bet your snatch ain't half as big as

REFRAIN

mine." All night long, All night long.

Three old whores in Mexico a-drinking cherry wine,
The first one said, "I'll bet your snatch ain't half as big as
mine."

REFRAIN:
All night long, all night long.

The first one said that hers was as big as all of the moon.
Two cowboys rode in in March and didn't come out till June.

The next old whore said that hers was as big as all of the sea.
A ship sailed in and turned around and waved its flag at me.

The third old whore said that hers was as big as all of the air.
An air-o-plane sailed right in and didn't touch a hair.

Field Collections and Manuscripts: Gordon (Inferno, Mss.), 2432, 2789;
Randolph (Mss.), pp. 78–81; Lomax (Mss.), folder 2E409; LC-AFC (Subject Collection), Bawdy Song Folder; LC-AFC 3323 A1, 2291 A3.
  References: Babad (1972), p. 133; Cray (1965), pp. 25–26, (1969), pp. 4–5,
191–93; Getz, 2 (1986), pp. TT 8–9; Laycock (1982), pp. 223–24; Legman (1964),
pp. 414–15.

29.*

"THE GAY CABALLERO"

Alternate Titles:
"The Spanish Nobilio" and "The Spanish Patrillo"

One of those bawdy songs with variants around the world, "The Gay Caballero" had to be known by many cowboys. Its theme is usually venereal disease or losing an ear and/or testicle to a jealous husband; sometimes, as in Ed Cray's version (1969), all themes are there. Riley Neal knew two variants—one about catching syphilis and the other about losing an ear. He said that he learned them from Martin Marcoot (see "Root, Hog, or Die") in the early 1920s.

Gershon Legman in *The Horn Book* described the melody as a favorite among those who enjoy trying to sing limericks, but too weak for anyone sober to enjoy repeating. Variants have appeared in many collections, with five verses being most common; however, in Harry Morgan's *More Rugby Songs* there are fourteen verses.

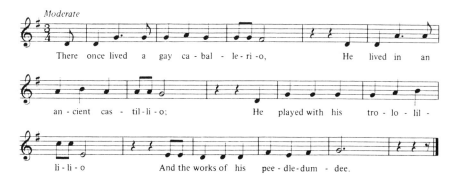

Moderate

There once lived a gay ca - bal - le - ri - o, He lived in an

an - cient cas - til - li - o; He played with his tro - lo - lil -

li - li - o And the works of his pee - dle - dum - dee.

A cow camp near Cimarron, New Mexico, in the late 1880s. The sleeping tents, chuck wagon, and remuda are seen in the background. (Courtesy of the Denver Public Library, Western History Department.)

Text A

There once lived a gay caballerio,
He lived in an ancient castillio;
He played with his trololillio,
And the works of his peedle-dum-dee.

One night he went to a dancillio,
He met a fair señoritio;
He asked her to be his wifillio,
Try the works of his peedle-dum-dee.

He took her into his castillio,
He laid her upon his sofillio;
He pulled out his trololillio,
Tried the works of her peedle-dum-dee.

In nine days he sat on his piassillio,
With cotton all around his trolillio;
He cursed this fair senoritio
And the works of her peedle-dum-dee.

He went to see his doctillio,
To get something done for his trolillio;
He said, "You've got a case of the siffillio,
In the works of your peedle-dum-dee."

Text B

I am a gay caballerio
Coming from Rio de Janerio;
With nice oily hair and full of hot air
I'm an expert at shooting the bullo.

I'm seeking a fair señorita,
Not thin, and yet not too much meata;
I'll woo her awhile in my Argentine style,
I'll carry her off of her feeta.

It was at a gay cabarrito,
While wining and dining I met her;
We drank one or two as other folks do,
The night was wet, but she got wetter.

She was a dancer and singer,
At me she kept pointing her finger,

And saying to me, "Si, si, senor, si, si,"
But I couldn't see a darn thinga.

She told me her name was Estrella,
"Please stick around me, young fella.
Mosquitoes do bite, and they're awful tonight,
And you smell just like sassafrailla."

She told me that she was so lonely,
So I climbed upon her balcony;
But her husband was there,
And I do declare—the bastard bit off my left earo.

Now I am a sad caballerio,
Returning to Rio de Janerio,
Minus my hair and beat up for fair,
Her husband chewed off my left earo.

Field Collections and Manuscripts: Gordon (Inferno, Mss.), 448, 402; Randolph (Mss.), pp. 519–21; Legman (TS VF), n.p.; Hickerson and Hitchcock, reel 2, side B, number 3; Reuss (1965), pp. 261–63.

References: Cray (1965), pp. 83–85, (1969), pp. 90–91, 200–2; Getz, 2 (1986), p. GG 2; Hart-*Immortalia* (1971), pp. 40–43; *Immortalia* (1927), p. 82, (1960), p. 128; Laycock (1982), pp. 224–25; Legman (1964), pp. 440–46; Morgan (1968), pp. 29–31; Silverman (1966), p. 65.

Non-bawdy versions are in the Fife Folklore Archives, and Frank Crumit recorded a clean version, RCA Victor V-2735. No doubt there are additional polite-society versions.

30.*

"CALIFORNIA JOE"

Original Title:
"California Joe and the Trapper Girl"

This song takes much time to sing. It is the nineteenth song that Riley Neal pulled out of his memory the morning of our first recording session. He did not remember all of the verses, but a few months later, when he sent his written version to me, he indicated that his sister had helped with lines that he had forgotten. During the recording session, Lew Pyle sang along with him, indicating that Lew once knew the song. At least four people in the Payson area knew it—Riley, his sister, Lew, and the unidentified person who taught it to them.

California Joe was a genuine frontier character who was immortalized by John Wallace "Captain Jack" Crawford. Although the exact identity of California Joe is not known, in *The Poet Scout* (1886) Captain Jack wrote that the poem was based on a campfire story told by Joe in mid-April 1876, and that Joe, while acting as a guide, was killed at Red Cloud, South Dakota, in December 1876. He also stated that Joe "was a brave, generous, unselfish man, and his only fault was liquor."

John Wallace "Captain Jack" Crawford was as unusual as California Joe. He was born in Donegal, Ireland on March 4, 1847, and at the age of thirteen arrived in Pennsylvania, where his father and mother had immigrated a few years earlier. There he worked in coal mines for $1.75 a week until he joined the Union Army in 1863. On May 12, 1864, while he was only seventeen, he was wounded, and during his hospitalization, was taught to read and write.

Approximately five years after the Civil War, Crawford moved to the Dakotas and became a scout for the army. He was also "captain" of the

Pitching camp on the Matador Ranch range, Texas, 1908. The men who worked the bed wagon duty have already scattered the cowboys' bedrolls around the area. (The Erwin E. Smith Collection of the Library of Congress on deposit at the Amon Carter Museum, Fort Worth.)

Black Hills Rangers (a small home-guard organized in Custer, Dakota Territory, for protection), thus, his title "Captain Jack." His experiences as a scout and prospector provided him with subject matter for poems and plays and provided Ned Buntline material in 1880 for a dime novel about Crawford: *Captain Jack; or the Seven Scouts.* He worked with Buffalo Bill Cody and with other wild west shows, and during his work and travels, he wrote poetry and called himself "The Poet Scout." Crawford's first collection of poetry was published in 1879 under the title *The Poet Scout* and was enlarged and revised in 1886. Other collections were printed before his death in 1917. Paul T. Nolan has written an excellent study of Crawford, *John Wallace Crawford* (1981). Nolan's approach to Crawford is primarily as a playwright rather than a poet; therefore, not much insight into "California Joe" is available. Nolan apparently was unaware that Crawford's immortality was through the folk acceptance of "California Joe," not through the plays that he wrote.

Who set the poem to music and when it happened are not known, but John A. Lomax included the song in his 1910 edition of *Cowboy Songs and Other Frontier Ballads*, however, it was not a complete text. When the 1938 edition appeared, a twenty-six verse text was used, along with credit given to Captain Jack Crawford. The only other collector to include "Cowboy Joe" in a printed collection was Margaret Larkin in her *Singing Cowboy.* In 1971, a California variant was published in *Western Folklore* as collected by Sunny Goodier, and in response to her solicitation for additional information, in 1973 Austin E. Fife provided bibliographical information about no fewer than twenty variants from at least eight states. Jack Thorp in his copy of Lomax (1916) indicated that he had collected the song, but he did not use it in his 1921 edition of *Songs of the Cowboys.*

Riley's version has only eighteen verses, but the story is intact. His memory retained the essential elements of action and love.

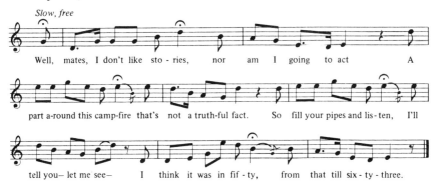

Slow, free

Well, mates, I don't like sto - ries, nor am I going to act A

part a-round this camp-fire that's not a truth-ful fact.   So fill your pipes and lis-ten,   I'll

tell you— let me see—   I   think it was in fif - ty,   from   that till six - ty - three.

Well, mates, I don't like stories, nor am I going to act
A part around this campfire that's not a truthful fact.
So fill your pipes and listen, I'll tell you—let me see—
I think it was in fifty, from that till sixty-three.

I think it was in fifty we camped on Powder River;
We killed a calf of buffalo and fried a slice of liver;
While eating, quite contented, we heard three shots or four;
Put out the fire and listened, and heard a dozen more.

You've all heard tell of Bridger, I used to run with Jim
And many a hard days scouting I've done along side of him.

'Twas near old Fort Reno, a trapper used to dwell;
We called him old Pap Reynolds the scouts all knew him well.
We knew that old Pap Reynolds had moved his traps up here;
So picking up our rifles and strapping on our gear.

We moved as quick as lightning—to save was our desire.
Too late; the painted heathens had set the house on fire.

The cabin burned so fiercely, the light showed all around,
We started looking all about for bodies on the ground.
And there among the bushes a little girl did lie.
I picked her up and whispered "I'll save you or I'll die."

Lord, what a ride! Old Bridger had covered our retreat;
Sometimes the child would whisper in a voice so low and sweet,
"Dear Daddy, God will take him to Mama up above;
There's no one left to love me, there's no one left to love."

The little one was thirteen and I was twenty-two;
I said, "I'll be your father and love you just as true."
She nestled to my bosom, her hazel eyes so bright,
Looked up and made me happy thru the close pursuit that night.

Three years had gone and Maggie—we called her Hazel Eye—
Was really going to leave us, was going to say good-by.
Her uncle, Mad Jack Reynolds, long since reported dead,
Had come to claim my angel, his brother's child, he said.

What could I say? We parted, mad Jack was growing old;
I handed him a bank note and all I had in gold.
They rode away at sunrise, I went a mile or two
And parting said, "God bless you, Mag, may God watch over you."

'Twas a dancing, laughing brook the little cabin stood,
And wearied by the long day's scout, I spied it in a wood.
The pretty valley stretched beyond, the mountains towered above,
And by its willow bank I heard the cooing of a dove.

'Twas one grand pleasure; the brook was plainly seen,
Like a long thread of silver on a cloth of lovely green.
The laughter of the water the cooing of the dove,
Was like a painted picture or some well told tale of love.

While drinking in the country and resting in the saddle
I heard a gentle rippling like the dripping of a paddle,
And turning to the water a strange sight met my view—
A maiden with her rifle in a little bark canoe.

She stood up in the center, her rifle to her eye;
I thought for just one moment my time had come to die.
I tipped my hat and told her, if it was just the same,
She'd better drop her rifle, for I was not her game.

She dropped the deadly weapon and leaped from the canoe.
Said she, "I beg your pardon, sir; I thought you were a Sioux.
Your long hair and your buckskins looked warrior-like and rough;
My bead was spoiled by sunlight, or I would have killed you
     sure enough."

She then began to look at me, she did not seem to know.
At last she said, "I know you, now, you are California Joe."
She then looked upon my fact, and she begin to cry.
I then knew it was Maggie, my long-lost Hazel Eye.

She said, "My dear old uncle in yonder cabin lies."
She said, "I know what ails him, but he is going to die."
We sat upon the mossy bank, her eyes began to fill.
The brook was babbling at our feet, the dove was cooing still.

I took her little hand in mine; she knew not what it meant,
And yet she drew it not away, but rather seemed content.
I put my arms around her, and drew her to my breast
And whispered, "Mag, my darling, once before there you did rest."

We buried her old uncle on a hill not far away;
Up behind the cabin he lies there until this day.
Every spring we visit him, Maggie—my wife—and I,
Sometime we're coming here to live and stay until we die.

Field Collections and Manuscripts: Fife Folklore Archives, FMC I 532, FMC I 540 (p. 6), FMC I 716, FMC I 866, FMC I 983 (p. 3), FMC I 1000, FAC I 210; Culwell (1976), p. 132; Scroggins (1976), pp. 58–61.

References: Crawford (1886), pp. 36–44; Fife (1973), pp. 49–51; Goodier (1971), pp. 133–37; Larkin (1931), 133–37; Lomax (1910 and 1916), pp. 139–46; Lomax and Lomax (1938, 1986), pp. 346–53; Nolan (1981), pp. 17–59; Wolfe (n.d.), pp. 7–8.

Recordings: Ray Reed, *Sings Traditional Frontier and Cowboy Songs*, Folkways FD 5329; Jim Ringer, *Waiting for the Hard Times to Go*, Folk Legacy FSI-47.

31.*

"THE DAYS OF FORTY-NINE"

It is possible that this song was written by a California vaudevillian, Charles Rhoades. In 1965, William L. Alderson conjectured in his study of the song that it could have been written by "the minstrel singer and banjo-artist Charles Bensell," but concluded that it "is probably Charley Rhoades' song."

It is a reflection or reminiscence about the "good old days" of gold mining on the West Coast; the characters are colorful and paint a vivid and humorous portrait of frontier personalities. The song has traveled many miles throughout the years without losing its vitality and humor. Variants retain most of the names, sins, and actions found in the version as printed in 1872 in *The Great Emerson New Popular Songster*. However, Riley Neal knew only five of the ten verses, and although he first heard his father sing it, he learned it "from Joe Gibson."

G. Malcolm Laws, Jr., classified it under "ballad-like pieces," finding it "disunified in narrative action."

Old Tom Moore they call me now, A rel - ic of by - gone days, And a

bum-mer, too, they call me now, But what care I for praise? And

as   I flit from town to town They call   me the ram - bling   sign   Of the

days   of old   and the days of   gold   And the days   of   For - ty - nine.

Old Tom Moore they call me now,
A relic of bygone days,
And a bummer, too, they call me now,
But what care I for praise?
And as I flit from town to town
They call me the rambling sign
Of the days of old and the days of gold
And the days of Forty-nine.

There was "Roaring John," the roaring man,
He could outroar a buffalo, you bet,
He could roar all day and roar all night,
And I guess he's roaring yet;
One night he fell in a prospect hole,
'Twas a roaring bad design,
And in that hole he roared out his soul,
In the days of Forty-nine.

There was "Windy Jake," the butcher boy,
He was always getting tight,
When he'd fill up on red eye,
He was longing for a fight.
One night he met a butcher knife
In the hands of old Bob Sine,
And over Jake they held a wake
In the days of Forty-nine.

There was old "Aunt Jess," that hard old cuss,
He never would relent,
He never missed a single meal
Nor paid a single cent;
When asked for his board bill,
He raised a hell of a whine,
And in his bloom went up the flume
In the days of Forty-nine.

Of all this rambling, gambling crew,
There's few who's left to boast,
And I am left in my misery
Like some poor wandering ghost;
And as I flit from town to town,
They call me the rambling sign
Of the days of old and the days of gold
And the days of Forty-nine.

Field Collections and Manuscripts: LC-AFS 1372 B2, 3694 A1, 3363 A1, 3365 A2; Fife Folklore Archives, FAC I 138, FAC I 205, FAC I 372, FAC I 490; Culwell (1976), p. 136; Scroggins (1976), pp. 110–12.

References: Alderson (1965), pp. 5–10; Allen (1933), pp. 152–54; Botkin (1951), pp. 735–36; Clark (1932), pp. 26–27; Davis (1935), p. 44; Dwyer and Lingenfelter (1965), pp. 189–90; Frey (1936), pp. 76–77; Glassmacher (1934), pp. 67–69; *Hobo News* (n.d.), p. 24; Hubbard (1961), pp. 297–99; Laws (1964), p. 277; Lingenfelter, Dwyer, and Cohen (1968), pp. 558–59; Lomax (1910 and 1916), pp. 9–14; Lomax and Lomax (1938, 1986), pp. 378–81, (1947) pp. 161–62, 180–83; Randolph, 2 (1948), pp. 221–22; Ridings (1936), pp. 334–35; Rogers, *Cowboy . . .* (n.d.), p. 8; Silber (1967), pp. 96–98; *Treasure Chest of Cowboy Songs* (1935), pp. 42–43.

Recordings: Jules Verne Allen, Victor 21627, reissued on *The Texas Cowboy*, Folk Variety FV 12502, reissued as Bear Family BF 15502; Bog Trotters, *Dance Music, Breakdowns and Waltzes*, Music Division, Library of Congress LBC 3; Glenn Ohrlin, *The Hell-Bound Train*, University of Illinois, Campus Folksong Club CFC 301, and *The Wild Buckaroo*, Rounder 0158; George S. Taggart, on *The New Beehive Songster*, Okehdokee OK 75003; Frank Warner, *Hudson Valley Songs*, Disc 661.

32.*

"JOE WILLIAMS"

This song is a parody of "The Son of a Gambolier," more widely known as "The Rambling Wreck from Georgia Tech." The tune has probably been used for a greater variety of lyrics, often bawdy, than any other melody. Sigmund Spaeth in *Read 'em and Weep* stated "variants are numerous, both in text and melody . . . (p. 89). There are many other sets of words to the universal tune, some of them of an unprintable vulgarity . . ."(p. 91). While the song is of probable Irish origin, it has traveled around the world, and George Milburn wrote in *The Hobo's Hornbook* that it "probably, is the earliest hobo song" (p. 183). The tune has not been limited to the life of the hobo, very few occupations have been spared from it and the parodist.

The protagonist of "Joe Williams" is a bull-puncher or ox-driver, apparently from lumbering country. His activities in town with the ladies of pleasure were and are of universal interest among men isolated from women for long periods of time. The problem of the "pox" or a similar irritation has often been proclaimed as an experience suffered by those who sexually "leap before they look." Cowboys certainly visited enough "houses" to inspire Charles Russell to depict a cowboy's work, pleasure, and its aftereffects in a sequence of four watercolors, The Sunshine Series, individually titled "A Little Sunshine," "A Little Rain," "A Little Pleasure, and "A Little Pain" (see pp. 62–63).

I found one variant of this song in the Library of Congress, Archives of Folk Culture, that Alan Lomax recorded in Newberry, Michigan in September 1938. This variant is similar to Riley Neal's but not as long

Cowboys loading bedrolls on the chuck wagon; smaller outfits had to carry their bedding and baggage along with their food in the chuck wagon instead of on a bed wagon, New Mexico, early 1930s. (Guy Logsdon—Jack Thorp Collection.)

and complete; both versions also have similar melodies. One significant variation in words is that the Michigan variant is localized with "driving an ox team in the Comstock lumber woods," whereas Riley's version is, "to punching bulls for the Stock and Lumber Wood." Other variations include reference to the penis as "old Ruben" in the Michigan version, whereas Riley says, "it"; the Michigan variant ends with "Fare well, all you chanty boys," and Riley's audience are "chippy girls." The Michigan version is more specifically a lumberjack song.

Lew Pyle knew "Joe Williams" and said that he had heard a Payson area cowboy, Jamie Holder, sing it "many years ago." However, Lew did not remember as much of the text as did Riley; both men apparently knew the song by 1920. Because logging in the Payson, Arizona, area was and is a major industry, it is possible that the song came to the area through migrant loggers.

Riley's comment when Lew asked him if he knew it was, "That one's awfully ugly." He was correct.

My name it is Joe Williams, my age is twenty-one,
I came out to this country a ramblin' son-of-a-gun.
Like all other old bull-punchers I love my whiskey tod,

I'm a ramblin' wreck of poverty and a son-of-a-bitch for grog.
I went to punching bulls for the Stock and Lumber Wood,
And to hear me cuss and swear, it would do your asshole good.

CHORUS:

> Whoa back, Broad, you long-horned son-of-a-bitch,
> Ballie, if you kick me, I'll slug you till you shit.
> Swamper cut that knot off, you cockeyed son-of-a-whore,
> You can suck my dirty asshole till your upper lip is sore.

I went down to town, I thought I was a man,
I run 'round the streets with my elick in my hand.
On Fifth Avenue I met a pretty lass,
I introduced her to my elick, and I shoved it up her ass.
When it went up in her little gut, she went off in a fit,
And when I pulled it out, it was all covered with blood and
    shit.
The drip ran down her legs, that would run a water mill,
If you was a-feedin' bacon-hogs, it would have made a barrel of
    swill.

CHORUS

> When I got to camp, I found I had the pock,
> I wished I had stayed at home and banged my old off-ox.
> I tied it up in axle grease, I washed it with a rag,
> And I bathed it in cold water, till I wished I was a stag.
> When I went to piss, my whole asshole was on fire,
> And if you think it didn't hurt, you are a goddamned liar.

CHORUS

> Now my song is ended, I'll sing to you no more,
> Farewell, all you chippy girls, farewell, all you whores.
> Now my song is ended, I'll sing to you my last;
> If you don't like my little song, you can suck my dirty ass.

Field Collections and Manuscripts: LC-AFS 2344 A1.

"The Son of a Gambolier":
    References: Milburn (1930); Sandburg (1927), p. 44; Shay (1927), pp. 106–7;
Spaeth (1927). For bawdy variants see Cray (1969), pp. 58–59, 67–69, 229, 243,
248.

33.*

"BAD COMPANY"

Alternate Titles:
"Young Companions" and "Bad Companions"

T his "young man gone bad" ballad could fall within a variety of subject or regional categories. Even though the young man met his fate in Chicago and had traveled no further west, it has been sung by cowboy singers as an outlaw frontier song. After relating the series of events that led him to the scaffold, instead of the usual "don't do as I did" admonition, he ends his tale with, "you may forget the singer, but don't forget the song." Also, he implies that his fate was sealed when he started "drinking." These elements within the song along with its structure imply that it was composed in the late nineteenth century as a temperance or sentimental moralistic song of the times.

Lomax included it in his 1910 edition, but how many years earlier it was composed and by whom are not known. Nothing is known about the murder, for the girl's name is not given, which is contrary to many ballads of this type. All that Riley Neal could say about it was, "It's an old song." It has been included in only a few printed field collections.

Moderate

Come all you young com - pan - ions, and lis - ten un - to

me, I'll tell you all a sad sto - ry of some bad

"The Thirsty Cowpuncher," a drink in hand, on his horse, in the doorway of a saloon. His angora chaps indicate that he is from the cold northern cattle states. (Prints and Photographs Division, Library of Congress.)

com - pa - ny.   I was born   in   Penn - syl - va - nia

a - mong   those beau - ti - ful   hills,   And the   mem - 'ries

of   my   child-hood   is   warm with - in   me   still.

Come all you young companions, and listen unto me,
I'll tell you all a sad story of some bad company.
I was born in Pennsylvania among those beautiful hills,
And the mem'ries of my childhood is warm within me still.

I had a kind old mother, who often would plead with me,
Often she would tell me, "My boy, my boy, I fear."
I had two loving sisters as kind and beautiful as could be.
And down on their knees before me, they prayed and wept for
    me.

I did not like my fireside; I did not like my home.
I had in view for rambling, and far away did roam.

    . . . .
    . . . .

It was then I took to drinking; I sinned both night and day,
And yet within my bosom that feeble voice would say.
"Fare thee well, my loved one, may God protect my boy,
And blessings always be with him throughout his manhood
    joy."

I courted a fair young maiden, her name I will not tell,
For I only disgrace her as I am doomed for hell.
'Twas on one beautiful evening, the stars were shining bright,
That with that fatal dagger, I bid her spirit flight.

But justice overtook me, as you can plainly see;
My soul is doomed forever, throughout eternity.
Now I'm on the scaffold, my moments are not long,
You may forget the singer, but don't forget the song.

Field Collections and Manuscripts: LC-AFS 4147 A2, 552 A, 5253 B1; Fife Folklore Archives, FAC I 496, FAC I 697 (pp. 1,2), FAC I 731 (pp. 4, 11); Scroggins (1976), pp. 264–65.

References: *American Cowboy Songs* (1936), pp. 50–51; Clark (1932), pp. 80–81; Frey (1936), pp. 66–67; Glassmacher (1934), pp. 42–43; Larkin (1931), pp. 103–5; Laws (1964), E 15, p. 183; Lomax (1910 and 1916), pp. 81–82; Lomax and Lomax (1938, 1986), pp. 212–14; Randolph, 2 (1948), pp. 139–41; Randolph and Cohen (1982), pp. 153–54; Rosenberg (1969), p. 144; *Treasure Chest of Cowboy Songs* (1935), pp. 4–5.

Recordings: Carter Family, Victor 40328; Vernon Dalhart, Cameo 8221, re-issued on other labels; Kelly Harrell, Okeh 40544; George Reneau, Vocalion 15150 and 5079; Carl T. Sprague, Victor 19747, reissued on *The First Popular Singing Cowboy*, Folk Variety FV 12001, in turn reissued as Bear Family BF 15002; Ernest Stoneman, Edison 51788; Marc Williams, Brunswick 274; there are additional hillbilly/country recordings of this popular song.

34.*

"HAUNTED FALLS"

Alternate Title: "Haunted Wood"

While one of the least known traditional ballads, this is one of the most powerful. Austin E. and Alta S. Fife wrote that it can be compared it with the greatest of the English and Scottish traditional ballads. It certainly has the tragedy found in many of the great ballads. Yet its origin and age are not known.

Olive W. Burt collected it in Utah, but her informant had learned it from a New Mexico cowboy. The belief was that the story of Indians murdering a mother and her children came from Minnesota, where in 1862, Little Crow, a Sioux chieftain, murdered a German family in revenge for Indians' mistreatment. Yet there are falls and woods throughout the nation that are said to be haunted, and there are numerous states in which such an incident could have occurred. In fact, J. Frank Dobie's informant learned the song in Texas from a grandmother from Alabama. Dobie sensed a "distinct literary flavor," a flavor that is very definite.

For two centuries, writers in this nation produced captivity and massacre stories to incite outbursts against Native Americans. The fictional accounts of brutality kept the flames of hatred leaping from one generation to another. Songs about Indian misdeeds were also composed; yet because no in-depth study of either the stories or the songs against Indians has been made, there is no exact proof that "Haunted Falls" was, indeed, an anti-Indian broadside ballad. It has the necessary ingredients, however.

Because this song has appeared in only a few collections, Riley Neal's version is important. It was recorded on the second day of my first

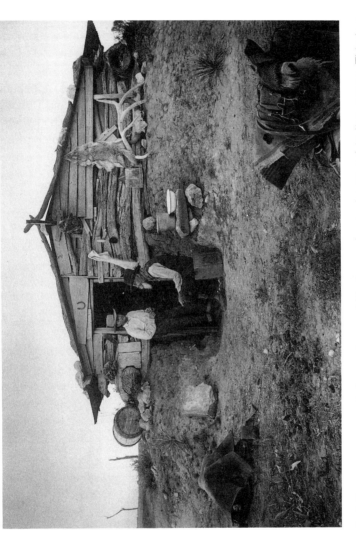

Isolation was an accepted experience of life for cowboys who stayed in line camps. This is a Matador Ranch line camp, Texas, 1908. Judge Henry H. "Paint" Campbell (seated) was the founder of the Matador, and this line camp was the original headquarters in the 1880s. George Patullo, a Boston writer turned cowboy, is visiting with Campbell. (The Erwin E. Smith Collection of the Library of Congress on deposit at the Amon Carter Museum, Fort Worth.)

session with him and was the forty-sixth song during that first visit. He had very little time to think about it and may have known other verses. Nevertheless, although it varies from the versions of the Fifes and of Dobie, the variations are not major. The Fife version has two children, whereas Riley and Dobie tell of three. Dobie has two Indians; Riley three; and the Fifes have "some Indians" as the killers. In Dobie's version the father went to town for meal, whereas in the others he went to get the mail—either purpose is plausible.

The length varies with nine verses in Burt (by far the least appealing variant), twelve in Riley's, and thirteen in both the Fifes' and Dobie's. But the Fifes and Dobie have a different additional verse, which indicates that there were probably at least fourteen verses. The absence of the two verses is not noticed because Riley's version moves into the action and tells the story as dramatically as the others.

Once in olden times a river
Flowed between two mountain walls,
And not far from where it started
Formed a place called Haunted Falls.

On the bosom of this river
There danced many a light canoe,
And there's many tribes of Indians
Scouted from this point of view.

On the bank there lived a white man
With his wife and children three.
And for many years the forest
Echoed back their shouts of glee.

It was one day while the father
To the town for the mail had gone,

Left his wife and little children
For one quiet hour alone.

Hark! the sound of trampling horses—
And the mother turned in fright,
Just in time to bolt the door to,
When three Indians came in sight.

Then she called her frightened children,
Bade them neither speak nor cry,
Locked them in the secret closet,
Then prepared herself to die.

With one angry push, the chieftain
Tore the bolt from off the door,
There he saw this weeping woman
Lying there upon the floor.

Then he shouted to his comrades,
Who had seized a heavy stick,
"Come and help, we'll drown the woman,
Lose no time, I say, be quick!"

Then they seized this weeping woman,
Dragged her there from off the floor,
Caught her by her long brown tresses,
Then they dragged her to the shore.

Cast her on the rocks below them,
Heeding not her piteous cry,
Threw her in the foaming waters,
There in agony watched her die.

'Twas revenge that they had wanted,
'Twas revenge that they had found,
So they burned these sleeping babies
And the dwelling to the ground.

Now the old man wanders lonely
Around the place where the dwelling stood,
And the people of that village
Called that place the Haunted Wood.

Field Collections and Manuscripts: Fife Folklore Archives, FMC I 581, FMC I 993, FAC I 170; LC-AFS 4145 A; Todd-Sonkin 58A.

References: Burt (1958), pp. 144–46; Dobie (1927), pp. 129–30; Fife and Fife (1969), pp. 118–19.

Recordings: Eva Ashley, on *Old Time Music at Clarence Ashley's*, Folkways FA 2355.

35.*

"JUANITA"

In sharp contrast with lost love and murder ballads in which the female is usually the unfaithful party and/or the murder victim, it is the cowboy in "Juanita" who loves and leaves and who is murdered by the young Mexican woman. The only dialogue is spoken by the cowboy, who expresses an extreme lack of concern and sensitivity toward the girl; with a dagger she returns his coolness. The only collection in which "Juanita" has appeared is Austin E. and Alta S. Fife's *Cowboy and Western Songs*; however, there is evidence that it enjoyed some popularity, at least west of the Rocky Mountains. Rosalie Sorrels included it in her album, *The Lonesome Roving Wolves: Songs and Ballads of the West*, and says that she has heard at least six variants.

Juanita Brooks, renowned Utah and western history scholar, wrote to the Fifes in 1956 and stated "Juanita" was a favorite of her mother's, who sang it often—"hence my name." She indicated that it had been popular in southern Nevada where she was born (FMC II 615).

Riley Neal learned "Juanita" from a boy named Henry Farrell. "We were boys together and grew up together," Riley told me. "He's dead now; he died several years ago. He was a good cowboy, a good fence builder and could do most any kind of ranch work such as breaking horses. He got his neck broke while working for a cowman named Hagen, who has a cow outfit near Globe, Arizona. He lived that way for several years before he died in the Globe hospital."

Riley's version has six verses, whereas the Fifes' has nine; Riley's version narrows the dialogue to the cowboy; the Fifes' variant allows

Juanita to speak her bitterness before killing him. Sorrels's variant is similar to the Fifes'. Riley Neal did not sing this for me; the melody appears in Austin E. and Alta S. Fife's *Cowboy and Western Songs* (1969).

"I must leave you, my Juanita,
Though it almost breaks my heart;
I have told you, my Juanita,
Sometimes true lovers have to part.

"I will miss you, my Juanita,
Though from you I'll be far away;
But you'll have another lover
Before, perhaps, another day.

"You will miss me, my Juanita,
For perhaps one day and then forget;
Crying? Why, my brave Juanita?
Like dew drops your eyes are wet."

Juanita left the shelter,
And she left the place alone;
In her eyes no teardrops glistened,
From her heart the love had flown.

In the morning two braceros
Paused to rest there in the shade,
For siestas sought the shelter
Which the clustering foliage made.

"Maria Dios!" cried one bracero
As he pushed the vines apart,
"Here lies one Americano
With a dagger in his heart."

Field Collections and Manuscripts: Fife Folklore Archives, FMC I 797, FAC I 121, FAC I 164, FAC I 352, FMC II 615.

References: Fife and Fife (1969), pp. 144–45.

Recordings: Rosalie Sorrels, *The Lonesome Roving Wolves*, Green Linnet SIF 1024.

36*

"OH! MY! YOU'RE A DANDY FOR NINETEEN YEARS OLD"

Alternate Titles: "A Daisy for Nineteen Years Old,"
"Only Nineteen Years Old," "A Virgin of Nineteen,"
and "She Was a Virgin Only Nineteen Years Old"

This song about the female who has too many artificial parts is similar to "The Old Maid and the Burglar" (Laws H 23) and "The Warranty Deed" (Laws H 24); in each song the male observer becomes overwhelmed by the removal of so many female parts. "You're a Dandy for Nineteen Years Old" is more closely related to "The Warranty Deed," in which a new husband, not a burglar, is the witness and warns all young men to get "a warranty deed." Whereas in this variant, the warning is to inspect one's "true love from her head to her toe."

Baxter Black learned this song from Albert Stone of Alder Creek Ranch, Nevada, in 1975. He said, "Albert wouldn't sing it in the cook house with the ladies present. He took me in the back room and played it and a couple of others. We played 'em til I learned them. Albert was the one who ran off with a Piute woman an' got married an' she gut shot him. Albert lives on in these songs."

Dallas "Nevada Slim" Turner sent a version to me and stated that he re-wrote it to get the rhyme, meter, and humor that he wanted. It does not vary significantly from Baxter's version. I have found no other printed variants from this country, but apparently it was known and sung by other cowboys.

Ron Edwards in *Australian Folk Songs* reported a variant, "A Virgin of Nineteen," similar to Baxter's version; it includes a refrain:

They said she was a virgin, a virgin, a virgin,
They said she was a virgin only nineteen years old.

Edwards collected a parody of "After the Ball" in which the "disintegrat-
ing damsel" comes apart like the ninety year old.

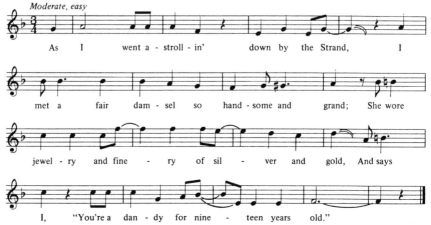

As I went a-strollin' down by the Strand,
I met a fair damsel so handsome and grand;
She wore jewelry and finery of silver and gold,
And says I, "You're a dandy for nineteen years old."

Her fingers were tapered; her neck like a swan,
Her nose alittle turned up an' her voice not too strong;
Six weeks we were married and wedding bells tolled,
I married my darlin', just nineteen years old.

After the wedding, we retired to rest,
Did my face change colors when my young wife undressed;
A bundle of padding from her form did unfold,
Says I, "You're a dandy for nineteen years old."

She took off her fingers, till I counted but three,
Unscrewed her cork leg plumb up to her knee,
Took out her glass eye, on the carpet it rolled,
An' says I, "You're a dandy for nineteen years old."

As I stood and I watched her, I thought I would faint,
She scraped from her pale face a bushel of paint;
She took off her wig an' her bald head then told
She was nearer to ninety than ta' nineteen years old.

So come all you young fellers when you courtin' to go,
Inspect your true love from her head to her toe,
Or else you'll be ruined like me and be sold
To a patched-up old geezer who's ninety years old.

Field Collections and Manuscripts: Fife Folklore Archives, FAC I 346,
FAC I 651; Turner to McCulloh, September 20, 1974.
References: Edwards (1972), pp. 123, 191; Turner (1977), p. 10.

For information about "Old Maid and the Burglar" and "The Warranty Deed," see
Laws (1964), H 23 and H 24, p. 241, and Randolph and Cohen (1982), pp. 333–35.

37.*

"SWEET SIXTEEN"

Young girls were not spared barbs from frontier singers; this song teases the young ladies about their vanity and feigned shyness. No doubt the song's greatest potential as humor could be realized only if sung in the presence of young ladies who would get mad. It is an excellent companion to another song with the same tune, "The Young Man Who Wouldn't Hoe His Corn."

The song as Riley Neal learned it from his father, appears below as Text A. I have found only one other variant, a holograph copy John A. Lomax received from Allen G. Wayt of Marshall County, West Virginia (Text B). The manuscript was not dated, but considering the material with which it was filed, Lomax probably received it before the 1930s.

Come all you good peo-ple and lis-ten to my song; There's not man-y vers-es and it will not take you long. It's all a-bout the girls who's al-ways to be seen, A-long a-bout the time of the sweet six - teen.

Text A

Come all you good people and listen to my song;
There's not many verses and it will not take you long.

It's all about the girls who's always to be seen,
Along about the time of the sweet sixteen.

They first begin to primp and then begin to lace
And buy paint and powder to put upon their face.
They will curl up their hair, and before the glass they'll preen,
Along about the time of the sweet sixteen.

Step up to one of them, "May I walk you home tonight?"
She'll be sure to tell you, "No," but her actions tell you right.
If you put your arm around her, she'll holler and she'll scream,
Along about the time of sweet sixteen.

They'll hug each other up, and they'll giggle and they'll laugh,
And they'll squirm and they'll wiggle like a little sucking calf.
But they'll never wash a dish, and they'll never boil a bean,
Along about the time of the sweet sixteen.

Oh, I think it's about time for this little song to end,
If there's any girls here who it might offend.
It's all about the girls who's always to be seen,
Along about the time of the sweet sixteen.

Text B

Come all you gentlemen, listen to my song.
It's might few verses, and won't detain you long,
It's all about the pretty girls who often may be seen
'Long about the time when they're sweet sixteen.

They first begin to comb and then begin to lace,
Make an artificious [*sic*] to wear upon their face.
Their necks is always bare, but very neat and clean,
'Long about the time when they're sweet sixteen.

Then to Sunday school they begin to run,
They'll laugh and talk about the boys and say they are so
        green,
They'll laugh and talk about the boys and say they are so
        green,
'Long about the time when they're sweet sixteen.

They'll laugh and talk about the boys all behind their back
If they had a chance, they'd give 'em all the sack.

When they're takin' arms they're always mighty keen,
'Long about the time when they're sweet sixteen.

Step up to them—see you home tonight?
They'll always tell you *No,* but they'll ask and tell you right.
They look as independent and sassy as a queen,
'Long about the time when they're sweet sixteen.

Throw your arm around them like a many a one does,
They're goin' to strike at you, and goin' to miss you, too.
But that is soon forgot when on you they will lean,
'Long about the time when they're sweet sixteen.

Field Collections and Manuscripts: Lomax (Mss.), folder 2E409.

38.*

"THE BOOGABOO"

Alternate Titles:
"The Foggy, Foggy Dew," "The Bugaboo," "The Weaver," and "The Bachelor's Son"

"The Foggy Dew" is widely known throughout the United States, it has been included for decades in popular folk song books and records, the repertoire of "folk revival" singers, and public school song collections. Very few, if any, in these audiences ever consider it to be a bawdy song, but when all verses are sung, its theme is premarital sex that produces a son; the ending varies from the young maid's death in childbirth and the narrator's memories of that night when he protected her from the "foggy dew" or "bugaboo," to the narrator marrying her and making her a virtuous wife. Riley Neal's version follows the latter pattern. Although many versions place the narrator as a weaver, Neal's is one of those that makes no mention of a trade, other than "a reckless trade."

G. Malcolm Laws, Jr., classified the song under the category of "Ballads of Faithful Lovers," but he made no mention of any bawdy consideration. Even in the shortened versions, what happens is left to the listener's imagination—a narrative technique that some literary figures, such as D. H. Lawrence, find more obscene than explicit detail.

Gershon Legman in *The Horn Book* wrote that "Foggy Dew" is a "corruption of 'The Bugaboo,' meaning demon or devil." With that knowledge, the words become more meaningful—the girl is, indeed, afraid of the darkness, and fear helps her into the narrator's arms. Obviously, he has a little of the "bugaboo" in him, which he readily gives to her. Riley Neal pronounced "bugaboo" as "boo-ga-boo."

James Reeves in *The Idiom of the People* compares and discusses more variants than has any other scholar, and his investigation of symbolism and innuendo in the words "foggy dew" is thorough. His final conclusions were that in the original context they meant "perpetual chastity," that during the passage of time and history of the song "its original symbolic significance was obscured in the popular mind," and that there is "hopeless confusion resulting from evident misunderstanding of traditional symbolism." Reeves also states that this song departs from traditional folk song by using the first-person narrative. My speculation is that the use of the first-person narrative may be more common in the United States than in Britain. The Neal variant reflects a disintegration of symbolism into a nonsense refrain.

In *Folksongs of Britain and Ireland*, Peter Kennedy includes an unusual variant with nine verses; it is the "Foggy Dew" type in which the "young maid" dies, and in which no mention of marriage is made. Kennedy provides an extensive list of field recordings and manuscript collections, and he, along with other scholars, credits Carl Sandburg (Kennedy also includes Burl Ives and Josh White) through commercial recordings with the song's popular revival in America and Britain; Sandburg sang two verses while Ives and White sang three. They successfully popularized a seduction song by expunging it—at least someone cleansed their versions.

Although controversy will continue about the meaning of "foggy dew" and "bugaboo," singers from folk to art song traditions will continue to sing it because it is still one of the most beautiful love songs in the English language.

fraid of the Boog-a - boo, boo, boo, She was a - fraid of the Boog-a - boo.

When I was a young and roving blade,
I followed a reckless trade.
But all the harm that ever I done
Was to court a pretty fair maid.

I courted her all summer and part of the winter, too.
My love she had but one weakness,
She was afraid of the Boogaboo, boo, boo,
She was afraid of the Boogaboo.

My love she came to my bedside,
Where I lay fast asleep.
My love she came to my bedside,
And bitterly did weep.

She wrung her hands and wept and cried, and she was full of woe.
"Oh! Jump in the bed, you pretty maid,
For there is the Boogaboo, boo, boo,
For there is the Boogaboo."

All in the first part of the night
How we did romp and play.
All in the latter part of the night
Within my arm she lay.

The night passed off, the dawn came on.
"Rise up young maid and don't be afraid,
For the Boogaboo is gone, gone,
For the Boogaboo is gone."

All in first part of the year,
My love grew thick around.
And in the middle part of the year,
She scarcely could sit down.

And in the last part of the year, she brought me a very fine son.
So you can see as well as I
What the Boogaboo has done, done, done,
What the Boogaboo has done.

I courted her and I married her,
And I loved her as my life.
I courted her and I married her,
And she made me a virtuous wife.

I never told her of her faults and be darn'd if ever I do,
But ever time she smiles on me,
I think of the Boogaboo, boo, boo,
I think of the Boogaboo.

Field Collections and Manuscripts: Gordon (Inferno, Mss.), 1752; Randolph (Mss.), pp. 227–29; LC-AFS 2280 A2, 2261 A2.

References: Brand (1960), pp. 54–55; Cray (1965), pp. 107–8, (1969), pp. 26–27, 191; de Witt (1970), p. 32; Emrich (1972), pp. 518–19; Getz (1981), F 15; Hubbard (1961), pp. 115–16; *Immortalia* (1927), p. 80, (1960), p. 124; Ives (1953), pp. 64–65; Kennedy (1975), pp. 393, 400–1, 428; Laws (1957), 0 3, pp. 227–28; Legman (1964), pp. 256–57, 411; A. Lomax (1960), pp. 89–90; McCarthy (1972), pp. 34–35; McGregor (1972), pp. 21–22; Pinto and Rodway (1957), pp. 370, 392; Purslow (1974), pp. 31, 109; Reeves (1958), pp. 45–57, 111–13; Sandburg (1927), pp. 14–15; Seeger and MacColl (1960), pp. 13, 20; Shay (1927), pp. 54–55; Silverman (1966), pp. 68–69, (1982), pp. 66–67.

Recordings: Oscar Brand, *Bawdy Songs and Backroom Ballads*, 2, Audio Fidelity AFLP 1806; Burl Ives, *The Wayfaring Stranger*, Asch 345 and *Ballads and Folk Songs*, 3, Decca Dl 5093; Bradly Kincaid, Decca 12024; A. L. Lloyd, *English Drinking Songs*, Riverside RLP 12-618; Milt Okum and Ellen Stekert, *Traditional American Love Songs*, Riverside 12-634; Carl Sandburg, *New Songs from the American Songbag*, Lyrichord LL4; Tom Scott, *Sing of America*, Coral CRL 56056; Josh White, *A Josh White Programme*, London H-APB 1005 and LL 1341; there are many more recordings of this popular song.

39.*

"RED WING"

Often thought to be an "old" song, "Red Wing" was a popular song published in 1907; the music was adapted by Kerry Mills from Robert A. Schumann's "The Happy Farmer" (Opus 68, No. 10, 1849). The lyrics, written by Thurland Chattaway, told of a young Indian maiden waiting in vain for the return of her brave. The sentimental song quickly entered the repertoire of folk singers and folk musicians nationwide, and it was perfect to parody.

The bawdy parody enjoys widespread popularity and is in that group of songs that young boys often learn—at least they learn the refrain:

Now the sun shines bright 'round pretty Red Wing,
As she lies sleeping, there comes a-creepin'
A cowboy brave with eyes a-gleamin',
His cock a-standin', with promised joy.

Riley Neal sang a different refrain:

Now the moon shines tonight on Charlie Chaplin,
His shoes are cracking, for the want of blackin';
His damned old britches, they need patchin',
Where he's been scratchin' the lice away.

John Brophy and Eric Partridge in *The Long Trail* include almost identical lines as a "ditty" popular among British soldiers during World War I. Brophy and Partridge believe that "Red Wing" had been sung by children before the troops used it. They made no mention of bawdy verses being sung, but they believe that it was inspired in 1918 by Charlie Chaplin's film, *Shoulder Arms*; however, no mention is made about the possibility of American troops introducing the song to British troops. It certainly would not predate Chaplin's popularity that started in 1916.

It is impossible to estimate the number of "Red Wing" parodies, but among folk song "revivalists" the best known is Woody Guthrie's "Union Maid." Guthrie changed the "Indian maid" to a "union maid" in 1940 when he wrote his humorous but serious tribute to the wives of union members.

Riley knew the original song as well as the bawdy parody. Text A is almost identical to the Mills and Chattaway text; a few words differ, but the story remains intact. Text B is the bawdy parody, and, other than the refrain, it is similar to other bawdy texts. Riley Neal not only sang the two versions, but he also played the melody on the harmonica and piano.

Text A

There once lived an Indian maid,
A shy little prairie maid,
She sang a lay, a love song gay,
While on the plains she'd while away the day;
This shy little maid of old,
She loved a warrior bold,
But far, far away he rode one day,
To battle in the fray.

CHORUS

Now the moon shines tonight on pretty Red Wing,
The breeze is sighing, the night bird's crying;
Far, oh, far beneath the star her brave is sleeping,
While Red Wing's weeping her heart away.

She watched for him day and night,
She kept all the camp fires bright,
While under the sky, each night she would lie
And dream about his coming by and by;
When all the braves returned,
The heart of Red Wing yearned,
But far, far away, her warrior gay,
Fell bravely in the fray.

Text B

There once lived an Indian maid,
She sat in the silent shade,
Afraid some buckaroo would ram it up her flue,
As she sat in the silent shade;
Then with her sunburned hand,
She crammed it full of sand,
So if some buckaroo did ram it up her flue,
He'd never reach the promised land.

CHORUS

Now the moon shines tonight on Charlie Chaplin,
His shoes are cracking, for the want of blackin'
His damned old britches, they need patchin',
Where he's been scratchin' the lice away.

"Red Wing"

The popularity of "Red Wing" and questions about its copyright status made it necessary for the staff at the Archive of Folk Culture, Library of Congress, to research the publishing history; their findings are in the Subject Collection folder "Red Wing." Also see: Fife and Fife (1969), pp. 142–43. There have been numerous hillbilly/country records including Buell Kazee and Sookie Hoffs, Brunswick 210; W. W. McBeth, Brunswick 443; the Blue Ridge Highballer, Paramount 3083; and many more.

Bawdy Parody: "Red Wing"

Field Collections and Manuscripts: LC-AFS 2291 B2; Hickerson/Hitch-cock, Reel 2, Side A, no. 5; Randolph (Mss.), pp. 619–20; Larson (Countryside), n.p.; Legman (TS VF), n.p.; Fife Folklore Archives, FAC I 60; "Apples of Eden" (n.d.), n.p.

References: Babad (1972), pp. 78–79; Brophy and Partridge (1965); Cray (1965), p. 49, (1969), pp. 69, 229–30; Getz (1981), p. L 8; Hart-*Immortalia* (1971), pp. 44–49; Laycock (1982), pp. 199–200; Morgan (1968), pp. 79–80.

Recordings: Oscar Brand, *Bawdy Songs and Backroom Ballads*, 3, Audio Fidelity AFLP 1824.

40.*

"THE LITTLE MOHEA"

This popular ballad has numerous title variants and has been collected throughout the nation. The Indian lass, rejected by the protagonist in favor of his true love at home is symbolic of native females
on any frontier. When the stranger returns home to find that his true
love has wed another, he longs to return to the Indian.

G. Malcolm Laws, Jr., in *Native American Balladry*, reviewed a variety of conjectures about the origin of "Little Mohea." It may be a re-
make of "The Indian Lass," a popular English broadside ballad, but the
English ballad may have been an adaptation of an American sea ballad.
No matter, it enjoyed, and enjoys, popularity that carried it to a Hawai-
ian setting as well as to a coastal United States setting. In recent decades
it has been a favorite among professional folk song singers such as Burl
Ives; therefore, numerous commercial recordings are available, as well
as variants in printed folk song anthologies and collections.

Riley Neal's version is short and to the point; it does not ramble,
and it has no extraneous detail. While he enjoyed singing about "Little
Mohea," Riley equally enjoyed playing it on the piano. He played it as a
waltz, with a heavy, left-hand rhythm at many dances in Gisela, Arizona.

I sat a - mus - ing my - self in the grass, Pray

whom should I spy but a young In - dian lass.

As I was out strolling for pleasure one day,
To view the creation and pass time away,
As I sat amusing myself in the grass,
Pray whom should I spy but a young Indian lass.

She came and sat by me and took up my hand,
Saying, "You are a stranger and not one of this land;
If you will agree, sir, and stay here with me,
I'll teach you the language of the little Mohea.

"Together we'll ramble, together we'll rove,
Till we come to my cottage in the coconut grove."

"Oh, no my dear maiden, this never can be,
For I have a true love in my own country;
And I'll not forsake her for I know she loves me,
Her heart is as true as the little Mohea's."

The last time I saw her, she stood on the sand,
And when my ship passed her, she waved me her hand,
Saying, "When you get over with the girl that you love,
Remember the Mohea in the coconut grove."

Now that I'm over on my own native shore,
With friends and relations around me once more,
With all that's around me, there's none that I see
That's fit to compare with the little Mohea.

The girl I had trusted proved untrue to me,
I'll turn my thoughts backward far o'er the blue sea;
I'll turn my thoughts backward and backward I'll flee,
I'll spend all my days with the little Mohea.

Field Collections and Manuscripts: LC-AFS has fourteen variants; Fife
Folklore Archives, FMC I 813, FAC I 826; most field collections contain variants;
Culwell (1976), p. 158; Gelber (1963), pp. 64–65.

Cowboys loved to dance; when no women were available, they danced with one another as seen in this photograph by Erwin E. Smith, taken probably between 1907 and 1910 in Texas. This is a "stag dance" that included young wranglers. (The Erwin E. Smith Collection of the Library of Congress on deposit at the Amon Carter Museum, Fort Worth.)

References: Botkin (1944), pp. 824–25; Brown, 2 (1952), pp. 340–42; Brumley (1970), no. 16; Burton, 2 (1969), pp. 39–40; Clark (1934), pp. 56–57; Colcord (1964), pp. 194–96; Fife and Fife (1969), pp. 134–36; Hood (1977), p. 35; Hubbard (1961), pp. 96–97; Ives (1953), pp. 256–57; Laws (1964), H 8, pp. 233–34; Lomax and Lomax (1934), pp. 163–65; Moore (1964), pp. 192–94; Rosenberg (1969), p. 71; Sherwin (1939), pp. 22–23; *The Songs You Hear No More* (n.d.), p. 19; *357 Songs We Love to Sing* (1938), p. 149.

Recordings: Wilf Carter, *My Heartache's Your Happiness*, RCA Camden CASX-2616; Hall Brothers, on *Native American Ballads*, RCA LPV 548; Burl Ives, *The Wayfaring Stranger*, Columbia CL 628, and *Return of the Wayfaring Stranger*, Columbia CL 5068; Buell Kazee, Brunswick 436; Bradley Kincaid, Gennett 6856, Supertone 9402, and Champion 15731; John Jacob Niles, *Sings American Folk Songs*, Camden CAL 245; Bunk Pettyjohn, on *In an Arizona Town*, Arizona Friends of Folklore AFF 33-3.

41.*

"SWEET BETSY FROM PIKE"

S weet Betsy was sung about more than any other frontier woman; although she was the outgrowth of the gold rush days, every other wave of frontier settlers picked her up and continued her sore-footed trek through song.

Frontier women must have empathized with Betsy's woes, and men found Ike to be a man of similar experience; but the humorous nature of the song helped its listeners laugh at their own situations. The universal frontier experiences of disaster, discouragement, irony, anger, and humor were captured by John A. Stone in approximately 1858 (no substantial evidence has been found to refute Stone's professed authorship).

Stone crossed the Plains in 1850, one who had gold madness, but his mother lode came in the form of verse. He wrote each of his songs to be sung to a familiar air or tune; "Sweet Betsy from Pike," for example, was to be sung to "Villikins and His Dinah." Stone claimed to have sung all of his songs at various times and places and occasionally with the assistance of a group of men known as the Sierra Nevada Rangers. With encouragement from friends, he published his songs as *Put's Original California Songster* (1855), which was followed by other "Put's" songsters that dealt with the mountains and California. "Sweet Betsy" appeared in the second edition of *Put's Golden Songster* (1858), and most collected variants have remained remarkably similar to that printed text. Riley Neal's version is no exception. In fact, the greatest variation appears in the different refrains, but Riley sang no refrain. It is possible that if indeed Stone did sing his songs before they were published, some may have entered oral tradition through that channel, but it is more likely that the widespread popularity of his songsters was the source of dissemination and, ultimately, tradition.

Vance Randolph in his "Unprintable Songs from the Ozarks" reported two slightly obscene verses, which seem to be isolated texts because no complete obscene variant is known—at least by this collector. C. W. "Bill" Getz in *The Wild Blue Yonder* (1986) includes five bawdy songs sung to the tune "Sweet Betsy from Pike," but they are not parodies of "Sweet Betsy."

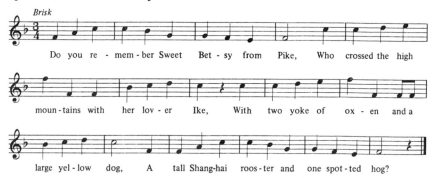

Do you remember Sweet Betsy from Pike,
Who crossed the high mountains with her lover Ike,
With two yoke of oxen and a large yellow dog,
A tall Shanghai rooster and one spotted hog?

One evening quite early they camped on the Platte,
Near by the road on a green shady flat;
Betsy, quite tired, lay down to repose,
While Ike gazed with wonder on his Pike County rose.

They soon reached the desert, where Betsy gave out,
And down on the ground she lay tumbling about;
While Ike in great wonder looked on with surprise,
Saying, "Betsy, get up, you'll get sand in your eyes."

Sweet Betsy arose in a great deal of pain
And swore she'd go back to Pike County again;
Ike walked up and they fondly embraced,
And they both walked along with his arm 'round her waist.

The wagon broke down with a terrible crash,
And out on the prairie rolled all sorts of trash;

A few little baby clothes done up with great care
Looked rather suspicious, but it's all on the square.

They went by Salt Lake to inquire the way,
Old Brigham insisted that they should stay;
Betsy got frightened and ran like a deer,
While Brigham stood pawing the earth like a steer.

The Shanghai ran off and the cattle all died,
The last piece of bacon that morning was fried;
Poor Ike grew discouraged, and Betsy got mad,
And the dog wagged his tail and looked wondrously sad.

One morning they climbed up a very high hill
And stood gazing down upon old Placerville;
Said Ike in great wonder, as he cast his eyes down,
"Sweet Betsy, my darling, we've got to Hangtown,"

Long Ike and Sweet Betsy attended a dance,
And Ike wore a pair of his Pike County pants;
Sweet Betsy all covered with ribbons and rings,
Quoth Ike, "You're an angel, but where are your wings?"

Said a Pike County miner, "Will you dance with me?"
"Oh! yes," said Sweet Betsy, "if you don't make too free;
If you want to know the reason why,
Doggone ye, I'm chock full of strong alkali."

Long Ike and Sweet Betsy got married, of course,
But Ike getting jealous obtained a divorce;
Betsy, well pleased, cried out with a shout,
"You great big lummox, I'm glad you backed out!"

Field Collections and Manuscripts: LC-AFS 3295 A1, 1697 A1, 5299 B2, 4099 A2; Todd-Sonkin 12A2; Randolph (Mss.), pp. 282–284; Fife Folklore Archives, FMC I 618, FAC I 185, FAC I 311, FAC I 312, FAC I 313, FAC I 644; Gelber (1963), pp. 63–64; Scroggins (1976), pp. 230–32.

References: *American Cowboy Songs* (1936), pp. 74–75; Belden (1940), pp. 343–45; Boni (1947), pp. 62–63; Botkin (1944), pp. 861–63; Brand (1961), pp. 146–47; Cheney (1968), pp. 184–85; Clark (1932), pp. 56–57, (1937), p. 30; Dwyer and Lingenfelter (1965), pp. 43–44; Fife and Fife (1969), pp. 48–49; Frey (1936), pp. 90–91; Getz, 2 (1986), pp. AA 2–3, AA 12–13, GG 7, SS 5–6; Glass and Singer (1966), pp. 18–20; Hood (1977), p. 374; Hubbard (1961), pp. 300–1; Ives (1953), pp. 256–57; Koon (1973), p. 72; Laws (1964), B 9, p. 137; Lingenfelter, Dwyer, and Cohen (1968), pp. 42–43; A. Lomax (1960), pp. 327, 335–36; Lomax (1910 and 1916), pp. 258–60; Lomax and Lomax (1934), pp. 424–26, (1938, 1986), pp. 388–91; Moon (1982), pp. 12–13; Moore (1964), pp. 319–21; *900 Miles* (1965), p. 59; Randolph, 2 (1948), pp. 209–10; Randolph and Cohen (1982), pp. 193–96; Rosenberg (1969), p. 121; Sandburg (1927), pp. 108–9; Silber (1967), pp. 14–17.

Recordings: Rex Allen, *Mister Cowboy*, Decca DL 78776; Bill Bender, *Frontier Songs and Cowboy Ballads*, Stinson SLP 18; Curley Fox and Texas Ruby, on *Songs of the West*, Glendale GL 6020; Cisco Houston, *Cowboy Ballads*, Folkways FA 2022; Burl Ives, *The Wayfaring Stranger*, Columbia CL 628; Bradley Kincaid, on *Native American Ballads*, RCA LPV-548; The Ranch Boys, Decca 2646; Riders in the Sky, *Saddle Pals*, Rounder 8011; Sons of the Pioneers, *Twenty-five Favorite Cowboy Songs*, RCA 1130; Nevada Slim Turner, *Songs of the Wild West*, 4, Rural Rhythm RRNS 165; and many more country/western/folk artists.

42.*

"THE COUNTRY GIRL"

This song, set to the tune of "Little Brown Jug," has the appearance of an old English-Scottish song. I believe that it is a shortened
and Americanized variant of "The Fair Maid of the West Who Sold Her
Maidenhead for a High-crown'd Hat," as printed in Pinto and Rodway's
The Common Muse.

Riley Neal said, "That's one of them old time ones; I learn't that
from old Uncle Ambrose Bull." The story is self-explanatory, but it is not
an isolated theme. The gullible or willing country girl is a common folk
character.

Oh, the coun-try girl, she went to the fair, She said to the mer-chant when she got there, "I want a bon-net for sum - mer wear, Some-thing nice to wear to the fair."

The country girl, she went to the fair,
She said to the merchant when she got there,
"I want a bonnet for summer wear,
Something nice to wear to the fair."

He looked at the girl and then did say,
"Do you have any money with which to pay?"

Cowboys at the turn of the century in front of a saloon in Glenrock, Wyoming. (Guy Logsdon Collection)

She smiled at the merchant, and then she said,
"All I have, kind sir, is my maidenhead."

He caught her around her slender waist,
Carried her to a room in back of the place,
And on a soft and downy bed,
He took away her maidenhead.

The country girl went home from the fair,
She said to her mother when she got there,
"In my heart I feel right glad,
To think what I got for my maidenhead."

Her Mother went out and cut a switch,
"I'll whip your ass, you dirty bitch;
Hike you back to that very same store,
And see that you act like a fool no more."

The country girl went back to the fair,
She said to the merchant when she got there,
"Me and my Mother, we never can agree
About that little old thing which you took away from me."

He caught her around the slender waist,
He carried her back to the very same place;
And on that soft and downy bed
He gave her back her maidenhead.

References: Pinto and Rodway (1957), pp. 365–67.

43.*

"THE OAKS OF JIMDERIA"

The words to "The Oaks of Jimderia" (pronounced *Jim Derry*) were received from Riley Neal on March 10, 1969. In August 1970, when I asked Riley to sing it, he was too tired and too far into his cups to sing a good melody and version. The extra line in the fourth verse and the added couplet in the fifth verse indicate additional verses now partially forgotten.

Vance Randolph collected two verses similar to the story in this song; he used the title "Formations of Nature." Otherwise, I found no other variant. However, the song is similar to "Walking in a Meadow Gren [Green]," as printed in *Loose and Humorous Songs from Bishop Percy's Folio Manuscript*, edited by Frederick J. Furnivall, and it is closely related to "The Pear Tree," a rarely collected song in England. "The Pear Tree" is not as explicit as this song, but it features a young boy in a pear tree watching a young couple below with voyeuristic delight.

> As I was out walking for pleasure one day,
> To the oaks of Jimderia I happened to stray;
> Found a green shady bower, climbed up in a tree,
> And waited the prospects of nature to see.

> I did not have to wait very long,
> Till I saw scenes and actions that prompted this song;
> I saw near approaching a man and a maid,
> Draw near to my tree and sit down in the shade.

"Oh! Nancy, fair Nancy, I've met you once more,
My prick is so hard that my balls they are sore;
I've fucked you before, and I'll fuck you now here,
There's no one in the valley, there's nothing to fear."

Down upon the ground these two they did lay;
He fucked her, and then he rose up to pray,
Saying, "God bless this white belly and curly black hair,
The rod of old Jacob may here lose its seed,
But a cunt that lies gaping shall ne'er gape in need."

Her legs twined around him, his motions she met;
My feelings were awful, I had to whet.
They rose from their pleasure and brushed off their clothes,
Whatever possessed them the Lord only knows,
But glancing around, they looked up and saw me,
Lord, God! How they got out from under my tree.

Field Collections and Manuscripts: Randolph (Mss.), pp. 36–37.

"Walking in a Meadow Gren":
    References: Farmer, 2 (1897, 1964), pp. 13–15; Furnivall (1868, 1963), pp. 3–5.

"The Pear Tree":
    References: Palmer (1980), pp. 37–38; Yates (1975), pp. 77–78.
    Recordings: Frank Hinchliffe, *In Sheffield Park*, Topic 12 TS 308.

44.*

"COUSIN HARRY"

Alternate Title: "Cousin Nellie"

Little can be said about "Cousin Harry," for I found only one version in other collections. That version was collected in Idaho by Kenneth Larson in 1932 and has fewer verses than Riley Neal's "Cousin Harry." It is similar in content and action, but Larson's informant used the title "Cousin Nellie." There is no internal evidence to associate it with rural or urban characters or to date it; however, because attitudes about cousins having sexual intercourse or marrying have become more critical during this century, the rather casual attitude of the narrator *might be* an indication of earlier composition.

Riley said, "I learned it from a fellow named Bill Davis who use to stay around here. He drank whiskey mostly, but he worked as a carpenter."

Moderate

As I sat with my cous-in Nel - lie 'neath the dear old lem-on trees, It was sweet to sit be - side her as her hair waved in the breeze. It was sweet to sit be - side her and watch the fleec - y clouds a - bove. She leaned and whis-pered to me, "Cous-in Har-ry, what is love?"

As I sat with my cousin Nellie 'neath the dear old lemon trees,
It was sweet to sit beside her as her hair waved in the breeze.
It was sweet to sit beside her and watch the fleecy clouds
    above.
She leaned and whispered to me "Cousin Harry, what is love?"

"Oh! Love is just a passion, a passion to be felt,
And once you have experienced it, you will care for nothing
    else."
She laid her little hand in mine, as gentle as a dove,
And whispered, "Cousin Harry, please teach me how to love."

She took my throbbing peter within her little hand;
She put it on her pussy though it needed no command.
And as she pushed up to me, I reached home with a shove.
She whispered, "Cousin Harry, my God! This must be love."

Next month as I sat with Nellie, beneath the same old lemon
    trees,
'Twas sweet to sit beside her as her hair waved in the breeze.
She stretched herself upon the grass and laid with her belly
    bare,
"Get on me, Cousin Harry, true love lies only there."

Field Collections and Manuscripts: Larson (Countryside), n.p.

45.*

"THE POOR GIRL ON THE TOWN"

A few months after I first visited Riley Neal in August 1968, he started sending his handwritten texts to me. This song was one of the first; it arrived on December 23, 1968. He included no statement about when or from whom he had learned it; I was unable to record the melody when I visited him in 1970. In his handwritten text he used the word "whorelet"; I have changed it to "harlot." The tone resembles that of late-nineteenth-century songs. I have found no variants.

> I had a dear old father once, who gave me this advice.
> He said, "My son, wherever you go, pray choose yourself a
>   wife.
> The world is wide before you, with honor and reknown.
> Wherever you go, pray never know the harlot on the town.
> Wherever you go, pray never know the harlot on the town."
>
> "Oh! Father, you give good advice, but sisters I have three.
> If fortune might upon them frown and whores they all might
>   be,
> Then they would smile upon the boys as the girls now smile
>   on me.
> Wherever I go, I'm sure to know the poor girl on the town.
> Wherever I go, I'm sure to know the harlot on the town."
>
> "If ever you meet one of those girls and you are hungry or dry,
> Ask her for a dollar note and you she'll not deny.

She'll take you to some closet room and with you there lie
    down.
Your heart's as gay as the flowers in May with the poor girl on
    the town.
Your heart's as gay as the flowers in May with the harlot on the
    town."

46.*

"THE OLD TOM CAT"

In the popular comic song tradition, animals have often appeared as the main characters. Songs such as "The Monkey's Wedding" were printed in sheet music form as early as the 1830s, but the origin of many of the comic animal songs may never be known. Were they taken from oral tradition and printed, or did they become so popular that they entered oral tradition?

Lester S. Levy, in *Flashes of Merriment*, reproduced a few animal songs that were printed as sheet music during the nineteenth century; among them was an 1836 song, "Our Old Tom Cat" or "The Cats March Out of the Ash Hole." The lyrics were written by an Englishman, William Clifton, who Levy credited with introducing cat songs to this country. As with most animal songs, at some point the sounds of the animal or animals are made, "Our Old Tom Cat" followed the pattern. Among the many nineteenth- century animal or fowl pop songs were "Pop Goes the Weasel," "The Monkey's Wedding," "The Cat Came Back," and "Listen to the Mocking Bird"; each entered traditional music in varying degrees of popularity. Cat songs seemed to be particularly popular; it was only natural for someone to create bawdy lyrics.

I have found no variants of Riley Neal's "The Old Tom Cat."

Lively

An old la-dy sat by the fire, And she thought no one was nigh her; There was

no one nigh but the tom cat by, And she pulled up her pet-ti-coat high - er.

An old lady sat by the fire,
And she thought no one was nigh her;
There was no one nigh but the tom cat by
And she pulled up her petticoat higher.

The old tom cat saw something naked,
And for a rat or a mouse did take it;
He made one spring at the old lady's thing
And so merrily did shake it.

The old lady fizzled and she farted,
The tom cat snarled and he snorted;
They made such a din that the neighbors rushed in
And the cat and the cunt were parted.

The woman's name was Florie,
And the tom cat's name was Tory;
The cat was drunk when he jumped at the cunt
And that is the end of the story.

References: Levy (1971), pp. 226, 235–37.

47*

"THE STINKIN' COW"

Late in the afternoon of November 2, 1962, Lew Pyle left the east door of his home in order to feed his burros and goats. I was helping him. Near the corral gate he started a song—actually, something between a song and a recitation, for his singing ability had been tempered by age. With a low chuckle, he rendered "The Stinkin' Cow." It was incomplete and it had no discernible melody, but to Lew it was a humorous, clever song. Because I had no portable tape recorder, and could not transcribe the musical monologue, I collected the words only.

"I heard this one around 1900," Lew exlained, "I think it was when I was in the Forest Service (circa 1905). Old Hank Winfield used to sing it over at Camp Verde. I heard him sing it around cow camps—never in a mixed crowd." It is probably of British origin; I have not found any variant.

> The sun came peekin' over the hills,
> To dry the dews of morning;
> The little birds in all the trees
> Rejoiced in its returning.

> Old McGee his daughter sees,
> Sing, "Molly, get you ready,
> For Johnny will bear you company,
> This lad so bold and steady."

> As they rode together,
> They first discussed the neighbors;

It warmer grew, and
So hot became the weather.

And there beside a barley mow,
. . . .
They saw a bull, so vigor full,
A-slippin' it to a cow.

"John," says Moll, "how can he tell
When she's in the humor for it?
Or is the cow by nature
So inclined to it?"

"Oh, no!" says John, "that is not it."
This was his explanation,
" 'Tis by the smell, the bull can tell,
For he knows her inclination."

She tells, "Like the cow, I'm stinkin' now,
Oh! Johnny, can't you smell me?"
On the ground he placed her,
And he did to her what the bull did to the cow.

48.*

"THE CUCKOO'S NEST"

This is another of Riley Neal's songs that remains elusive. Oscar Brand recorded a version, and in his song notes he referred to it as a "Scottish ballad heard in Scotland widely from tinker (wandering) families." Harry Babad used Brand's version in *Roll Me Over* and claimed it might be an Elizabethan song. Tony McCarthy used a similar version in *Bawdy British Folk Songs*, but he supplied no source data. It may be as widely sung as Brand asserted, but "The Cuckoo's Nest" has not been widely reported. Herbert Halpert (a folklorist, author, and professor emeritus at Memorial University of Newfoundland) collected fragmentary versions in which Riley's first verse is sung as a refrain and the last two lines of the refrain are different:

> But I like one that will lie still
> And cock up her legs (ass) like a whippoorwill.

In the Scots version (Brand), the young lassie is willing to aid the narrator in his quest:

> I met her in the mornin' and I had her in the night;
> I'd never gone that way before and had to do it right.
> I never would have found it and I never would have guessed
> If she hadn't showed me where to find the cuckoo's nest.

In the Americanized version, the girl is not cooperative, and only two verses actually appear in narrative sequence. Riley's version is Americanized, almost into a different song; the unifying thread for the verse is the "cuckoo's nest." Each verse can stand alone, and it has lost any ballad characteristics that it may have had.

Some like a girl that's pretty in the face,
Some like a girl that's slim around the waist;
But I like a girl with the bubbies on her breast,
And a road that's easy travelled to her cuckoo's nest.

I took my little girl for a stroll in the fall;
All that I thought about was a piece of tail.
In a nice shady bower she agreed to take a rest,
And I gently slipped my hand upon her cuckoo's nest.

"Oh! No!" she cried, and began to scream and bawl,
"That's one thing, sir, you mustn't do at all,
Because my aged mother, she would never be at rest,
If you ruffled up the feathers on my cuckoo's nest."

Along came a pigeon and a rabbit through the grass,
Along came a rattlesnake with a shell on its ass;
Of all the birds and poultry, they all have a nest,
It takes nine months to hatch out in the cuckoo's nest.

I had another girl, and her name was Bess,
I loved her better than any of the rest;
She would wiggle and she'd giggle, and she'd heist up her
    dress,
And I'd make a double circle of her cuckoo's nest.

Some like coffee, and some like tea,
But I like rotgut as strong as it can be.
That's the last of my song, and you'll never know the rest
Of the stories I could tell about the cuckoo's nest.

Field Collections and Manuscripts: Halpert to Logsdon, June 6, 1985.
References: Babad (1972), p. 36; McCarthy (1972), pp. 28–29.
Recordings: Oscar Brand, *Bawdy Songs and Backroom Ballads*, 4, Audio Fidelity AFLP 1847.

49.*

"OLD HORNY KEBRI-O"

Riley Neal could remember only that he had heard "some old cow-boy" sing this song. It has not appeared in any printed collection, and to my knowledge, only one other collector has recorded it. Herbert Halpert found a version in New Jersey, with this variant last line: "With my old horny knickabriney-o."

Lively, free

When I left home I had good luck, Four-teen maid-ens I did fuck;

Thir-teen of them I knocked up With my old horn-y ke - bri - o.

Shag-gin', shag-gin', shag-gin' a-way, Shag-gin' a lit-tle bit ev-'ry day;

Just from the whore-house and don't give a damn, With my old horn-y ke - bri - o.

When I left home I had good luck,
Fourteen maidens I did fuck;
Thirteen of them I knocked up
With my old horny kebri-o.

Branding time on the open range in New Mexico, around 1893. (Courtesy of the Museum of New Mexico, Santa Fe.)

CHORUS

    Shaggin', shaggin', shaggin' away,
    Shaggin' a little bit every day;
    Just from the whorehouse and don't give a damn,
    With my old horny kebri-o.

I took them down to the river side,
And on their bellies I did ride;
It was pretty slick, but they couldn't slide,
With my old horny kebri-o.

CHORUS

When I got back home, I had bad luck,
I fucked an old yearling that did suck,
And then jacked off on a damned old duck,
With my old horny kebri-o.

CHORUS

Field Collections and Manuscripts: Halpert to Logsdon, June 6, 1985.

50.*

"OLD MAN'S LAMENT"

The tune used for this "Lament" is "Little Brown Jug." The lyrics indicate that it is a bawdy parody of the popular song, which was composed by Joseph Eastburn Winner in 1869. The broken rhyme pattern in some verses suggests either that they were poorly reconstructed from a faulty memory or more likely, that fragments of additional verses were combined to make what we have here (the original song had six verses). The song expresses through humor the concerns and fears of many males—both young and old—of impotence. I found no other versions similar to this one, sung by Riley Neal; however, C. W. "Bill" Getz in *The Wild Blue Yonder* (1981) has three verses titled "Old Man's Lament." No tune is indicated, but the theme is the same.

When I was young and in my prime
I could get a hard on any old time;
Now I'm old and my balls are cold,
And I can't get a hard on to save my soul.

"Cowboys at Home" on the range, showing off for the camera. These cowboys worked for the 101 Ranch and Wild West show, Oklahoma. (Guy Logsdon Postcard Collection.)

When a man gets old his balls get cold,
And the head of his prick turns blue;
When he goes to diddle, it bends in the middle—
Did it ever occur to you?

I used to go out on Saturday night,
I would drink and carouse until after midnight;
I would then go home, crawl in bed with my wife,
Stay there and screw her until after daylight.

I now go to bed as soon as its dark,
I lie there and snore and groan and fart;
If my wife moves over and tickles me
I always have to get up and go pee.

If you are young and full of life,
Pray listen to me and take my advice;
Do it all that you can while you are young and spry,
For the time soon will come when you'll be the same as I.

References: Getz (1981), p. O 5.

51.*

"LONDON TOWN"

Alternate Titles:
"The Ring Dang Doo," "The Doo-Gee-Ma-Doo,"
"The Rang-a-Tang-Too," and "The Ring-a-Rang-Roo"

A widely traveled song, "London Town" (more commonly titled "Ring Dang Doo") has been sung by generations of men in this country. Ed Cray in *The Erotic Muse* stated that, "Sometime around the age of twelve or thirteen, boys seem to learn this song, just as their fathers did before them, and their fathers before them" (p. 60). And as it has traveled, the song has changed; however, the common verse essential to each version is the description of the "doodle-doo" or "ring dang doo" or whatever it is called.

The common description is "soft and round like a pussy cat" with "a hole in the middle" or "fringed all around" and "split in two." The song has two common endings. Either the young maiden passes her venereal disease to those who use her talents, or she dies of the "pox" or "clap" as passed to her by a wild man, usually a sailor or soldier. Riley Neal's version includes a moralistic regret spoken by the maiden; a complete departure from the usual progression of verses. Such a maiden's regret is common in other songs, however.

Even though the song has been collected in other English-speaking countries, it probably is a product of the United States that has been exported. Ewan MacColl and Peggy Seeger collected it from a Gypsy woman in England and in *Travellers' Songs from England and Scotland* state that it is "rarely found in the repertories of English and Scots traditional singers."

As I walked out on London's street,
A pretty maid I chanced to meet.
She offered me gold and silver, too,
Just to crawl right onto her doodle-doo.

"Your doodle-do and what is that?"
"It's something like old granny's cap;
It's fringed all around and split in two,
And that's what I call my doodle-doo."

She went into her father's house,
Just as quiet as a little mouse.
She barred the doors and windows, too,
Just to give me a shake at her doodle-doo.

She climbed upon her maiden's bed,
She took the pillow from beneath her head,
She tossed the quilts and the blankets, too,
And I crawled right on to her doodle-doo.

She went into her father's hall
And down upon her knees did fall.
"Oh! dearest father and mother, too,
I've been too free with my doodle-doo."

"You nasty, stinking, dirty bitch!
I wish I had a thorny switch.
I'd beat your back and belly, too,
And drag it through your doodle-doo."

"Oh! dearest Mother, don't be enraged.
Before you were sixteen of age,

THE WEST 30 YEARS AGO.

101 - Copyright 1909 by W.H.Martin

"The West 30 Years Ago" as photographed in 1909 on the 101 Ranch, Oklahoma. These steers are Texas longhorns, the type of cattle trail herded for two decades from Texas to northern markets. (Guy Logsdon Postcard Collection.)

You left your father and mother, too,
And followed dad for his doodle-doo.

"Oh! I oft times wished, and I've wished in vain,
I've wished I were a maid again;
But a maid I'm not or ne'er can be,
For the man I love has ruined me.

"I wish to God my babe was born,
And laid upon its father's arm,
And I, poor girl, was dead in the grave,
And the green grass over me."

Field Collections and Manuscripts: LC-AFS 1484 A1, 1486 B1; Gordon (Inferno, Mss.), 1763, 3913; Randolph (Mss.), pp. 175–79 and 118–22; Larson (Countryside), n.p.; Legman (TS VL), n.p.; "Immortalia" (1927), p. 45.

References: Babad (1972), p. 122; Brand (1960), pp. 80–81; Cray (1965), p. 52, (1969), pp. 60–61, 230–31; Getz, 2 (1986), pp. RR 4–5; Hogbotel and ffuckes (1973) p. 17; Hopkins (1979), pp. 140–41; *Immortalia* (1960), p. 68; Laycock (1982), pp. 128–29; MacColl and Seeger (1977), pp. 159–60; Silverman (1982), p. 142.

Recordings: Oscar Brand, *Bawdy Songs and Backroom Ballads*, 3, Audio Fidelity AFLP 1824; Glenn Ohrlin, on *Just Something My Uncle Told Me*, Rounder 0141; *The Unexpurgated Folk Songs of Men*, Raglan R-51.

52.*

"THE SEA CRAB"

Alternate Titles:
"Good Morning, Mister Fisherman," "The Crab Fish,"
"The Jolly Fisherman," "Fisherman, Have You Any
Sea Crabs," and "John Henry and the Crab"

"The Sea Crab" is one of the oldest bawdy songs still being sung by
traditional singers. It is known to be more than three hundred years
old, for it appeared in *Bishop Percy's Folio Manuscript.* As a folktale
it is even older; according to Gershon Legman in *The Horn Book,* it
developed in song "from a joking tale of Levantine origin recorded first
in Italy by Sacchetti about 1400." The story recounts a humorous series
of events that occur when a man takes a sea crab home and, for lack
of a better place, puts it in the chamber pot. Unaware of the guest in
the pot, his wife relieves herself only to be bitten by the crab. While
attempting to rescue her, the husband, too, is bitten; the crab holds
him in an embarrassing position. The folktale is based on the "Bungling
Fool" motif, J 2675 in Stith Thompson's *Motif-Index of Folk Literature.*
Guthrie T. Meade, Jr.'s historical study and analysis (1958) provides an
extensive lineage for "The Sea Crab."

Not only does "The Sea Crab" have an impressive genealogy, but
also it apparently enjoyed widespread popularity across this country.
Meade listed two oral tradition sources; Ed Cray had two versions in his
1969 collection but cited other variants; Vance Randolph collected two
versions and a fragment in the Ozarks; and Robert W. Gordon received a
version from New York in 1923 and another in 1926, as well as a version
that carried no date or place. There are variants in the Wilgus–Western
Kentucky Folklore Archives, and Peter Kennedy includes in *Folksongs of
Britain and Ireland* an English variant and cites additional collections in

which variants are found. However, the Kennedy variant is not nearly as
explicit as this variant sung by Riley Neal.

Riley's version does not differ significantly from most variants, except that he whistled the melody of the first line of each verse after
singing it and used "Sing ho, sing ha" as a short refrain. Most variants
have a longer refrain of nonsense syllables.

Riley stated, "I learned this when I was a boy, from an old Texas
trail driver named Ambrose Bull. I sang 'Nearer My God to Thee' at his
funeral."

"Good morning, mister fisherman, I wish you mighty well,
    (whistle)
Good morning, Mister Fisherman, I wish you mighty well.
Say, kind sir, have you any crabs to sell?"
Sing ho, sing ha.

"Yes sir, yes sir, I have three, (whistle)
Yes sir, yes sir, I have three,
And the best of them I'll sell to thee."
Sing ho, sing ha.

He picked up a sea crab by the back bone, (whistle)
He picked up a sea crab by the back bone,

And like a damned fool went a-waggin' off home.
Sing ho, sing ha.

When he got home his old woman was asleep, (whistle)
When he got home his old woman was asleep.
He put it in the piss pot safe for to keep.
Sing ho, sing ha.

The old woman got up the piss pot to hunt, (whistle)
The old woman got up the piss pot to hunt.
The sea crab nailed her right by the cunt.
Sing ho, sing ha.

"Oh, John! oh, John! just as sure as you are born, (whistle)
Oh John! oh, John! just as sure as you are born,
The devil's in the piss pot a-sticking out his horn."
Sing ho, sing ha.

John got down and he peeped up her clothes, (whistle)
John got down and he peeped up her clothes.
The sea crab nailed him right by the nose,
Sing ho, sing ha.

"Oh, Sal! Oh, Sal! Can't you let a little fart? (whistle)
Oh, Sal! Oh, Sal! Can't you let a little fart,
To blow my nose and your ass apart?"
Sing ho, sing ha.

Sal, oh, Sal, she tried a little bit, (whistle)
Sal, oh, Sal, she tried a little bit,
She filled John's face plum full of shit!
Sing ho, sing ha.

"Oh, Jackie, oh, Jackie, get the horse and the cart, (whistle)
Jackie, oh, Jackie, get the horse and the cart,
To pull my nose and Mammie's ass apart."
Sing ho, sing ha.

It tickled those children plum to the heart, (whistle)
It tickled those children plum to the heart,
To see the horse pull and to hear Mammy fart.
Sing ho, sing ha.

Now my song is ended, and I'll sing to you no more, (whistle)
Now my song is ended, and I'll sing to you no more,

I've got a risen on my ass and you can suck the core.
Sing ho, sing ha.

Field Collections and Manuscripts: LC-AFS 4169 B2; Gordon (Inferno, Mss.), 474, 2188, 3913; Randolph (Mss.), pp. 38–43; "Immortalia" (1927), pp. 38–39.

References: Babad (1972), p. 101; Cray (1965), pp. 75–78, (1969), pp. 2–4; Farmer, 4 (1897, 1964), pp. 14–16; Furnivall (1868, 1963), pp. 99–100; *Immortalia* (1960), pp. 58–59; Kennedy (1975), pp. 452, 476; Laycock (1982), pp. 236–37; Legman (1964), pp. 188, 221, 346, 363, 413–14, 446, 471; Meade (1958), pp. 91–100; Thompson (1955).

53.*

"ONE-EYED RILEY"

Alternate Titles:
"The One-Eyed Riley," "O'Reilly's Daughter,"
and "One Ball Riley"

Known to be well over one hundred years old, "One-Eyed Riley" still enjoys popularity across the nation—particularly among male college students. As a British import, the American spelling and pronunciation are often "Old Riley" instead of "O'Reilly."

In 1949, T. S. Eliot had the Unidentified Guest, Sir Henry Harcourt-Reilly, sing one verse in *The Cocktail Party*. Yet the song seldom appeared in print before Eliot's use. Oscar Brand included it in his *Bawdy Songs and Backroom Ballads*, and it has been included in most bawdy collections printed since then. Usually, there are four to seven verses, and the use of the euphemism for sexual intercourse—"shag"—appears in most versions. The primary theme is "shagging" Riley's daughter; in some versions the narrator is caught by Riley, who gets treated roughly for catching his daughter enjoying herself. The version Riley Neal sang may be the most complete version to be recorded; it is a ballad of ten verses in which the narrator "rolled and tossed" the daughter, scared and "fucked" the mother, abused the father, and when the "old tom cat" ran by he "fucked the hole where the cat went under." Even though the daughter consented to sex, the mother called it rape. Most other versions have a longer nonsense refrain than does Riley's. In cleansed versions, O'Riley is interested only in marrying the daughter, not in premarital "shagging."

When Riley finished singing the song, he said with a gleam in his eye and a chuckle, "That one was about me. No, not really, it just happened that way."

Cowboys relax at night around the campfire and lantern light by singing songs, swapping stories, smoking, listening to fiddle music, and dancing, O R Ranch, Arizona, 1910. (The Erwin E. Smith Collection of the Library of Congress on deposit at the Amon Carter Museum, Fort Worth.)

I was a-sitting in my easy chair,
A-viewing the landlord's daughter;
I took a notion in my head,
I'd like to feel her hindquarter.

REFRAIN (after each verse):
    Turry-tink to Wiley,
    Dury-dink and One-Eyed Riley.

Mary went up to her room,
Left her door about half open,
After giving me a hint,
To fill all cracks that I found open.

I took my shoes in my right hand
And crept to Mary's chamber.
"Oh! Mary, Mary, dearest Mary,
Have you lodgings for a stranger?"

I took her lily white hand in mine,
And I threw my left leg over.
We rolled and tossed all over the bed,
Then I lay in her lap when the jig was over.

As I was sneaking from the room,
Who should I meet but her damned old mother.
She threw her hands up over her head,
And hollered, "Rape and bloody murder!"

As I was running down the stairs,
Who should I meet but her damned old father,
With a sword and a pistol by his side
To kill the man who raped his daughter.

I caught him by the ass of his pants,
Shoved his head in a tub of water,
I shoved the pistol up his ass
And fucked the old lady and not the daughter.

I ran out in the middle of the yard,
Shook my prick at old dog Towser.
The old tomcat came around the house
A making forty miles an hour.

I chased the tomcat around the house,
He ran under a pile of lumber.
I had my prick out in my hand,
So I fucked the hole the cat went under.

As I was a-goin' down the street,
I could hear at every quarter,
"There goes the one-eyed son-of-a-bitch,
Who fucked old Riley's wife and daughter."

Field Collections and Manuscripts: LC-AFS 3640 A1, 3674 A1, 2322 A3 and A4; LC-AFC (Subject Collection), Bawdy Song Folder; Gordon (Inferno, Mss.), 3803; Larson (Countryside), n.p.; Legman (TS VF), n.p.; "Apples of Eden" (n.d.), n.p.; *Shitty Songs of Sigma Nu* (n.d.) n.p.

References: Babad (1972), p. 134; Brand (1960), pp. 22–23; Cray (1965), pp. 105–7, (1969), pp. 28–29, 228–29; Eliot (1950), p. 30; Getz, 2 (1986), p. OO 16; Healy (1968), pp. 98–99; Hogbotel and ffuckes (1973), p. 44; Hopkins (1979), p. 158; Laycock (1982), pp. 185–86; Legman (1964), p. 446; McGregor (1972), pp. 71–72; Silverman (1982), p. 128.

Recordings: Oscar Brand, *Bawdy Songs and Backroom Ballads*, 1, Audio Fidelity AFLP 1906; Jim Garland, on *Just Something My Uncle Told Me*, Rounder 0141.

54.*

"THE KEYHOLE IN THE DOOR"

Versions of this song vary from explicit sexual action to peep show or strip-tease voyeurism; Riley Neal's version is explicit. The song is probably related to "The Whummil Bore," number twenty-seven in Francis James Child's *The English and Scottish Popular Ballads.* In this ballad, a servant of the king tells of looking through a small hole and seeing the princess nude as her maids dress her. The "peeping Tom" in Riley's "Keyhole in the Door" is a guest in the house, and the maiden is no longer a princess.

In Oscar Brand's version, a sailor not only peeks through the keyhole but also enters the room and has sex with the girl; his reward is "the pox." In Riley Neal's version, the narrator "jabbed it through the keyhole in the door." Thomas E. Cheney in *Mormon Songs from the Rocky Mountains* provides a variant in which the humor is in the number of clothes "Fair Jennie" removes; the Brand and Cheney variants have a refrain, but Riley did not sing one. The most complete variant, sent to Robert W. Gordon by a California man in 1924, is composed of nine verses and a two-line refrain; each verse follows the logical progression of a female disrobing, along with the appropriate thoughts of a man who can look but not touch. Gale Huntington found a similar variant in the 1879 logbook of the ship *Andrew Hicks;* it is reprinted in Huntington's *Songs the Whalemen Sang.*

Last night she left the par-lor, I think 'twas scarce-ly nine, And
by some hap-py for-tune, Her room was next to mine.

Last night she left the parlor,
I think 'twas scarcely nine,
And by some happy fortune,
Her room was next to mine.

And I being like Columbus
Had regions to explore;
I took a snug position
By the keyhole in the door.

Up before the mirror
She proceeded to undress,
She removed her outer garments,
There were forty, more or less.

She removed her undergarments,
I guess there was a score,
I could not be real certain
Through the keyhole in the door.

Down upon the hearth rug
Her little feet to warm,
With nothing but a chemise
To hide her perfect form.

I could see a sky-blue garter
On either leg she wore,
She was a perfect picture
Through the keyhole in the door.

If she'd only remove that chemise,
I'd ask for nothing more.
"Great God!" I saw her do it
Through the keyhole in the door.

I could feel my hair a-raising
Like the bristles on a boar;

"My God!" I felt like jumping
Through the keyhole in the door.

If I were like Samson,
I'd tear that damn door down!
I'd jazz that pretty maiden,
Or I'd wake this whole damned town!

But, as I am not like Samson,
Like any other boar,
I'll simply squirt my gun off,
Through the keyhole in the door.

When I awoke this morning,
My jock it was sore;
I think I must have jabbed it
Through the keyhole in the door.

Field Collections and Manuscripts: LC-AFS 4204 A2, 1635 B2, 2322 B4, 980 A1; Gordon (Inferno, Mss.), 3914 and (Davids, Mss.), 35; Randolph (Mss), pp. 610–11; Larson (Countryside), n.p.

References: Cheney (1968), pp. 16–18; Fowke (1966), pp. 47–48; Getz (1981), pp. JK 4–5; Huntington (1964), pp. 315–17; Laycock (1982), pp. 104–6; Legman (1964), p. 181.

Recordings: Oscar Brand, *Bawdy Sea Shanties*, Audio Fidelity AFLP 1884; Holland Puckett, Gennett 6271; and there are other hillbilly/country recordings of suggestive versions.

"The Whummil Bore"
Coffin and Renwick (1977), pp. 48–49, 223.

55.*

"THE BUTTONS ON HIS PANTS"

Alternate Titles:
"When I Was Young" and "An Inch Above Your Knee"

This song is an Americanized variant of the popular British song "Bell Bottom Trousers." However, the changes are sufficient enough to have created a separate song that travels side by side with its parent.

Very little variation is found among the collected versions of "The Buttons on His Pants." The major variation occurs in the final verses. One ending has the sailor pay the girl "For the damage I have done"; he has no interest in the possibility of fathering a child. In Riley Neal's version the ending warns single girls never to let "a sailor get an inch above your knee."

In this variant the female is the narrator. There is a similar song in which the sailor narrates his experience—"The Fire Ship," also known as "The Roving Kind" and "She Was One of the Roving Kind." While seduction by a sailor is the mutual theme, the songs do not appear to be related.

Moderate

When I was young and fool - ish, It was my heart's de - light To go to balls and par - ties And stay out late at night.

When I was young and foolish,
It was my heart's delight
To go to balls and parties
And stay out late at night.

'Twas at the ball I met him,
He asked me for a dance,
I could tell he was a sailor
By the buttons on his pants.

His shoes were nicely polished;
His hair was neatly combed;
He danced with me all evening,
Then asked to take me home.

As we were homeward strolling,
I heard some people say,
"There goes another girlie
Being led astray."

'Twas in my father's hallway,
Where first I met my fate;
It was in my mother's bedroom,
Where I was forced to lay.

He laid me down so gently,
He pulled my dress so high;
He said, "Now Madge, my darling,
I'll have it, or I'll die."

Come all you single girlies
And take a tip from me,
Don't ever let a sailor
Get an inch above your knee.

They'll hug you and caress you.
They'll promise to be true;
But when they've got your cherry,
They'll say, "To hell with you."

Field Collections and Manuscripts: LC-AFS 436 B1; Gordon (Inferno, Mss.), 482; Larson (Countryside), n.p.; "Immortalia" (1927), p. 58.
References: Brophy and Partridge (1965), pp. 68–69; Cray (1965), pp. 103–5, (1969), pp. 21, 251–60; *Immortalia* (1960), pp. 88–89; Wannan (1972), p. 31.

56.*

"DOWN, DERRY DOWN"

In *The Horn Book*, Gershon Legman devotes a lengthy, detailed, and scholarly section to Robert Burns and *The Merry Muses of Caledonia*, in which he quickly puts aside any doubt that Burns was both a collector and writer of bawdy songs. Legman's primary purpose is to discuss *The Merry Muses* as a source of folk songs, many of which were bawdy.

According to Legman, an edition of *The Merry Muses* published in approximately 1825, the only copy of which is in the British Museum, had a number of songs from other sources that had been added to the text. Legman refers to two of the songs as "tales-in-verse," one of which was "The Cricket and Crab-Louse." Its story came from "the profound and widely-dispersed folk motif of an insect—or sometimes the unborn child—lost inside the vagina and terrified by the intrusion of the penis, the fantasy underlying *Tristram Shandy*" (p. 183).

This song as sung by Riley Neal is probably more than two hundred years old, and, if not of Scottish origin, at least it was popular enough to have been considered by the Scots as one of their songs. However, it appeared only in the [circa] 1825 edition of *The Merry Muses*. I do not know if other versions are in unpublished collections in Scotland, but in this country it has not appeared in printed collections or in the field collections to which I had access. The folktale motif as mentioned by Legman is not in Thompson's *Motif-Index of Literature*, although it should be noted that other bawdy motifs are also missing from the *Motif-Index*.

Riley stated simply, "I heard it from a man named Jess Jackson."

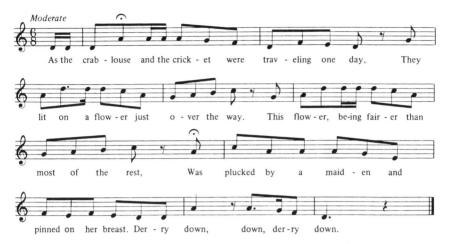

As the crab-louse and the cricket were traveling one day,
They lit on a flower just over the way.
This flower, being fairer than most of the rest,
Was plucked by a maiden and pinned on her breast.
Derry down, down, derry down.

At the dead hours of midnight as this maid lay asleep,
The crab-louse and the cricket down her backbone did creep.
Said the cricket to the crab-louse, "I think I'll stop here."
Said the crab-louse to the cricket, "I'm bound for the hair."
Derry down, down, derry down.

Next day as the crab-louse was passing that way,
He met his friend cricket and to him did say,
"Come sit here beside me in the shade of this tree;
I'll tell you the trouble which happened to me."
Derry down, down, derry down.

"Along came a traveler, traveling on his way,
His head was as red as the sun at noon day.
He pushed me before him, he pushed me right in;
By puffing and swelling he took off the skin."
Derry down, down, derry down.

"By puffing and swelling much larger he grew,
Till his red head it bursted, and his brains at me flew."

   .   .   .   .
   .   .   .   .

Derry down, down, derry down.

"All beslimed and begrimed I followed him out;
I sat on a bedpost until I dried out.
Come listen, friend cricket, come listen to me,
I'll give you a warning that'll always help thee."
Derry down, down, derry down.

"Down under that mountain there was a dark cave,
'Twas dark as a dungeon and silent as the grave.
With brown and black hair, it's befringed all about,
And if you get in there, you'll never get out."
Derry down, down, derry down.

References: Legman (1964).

57.*

"THE JOLLY BAKER"

In the first verse after the "jolly baker" establishes that he is a baker who bakes his "bread brown," he uses the double entendre to brag about the size of his penis—"I've got the biggest rolling pin of any man in town." The succeeding verses depart radically from the humor and sophistication of double entendre; the song becomes a man's graphic expression of his own sexual prowess—similar to any brag story or song.

The refrain, "Latin derry," indicates a song's origin in England or Scotland many years ago. Yet I have found no additional text or reference for comparison or for an indication of age. There are other "jolly" songs however: "The Jolly Tinker," "The Jolly Beggar," "The Jolly Ploughboy," and "The Jolly Tradesman." In Burns's *The Merry Muses of Caledonia* (1964 reprint) there is "The Jolly Gauger," but none of the songs is as graphic as "The Jolly Baker," and none has the "Latin derry" refrain. This is another Riley Neal song.

Brisk

I am a jol - ly bak - er, and I bake my bread brown,

Lat - in der - ry, lat - in der - ry day. I

am a jol - ly bak - er, and I bake my bread brown, I've

got the big - gest roll - ing pin of an - y man in town.

Lat - in der - ry, lat - in der - ry, lat - in der - ry day.

I am a jolly baker, and I bake my bread brown,
Latin derry, latin derry day.
I am a jolly baker, and I bake my bread brown,
I've got the biggest rolling pin of any man in town.
Latin derry, latin derry, latin derry day.

Oh! there was a little maid, and she lived in our town,
Latin derry, latin derry day.
There was a little maid, and she lived in our town,
She was always a-teasin' me to buy her a gown.
Latin derry, latin derry, latin derry day.

She woke me one morning a-knockin' at my door,
Latin derry, latin derry day.
She woke me one morning a-knockin' at my door,
Shoes and stockings in her hand and chemise up before.
Latin derry, latin derry, latin derry day.

I took her around the slender waist and gently laid her down,
Latin derry, latin derry day.
I took her round the slender waist and gently laid her down;
According to the contract, I wore the curly crown.
Latin derry, latin derry, latin derry day.

I fucked her in the kitchen, and I fucked her in the hall,
Latin derry, latin derry day.
I fucked her in the kitchen, and I fucked her in the hall,
I fucked her in the shit house, the damndest place of all.
Latin derry, latin derry, latin derry day.

I took her to the grave yard and laid her on a stone,
Latin derry, latin derry day.
I took her to the graveyard and laid her on a stone;
Every time I'd heave her up I'd hear the dead groan.
Latin derry, latin derry, latin derry day.

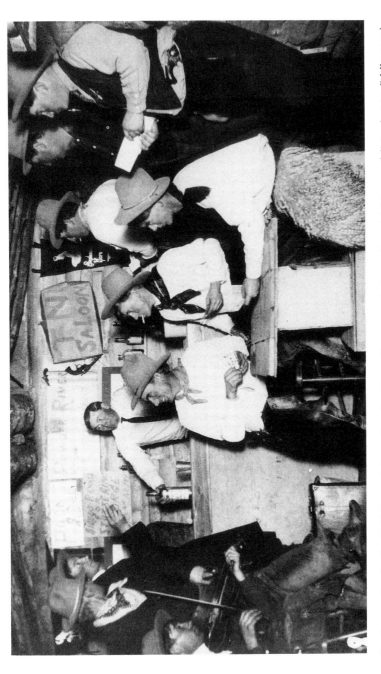

Cowboys relax in the T N Camp Saloon, Powder River, Montana, playing poker, drinking, and listening to fiddle music. (Photo by Evelyn Cameron; courtesy of the Montana Historical Society, Helena.)

I've fucked fillies, and I've fucked mules,
Latin derry, latin derry day.
I've fucked fillies, and I've fucked mules;
I'm going down to hell and teach a-fuckin' school.
Latin derry, latin derry, latin derry day.

Oh! I went down to hell, and the devil wasn't well,
Latin derry, latin derry day.
I went down to hell, and the devil wasn't well;
I fucked his damn daughter, and I fucked her well.
Latin derry, latin derry, latin derry day.

The old lady come in with a ten-foot pole,
Latin derry, latin derry day.
The old lady come in with a ten-foot pole;
I exercised my prick around her damned ass-hole.
Latin derry, latin derry, latin derry day.

Now I'm down to hell and got up my sign,
Latin derry, latin derry day.
Now I'm down to hell and got up my sign,
If you want to learn to fuck just give me a dime.
Latin derry, latin derry, latin derry day.

58.*

"THE SADDEST FACE IN THE MINING TOWN"

This "lost love" ballad has the tone of an old ballad, yet I have not found it in any printed or recorded collections. Perhaps it was a broadside that through time was shaped into a traditionally structured ballad, or it could have been a sentimental music hall song. In any event, it is a good example of older traditional singers' love for the sentimental. They didn't care about the age or origin of a song—it was its sentiment that gave it life to them. Traditional cowboy singers were no different; tragedy and sentiment were no strangers. All too often, the imagined or remembered love could be the only reality of home, marriage, and family. Yet to offset such sentimentality, the stark blatant rejection of sentiment in cowboys' bawdy songs was a contrast of emotion and relief from the absence of shared love.

Riley Neal loved the song and wiped away tears as he sang it and others like it. He said, "This was always one of my favorites. I learned that from the Peach family, Bill Peach. They lived up here at Strawberry —old, old-timers up there."

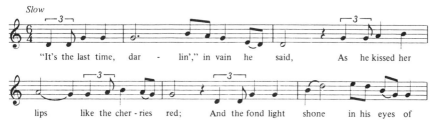

Slow

"It's the last time, dar - lin'," in vain he said, As he kissed her lips like the cher - ries red; And the fond light shone in his eyes of

brown,   "My love   is the   pret-ti - est girl in   town."

"It's the last time, darlin'," in vain he said,
As he kissed her lips like the cherries red;
And the fond light shone in his eyes of brown,
"My love is the prettiest girl in town.

"Tomorrow high up the bells shall ring
The most joyous peace that ever a-came;
No king is more blessed on his royal throne
Than I shall be when I claim my own."

With a fond farewell and a sweet good-bye,
She let him go with a troubled sigh;
Into the bucket that swayed and swung
O'er the glowering abyss he lightly sprung.

But the joy of her heart seemed turned to woe
As they lowered him into the depth below;
The fond fair face with the tresses brown
Was the fairest face in the mining town.

High up in the tower the marriage bells
On their wedding day pealed a mournful knell;
But the true heart was buried beneath earth and stone
Way down in the depth of the mine alone.

The years rolled on in a weary way
Till fifty years with its shadows gray
Had changed the light of her eyes to glow
And turned the brown of her hair to snow.

But never the touch of a husband's lips,
Nor the clasp of a child's sweet finger tips
Had come to lighten the shadows brown
Of the saddest face in the mining town.

Way down in the depth of the mine one day
In the loosening earth they were digging away,
They discovered a figure so young and fair
From the silent lips to the light brown hair.

Untouched by fingers of time's decay
As they drew him up to the light of day,
The wondering people all gathered around
To gaze on the man so strangely found.

There came a woman from among the crowd
With snowy hair and her old head bowed;
She silently kneeled by the form of clay
And kissed the lips that were cold and grey.

The fond old head with the snowy hair
On his youthful breast lay pillowed there;
He had found her at last, his waiting bride,
And the people buried them side by side.

59.*

"THE IRISHMAN"

Riley Neal sent the words of this song to me and sang it during my second visit in 1970. I have not found it in any field collections, printed song collections, or nineteenth-century song books; however, my access to American-Irish songsters has been limited. I assume, based on its content and structure, that it is a nineteenth-century music hall comic song. Yet the humor is a bit keener than straight burlesque humor, and the last episode is a folktale motif.

The Irishman sees a wagonload of pumpkins and is told that they are mule eggs; he buys one and tries to hatch it. After four weeks of sitting on it, in disgust he throws it away and scares a rabbit out of the brush; he sees the rabbit and yells "Come back! Don't you know I'm your dad?" This traditional "numbskull" motif is J 1772.1 in Thompson's *Motif-Index of Folk Literature* and tale type 1319 in Aarne and Thompson's *The Types of the Folktale*.

The Irishman experiences three numbskull episodes or jokes, which an imaginative singer and/or song-writer evidently adapted in a poetic format and set to music.

Riley learned this "from old John Hughes—use ta be around here in the 1920s. He was a blacksmith—a drunk."

'Twas in the mer - ry month of May An I - rish-man here land - ed; He

start - ed out to see the sights, An I - rish-man so can - did. He

had some fun - ny hap -pen-ings, He made some fun - ny slips; I'll

tell you of his trou - bles since Old Pad - dy left his ship.

'Twas in the merry month of May
An Irishman here landed;
He started out to see the sights,
An Irishman so candid.
He had some funny happenings,
He made some funny slips;
I'll tell you of his troubles since
Old Paddy left his ship.

As he was strolling around the dock
He spied a great big anchor;
He had no idea what it was
And for information hankered.
He asked a man in uniform
By the name of Johnny Max
To point him out the son-of-a-gun
Who used that great big axe.

As he was going up the road
In a tree he spied a parrot;
Says, "Ain't that a pretty bird?
I'll catch it, or I'm a coward."
He started climbing up the tree,
The parrot says, "What's the word?"
Pat says, "I beg your pardon, sir,
I thought you were a bird."

Just then the parrot begun to sing,
"God Save the Queen."
Old Pat would-a killed it then and there,
But its feathers they were green.

He couldn't harm that color,
And his anger held in check;
"Oh! if you were a canary bird
I'd wring your yaller neck."

As he was going down the street,
He saw some pumpkins in a wagon;
He asked the man who was in the seat,
What the horses were a-dragging.
He told him they were donkey eggs,
He believed it like a fool;
He bought him one and took it home
To hatch a little mule.

He sat on it for four long weeks,
Until the pumpkin did decay;
He got disgusted with the thing
And flung it far away.
He scared a rabbit out of the brush,
He saw what ears it had;
"Oh! come back here you son-of-a-gun,
Don't you know that I'm your dad?"

References: Aarne and Thompson (1964); Thompson (1957).

60.*

"PETER PULLIN' BLUES"

This is a song about sex education—a father's rather memorable method of introducing his son to sex, along with the fears of masturbation. Dallas Turner, contributed this text:

> I first heard this song in the summer of 1940. We hired a cowboy named Jack Steele to drive buck rake during haying season. Jack claimed to be from Lone Pine, California and was (so he said) a bosom buddy of Tex Fletcher. Jack wasn't a singer but he knew a passel of bawdy songs. This is one of them. Jack said he learned it from Tex Fletcher who (he claimed) wrote it. It is sung to the traditional tune of "Hungry Hash House Blues" and "Harding County Home"—two songs that are identified with Tex Fletcher.
>
> While none of us believed that he knew Tex Fletcher, years later, I discovered Tex Fletcher had spent some time near Lone Pine where he and Wilford Cline had a small ranch.

Tex Fletcher was a New Yorker who moved to South Dakota during the 1930s and became a cowboy, entertainer, and song writer. Glenn Ohrlin sings a few of Fletcher's songs, including "My Harding County Home," which appears in *The Hell-Bound Train*, along with more information about Fletcher. It is not definitely known that Fletcher wrote "Peter Pullin' Blues."

Cowboy saloons or drinking holes were seldom places of grandeur as commonly depicted by Hollywood. The name "Nigger Bob Saloon," Ismay, Montana, was derived from the owner's hatred and bigotry. (Photo by John A. White, 1896; courtesy of the Montana Historical Society, Helena.)

Papa caught me in the loft, I'd just finished jackin' off,
And he grabbed me by my leg and pulled my down;
Papa said, "You gawdamned fool, stop this playin' with your
  tool,
And I'll take you to the whorehouse up in town."

CHORUS
  If you're playin' with your prick, well you'd better stop it quick,
  It will soon hang down and watch you shine your shoes;
  I have fucked my final cow, and I'm in the 'sylum now,
  That is why I've got the peter pullin' blues.

Papa said, "Now just how long have you jerked your fuckin'
  dong?
It has made a lot of fellers climb the walls;
Son, this damned jack-offin' bull, it has the 'slyums full,
They'll put acid on your cock, cut out your balls."

Papa scared me half to death, he was cussin' ev'ry breath,
And I never had fucked nothin' but a cow;
But that practice I had quit 'cause a heifer took a shit
On my prick, and that is why I'm jackin' now.

We knocked at the whorehouse door, greeted by the madam
  whore,
She was drinkin', I guess whiskey from a glass;
Papa said, "This is my son, and this bastard's twenty-one,
Annabelle, it's time he had a piece of ass."

So she led me from the room, I could smell her damned
  perfume,
And she said, "Sweetheart, you must take off your pants";
When she grabbed me by the cock, it got harder than a rock,
'Cause to fuck a girl at last I had the chance.

Then she led me to a stand, an eye dropper in her hand,
And she squirted something red into my prick;
Well, it hurt so gawdamned bad that the hard on that I'd had
It was gone and I was stranded up shit crick.

So she skinned my peter back, and that bitch began to jack,
She said, "Honey, you have got a pretty rod;
Let me get it hard again, then sweetheart, I'll put it in,
It will feel good when you're shootin' off your wad."

But she couldn't get it hard, though she rubbed the head with
    lard,
The bell rang and she said, "I gotta go;
Babe, your gawdamn jackin' off, it has left your peter soft,
Pay your bill and then you mother fucker, blow!"

61.*

"HONKYTONK ASSHOLE"

Baxter Black is a hard-working, creative individual who has a rapport with the everyday working cowboy. I offer this song of his as an example of current bawdy song writing. The tune and the words are memorable, and the theme could apply to many young and old cowboys —at least it appeals to those who think that some element of the song was written about them. Its popularity in the West is growing.

Baxter wrote it for his friend from Idaho, Pinto Bennett, "The Famous Motel Cowboy." Pinto asked Baxter for his worst song; Baxter replied, "I haven't written it, yet," then wrote this song for Pinto. Pinto Bennett and His Republicans, now known as "The Famous Motel Cowboy Band," close each show with it.

I hang out in bars, both-er the dol - lies,
Speak when I'm not spo - ken to, Bum cig-ar-
ettes, flirt with the wait-ress, Wear-ing a mir-ror on my
shoe. I sing all the songs

a-long with the juke-box, Tell jokes that ev-'ry-one's heard,

Then late in the eve-ning the bar-tend-er calls me— I've

CHORUS

nev-er for-got-ten his words. "Honk-y-tonk ass -

hole, I'm talk-ing to you, I've told you and

told you, but there's no get-ting through; You're bad for my

busi - ness, you both-er and bore; Honk - y-tonk

ass - hole, git yer ass out the door."

I hang out in bars (and) bother the dollies
(And) speak when I'm not spoken to,
Bum cigarettes (and) flirt with the waitress,
(I'm) wearing a mirror on my shoe.
I sing all the songs along with the jukebox,
Tell jokes that everyone's heard,
Then late in the evening the bartender calls me—
I've never forgotten his words.

CHORUS
    "Honkytonk asshole, I'm talking to you,
    I've told you and told you, but there's no getting through;
    You're bad for my business, you bother and bore,
    Honkytonk asshole, git yer ass out the door."

I write on the walls, throw butts on the floor,
Brag about horses I've rode;

Dance with a darlin' and step on her feet;
They think I'm one brick shy a load.
But I do right well feelin' up dollies,
Tellin' my stories out loud,
Until that bartender figgers me out
And calls to me over the crowd.

CHORUS

IV

A SINGING COWBOY ROUNDUP

When cowboys trail-herded their range cattle north out of Texas across Indian Territory into Kansas during the late 1860s, they burned their brand deeply into the culture of the United States and ultimately the world; they left a vast, almost immeasurable trail across the lives of generations who lived and died since that first herd was started northward. With the passing of time and with the help of romanticizers in the fields of literature, history, journalism, and music, along with Hollywood and television, the cowboy became a folk hero, developed into a national legend, and ultimately was transformed into an American myth. But while the imaginary cowboy became more unreal, generations of *working* cowboys—or real cowboys—have nourished and kept alive their way of life, their work ethic, and their occupational techniques and customs from which the myth emerged. There are still many cowboys and ranchers who are not radically different from their nineteenth-century counterparts, whereas the "urban" and "reel" cowboys have only a "cloth" resemblance. As Baxter Black has written, there are cowboys out there, but "You just can't see them from the highway." It is among the real cowboys that the traditional folk songs can still be found and by whom new poems and songs are written each year. The "old songs" found in modern times form much—but not all—of this collection.

The cowboys' musical brand became a distinctive mark by the 1890s, but the first generation of range cattle industry cowboys loved and sang the songs that they carried from home; "home" to most of them was within the South. Therefore, their musical lineage was English-Scottish folk songs mixed or cross-bred with minstrel and popular music hall sentimental songs. J. Frank Dobie believed that the songs from the Civil War, particularly Confederate songs, "have a legitimate place in any collection of balladry of the Southwest."[1] And the early range cattle industry cowboy did indeed, sing Confederate songs along with music hall, minstrel, and folk songs, however, songs that used cowboy experiences and philosophy for themes did not appear until the 1870s.

It is strange that cowboy songs took so long to emerge, for contrary to popular belief, the Texas cattle industry was in existence during the 1840s and 1850s. Drovers trail-herded Texas longhorns to northern cities for years before the Civil War. During those years the terminology, tools, clothing, and work techniques that are still used were being developed. Yet that era of the cattle industry was not romanticized, and little has been written about it. The cowboy, or the cowboy myth as known today, was and is a reflection of the post-Civil War cowboy, and cowboy-theme songs are about that and subsequent eras.

The reason for the absence of songs and the dearth of reminiscences of the pre-Civil War cattle industry probably resided in the attitudes of the cowboys' contemporaries. Texas cattle were often ridiculed in newspaper accounts; they were hated by farmers in states through which they were herded because they often carried dreaded and deadly Texas fever.

The cattle markets paid little for Texas cattle compared to the price paid for cattle raised in northern states. Therefore, resistance from farmers and low prices made the trail drives before the Civil War either marginally profitable or else unprofitable—often a major loss to the cattlemen.[2]

Post-Civil War growth of the range cattle industry was spurred by Joseph G. McCoy in 1867, when he persuaded officials of the Eastern Division of the Union Pacific Railroad to build a spur to Abilene, Kansas. McCoy's decision to ship cattle from western Kansas was pragmatically based on laws that were either still in effect from the 1850s or recently passed in the mid-1860s in many midwestern states that prevented Texas cattle from being trail-herded across their borders. Kansas made an exception to its law when in February 1867, it specifically opened a portion of Kansas to Texas longhorn cattle. With entrepreneurial vision and skill, McCoy first sold his idea of "shipping yards" in the area to

Union Pacific officials and then selected Abilene as the location for the pens.

Earlier in the year other promoters had spread circulars in Texas in which they encouraged cattlemen to drive their cattle toward Kansas, where buyers would purchase them. But no buyers waited, and the drovers were stranded in Indian Territory with thousands of cattle. McCoy sent a rider into the Territory to tell the drovers to drive their cattle to Abilene. As a result, the first shipment of Texas longhorns left Abilene on September 5, 1867, and by the end of the year approximately thirty-five thousand head of cattle had been trail-herded to Abilene.[3] The legendary range cattle industry and trail drives were underway.

Trail Herd Era

McCoy's experiences in the cattle business and in Abilene were published in 1874 under the title *Historic Sketches of the Cattle Trade of the West and Southwest*, the first book to be published about the range cattle industry. It is considered to be one of the essential books about the industry, and it also contains the first mention, in print, of cowboys singing to cattle. McCoy wrote:

> Drovers consider that the cattle do themselves great injury by running round in a circle, which is termed in cow-boy parlance, "milling," and it can only be stayed by standing at distance and hallooing or singing to them. The writer has many times set upon the fence of a shipping yard and sang to an enclosed herd whilst a train would be rushing by. And it is surprising how quiet the herd will be so long as they can hear the human voice; but if they fail to hear it above the din of the train, a rush is made, and the yards bursted asunder, unless very strong. Singing hymns to Texan steers is the peculiar forte of a genuine cow-boy, but the spirit of true piety does not abound in the sentiment.
>
> We have read of singing psalms to dead horses, but singing to a lot of Texan steers is an act of piety that few beside a Western drover are capable of. But 'tis said that "Music hath charms that soothe the savage breast," or words to that effect, and why not "soothe" a stampeding Texan steer? We pause, repeating, why not?[4]

McCoy made other observations about the cowboys. Their life in the cow camp "is routine and dull"; with thousands of cattle around them milk and butter were never available because of "pure shiftlessness and the lack of energy." McCoy ascribed other privations such as sleeping in the open without the cover of a tent to the same characteristics. He saw most, but not all, cowboys as boys who enjoyed "frolic and debauchery"; whose eyes, while they dance, light up with "excitement liquor and lust."[5] He wrote about cowboy life:

> It is hard and full of exposure, but is wild and free, and the young man who has long been a cow-boy has but little taste for any other occupation. He lives hard, works hard, has but few comforts and fewer necessities. He has little, if any, taste for reading. He enjoys a coarse practical joke or a smutty story; loves danger but abhors labor of the common kind; never tires riding, never wants to walk, no matter how short the distance he wants to go. He would rather fight with pistols than pray; loves tobacco, liquor and women better than any other trinity.[6]

Cowboys did not arrive at that condition without assistance, for Abilene quickly attracted saloon keepers, gamblers, and prostitutes—all of whom were ready and waiting to help a cowboy part with what in some instances amounted to six months' or a year's wages. In the early years, there were at least seven saloons, of which the Alamo was the most popular.[7] But by 1870, thirty-two saloons were licensed in a town that had an off-season population of about five hundred citizens.[8] Most of the prostitutes arrived in Abilene each year when the trail herd season opened and departed when the last cowboys returned to the ranches. The Abilene citizenry, particularly the women, became incensed at the blatant openness of the brothels. In 1870, an ordinance was passed to eject the prostitutes and all individuals connected with the enterprise. So pimps and madames set up house about one mile out of town. The following year the city fathers, recognizing that they could not stop the trade, placed the women and houses on a plot of land southeast of town, which became known as "The Devil's Addition to Abilene."[9] That same year Abilene ceased to be a cattle-trade center, and the prostitutes took their wares to Wichita, the new center of trade. Where cowboys gathered, so did the prostitutes.

While McCoy painted a rather severe picture of the trail herding cowboys, not all eye-witnesses saw the same image. The most important book for the study of the range cattle industry is *Prose and Poetry of the Live Stock Industry* (1905), edited by James W. Freeman and sponsored by the National Live Stock Association and the National Live Stock Historical Association. The text was written by at least two different men who obtained their information from printed sources as well as from eye-witness accounts; however, because Freeman was the editor, the bibliographical entries are listed under his name.

The authors agree with much of McCoy's description of cowboys during the "wild and woolly" days, but they rationalize their actions with: "They were hardy, fearless, and reckless, products of the conditions by which they were surrounded, but not vicious as a body. Their life was one of hardship, isolation, and self-denial. . . . Truly, it was a lonely life. . . . Is it any wonder that the cowboy who went with a trail-herd to one of the old wild and woolly cowtowns after months, maybe a year, of such isolation as this, 'turned loose,' as he called it . . . ?"[10]

Indeed, the only forms of recreation and amusement in the cowtowns were drinking, gambling, dancing, and visiting prostitutes, but "not all the men took part in the orgies and debaucheries of the cowtowns, or forgot themselves at other times or in other places." The implication in *Prose and Poetry* . . . is that in most cases the town made the cowboy wild, instead of accepting the fact that without a customer there could be no sale. However, it should be accepted without question that not all cowboys were "wild and woolly and full of fleas."

The Freeman text also substantiates singing in cow camps as a form of diversion, as well as singing on the range to cattle: "Occasionally a strong-lunged brother would break forth in song, dealing with the deeds of some hero of the range, or with adventures on the trail, or with the charms and accomplishments of some imaginary 'dulce,' or in a 'cow-puncher's lament.' Whatever the burden of his song, and however harshly and discordantly it might be sung, he was heard without interruption . . ."[11]

Freeman writes about singing to cattle:

he also had vocal resources other and quite different from those of profanity for use in his rough business. Often at night when his cattle became restive under the mutterings of a coming storm, or uneasy from some unseen cause, or from the darkness of an overclouded sky, and even when on stampede, he would sing to them. . . . The cowboy made no pretensions to an elaborate *repertoire* . . . he sang, or tried to sing such songs as he happened to know . . . usually he knew some "church tunes" —lingering reminiscences of his boyhood away off somewhere toward sunrise . . . "Old Hundred," and the music and words of "I Would Not Live Alway" were favorites. . . . But oftener the cowboy improvised words for these and other church-tunes, or adopted to them those of some doggerel song he knew. . . .[12]

Another of the major sources for range cattle-cowboy history is James Cox's *Historical and Biographical Record of the Cattle Industry and the Cattlemen of Texas and Adjacent Territory*, published in 1895. Cox challenges McCoy's description by quoting the somewhat romantic statement of W. S. James:

The title "cowboy" is not intended to apply to all men who have taken an active part in handling cattle, but to those only who have proven themselves worthy the name of genuine, because of the nobility of character they possess. . . . the cowboy might properly be divided into three classes. . . . No. 1, the genuine, because of his true manhood . . . a man who is strictly honest, one whom it does not affect in his general health to eat a piece of an animal of his own mark and brand. . . . No. 2, . . . true type of Western hospitality, liberal to a fault, especially in his moral views; so much so that his conscience is possessed of such elasticity as to serve him in any emergency . . . peculiarly fortunate in his education. It often assists him in his interpretation of the brands of cattle from the Northern range, and enables him to appropriate the same. . . . No. 3, is the roaming, "come day, go day, God send Sunday, good-natured, easy-going cowboy," who is just as happy where he is as where he is not; who cares for nothing but a good saddle, spurs and quirt and a forty-dollar job; who seldom aspires to accumulate for himself, but is satisfied to spend his life in working for some one else, and when the season for working cattle is over repairs to the nearest town and spends what he has earned in having a good time.[13]

No doubt, most of the *cowboys* were of the "No. 3" classification; however, James progresses to a dogmatic statement that the "cowboy is a big-hearted, whole-souled bundle of humanity, kind-hearted, generous to a fault, possessed of all the frailties common to mankind, and not the biggest rascal on earth by a jug-full."[14]

Cox demonstrates his own flair for words when he writes: "Just as the snake-charmer lulls into innocuous desuetude the poisonous reptile before him, so did the old-time cattle drover and cowboy quiet many a stampeding steer, by night as well as by day, by singing as well as shouting."[15]

But no one has ever explained the genius of a cowboy who could ride at a full run in a driving rainstorm, try to turn or control cattle, and sing a hymn—all at the same time. Yelling was and is possible; it was possible that the quality of the average cowboy's singing and the aesthetic appreciation of the listeners was such that yelling often was thought to be singing. Cox and other second-generation chroniclers, along with first-generation cowboys who had grown old and basked in glory, told tales of quelling a stampeding herd with "music." The cowboy endowed with a voice of the volume that would have been required— when even the sounds of gunshots were drowned—had a remarkable voice and mind.

An Englishman also wrote about singing to cattle. Reginald Aldridge became a "partner" in the cattle business in 1877, and in 1884 his observations were published in *Life on a Ranch: Ranch Notes in Kansas, Colorado, the Indian Territory, and Northern Kansas*. Although according to many "cowboy scholars" it is not considered to be a major book in range cattle history, it is of value as one of the early witness, not cowboy participant, accounts. Aldridge wrote that "A herd of steers is especially liable to 'stampede' at night, often from the merest trifle, such as the horse of the herder snorting or stumbling, or even without any apparent cause. When on night-herd the men usually keep singing all the time as they ride around, that the cattle may know what is going on and not be suddenly startled by the sound or sight of a passing horseman. It is astonishing how instantaneously a whole herd are on their feet when they get a scare."[16]

The Cowboy Romanticized

It is important to recognize differences in terminology—distinctions between *cowboy* and *cattleman* and *rancher*. The owner or lease-holder of ranch land and cattle was and is the *rancher;* although ownership is often implied, a *cattleman* was and is a man who knows and works with cattle but does not in fact always own the property and/or cattle; *cowboy* implied and implies a working man on a ranch. Not all ranchers were cattlemen or cowboys; in fact, there were many absentee ranchers and corporate owners of ranches. And not all cowboys were or are cattlemen. However, some cowboys became ranchers and changed from the "wild and woolly" image to that of respected rancher-cattleman. Therefore, the cowboy image as depicted by McCoy and modified by Freeman and Cox did apply to "cowboys"; that is, they portrayed the "working cowboy."

In later years, strong disagreement with McCoy's description was voiced by many who were either always cattlemen and/or ranchers who let time and respectability alter their memories. Nevertheless, the trail herd generation of cowboys was a rough, hard-living group of men, although by 1890, through the extension of rail lines into Texas and through the growth of "fencing off" ranges, the practice of trail-herding cattle to market was basically dead. An exciting and colorful phase of cowboying ended, and the folk hero emerged along with songs that helped support the new image.

Journalists and writers of dime novels were quickly swept into the excitement and romance of the trail drives and the cowboy's ranch and range life. One writer, Louis C. Bradford, spent eighteen months in Texas "with these wild riders of the plains." In 1881, he wrote an article, published in *Lippincott's Magazine*, in which he greatly romanticized the excitement of cowboying. He observed that cowboys often spent "thirty-six hours continuously in the saddle. . . . With a piece of bread in one hand and some jerked beef in the other, he will ride around a stampeded herd, eating as he goes, and as happy as a king on his throne." Bradford made cowboy singing sound like a men's glee club: "At night the voices of the men singing to their sleeping cattle could be heard all along the line. . . . Sometimes the music of a violin, sounding strangely shrill in the calm night air, would mingle with the deep tones of voices singing 'The Maid of Monterey,' or 'Shamus O'Brien,' the cow-boy's favorite tunes."[17]

Obviously, the public's romance with the cowboy was in full bloom, but none of the early chroniclers mentioned any songs that used cowboy themes—for the most part, the songs were folk and music hall songs. However, cowboy poems and songs without music notation started appearing in small community newspapers. Examples are found in a small Indian Territory (now Oklahoma) newspaper, *Cheyenne Transporter*. This newspaper was published at the Darlington Agency on the Cheyenne and Arapaho Reservation. Although it was originally an Arapaho school newspaper, it became an "Indian and Stock Journal" that published information about Indian livestock associations and brands used in the area. Because cattle were trail-herded and grazed nearby, the paper also regularly provided the count of cattle driven to Kansas. The paper apparently enjoyed readership among Texas as well as Indian cowboys. In March 1882, a poem, "The Stockman," was given a front-page printing; in November 1884, "The Cowboy," an anonymous poem appeared; and in August 1886, the editor printed another poem, "The Cowboy's Lament" (later known as "The Campfire Has Gone Out"). These small newspaper poems did not often enter tradition, but because cowboy-theme ballads had their origins as individually composed poems or parodies, they traveled as much (or more) in small newspapers as they did by oral tradition.

Cowboy Poetry

A characteristic of cowboy life, both past and present, is an abundance of poets. It can be speculated that loneliness and the pastoral setting in which the cowboy spent much of his time inspired him to poetic expression, but whatever the reason, it is probable that no other occupation either produced such an abundance of poets or inspired as many poems. Some of the poets wrote parodies; some re-wrote or personalized and localized older poems; whereas others wrote poems with a structure that allowed them to be sung to a specified familiar melody. Unknown singers who liked a poem would find a melody for it.

An early example dates back to 1876, when "The Cowboy's Lament" supposedly was written. The claim for having written it was made by Francis Henry Maynard in a Colorado Springs newspaper article. When he was seventeen, Maynard moved from his home in Iowa to Kansas, where he worked as a trader, buffalo hunter, and cowboy. In 1876, he was working for "a Grimes outfit" with a herd from Matagorda Bay, Texas:

> We were wintering the herd on the Salt Fork of the Arkansas River on the border of Kansas and Indian Territory, waiting for the spring market to open at Wichita.
>
> One of the favorite songs of the cowboys in those days was called "The Dying Girl's Lament." . . . I had often amused myself by trying to write verses, and one dull winter day in camp to

while away the time I began writing a poem which could be sung to the tune of "The Dying Girl's Lament." I made it a dying ranger or cowboy, instead of a dying girl, and had the scene in Tom Sherman's barroom instead of a hospital.[18]

Tom Sherman's barroom was a popular cowboy dance hall and bar in Dodge City, Kansas, and Maynard's original locale. The cowboys to whom he sang his new version apparently liked it well enough to carry it back to Texas, where with the passing of time the locale was changed to the streets of Laredo. A few changes occurred within the verses, as is the case with most folk songs, that smoothed the meter and words into a more easily sung song than the original poem. Maynard wrote eight verses and one chorus, but different informants have claimed that at one time there were as many as seventy verses, most of which were obscene, in oral tradition. There is no evidence to indicate that "The Cowboy's Lament" ever varied much from the versions that are currently known nor is there evidence to either support or refute Maynard's claim to authorship.

Nevertheless, during the 1870s a few cowboy poets were composing ballads and lyrics about cowboy life and experiences, and the once-prevalent theory that cowboy songs came from communal or group composition can be applied only to a few lyrically disjointed songs such as "The Chisholm Trail" verses, most of which were obscene. Individual cowboy poets wrote most of the cowboy-theme songs.

The first published volume of cowboy poetry that I have found was L. [Lysius] Gough's *Western Travels and Other Rhymes*, published in Dallas in 1886. The poems were written from 1882 to 1884 while Gough cowboyed in Texas; apparently none entered oral tradition.

In 1893, approximately three years after the trail drive era ended, *Ranch Verses*, a volume of cowboy poetry written by William L. Chittenden, was published by G. P. Putnam's Sons. Chittenden's poem "The Cowboy's Christmas Ball" was popular enough among cowboys to be adapted into a song and become a part of cowboy lore. Other cowboy poetry books followed, from which many poems were adapted to music and entered oral tradition. Poets such as D. J. "Kid White" O'Malley, N. Howard "Jack" Thorp, Owen Wister, Charles Badger Clark, James Barton Adams, Arthur Chapman, Gail Gardner, Romaine Lowdermilk, Curley Fletcher, and others had volumes published either by major publishing firms or vanity presses, as well as poems published in newspapers and agriculture and livestock journals. They also enjoyed the satisfaction of seeing some of their poems become traditional songs loved by cowboys.

Songs in Print

Although 1886 was when the cowboy poets began publishing volumes of personal poetry, it was twenty-two years later before any attempt was made to publish a collection of songs sung by cowboys. And it was seventeen years before any texts were printed in popular magazine articles. However, the earliest inclusion that I have found of cowboy song texts that were actually learned from cowboy singing or recitation came through the efforts of Mary J. Jaques in her recollections and experiences that were published in London in 1894, *Texan Ranch Life*. She included a nearly complete text for "The Jolly Cowboy" and a lengthy variant of "The Dying Cowboy." Her experiences in hearing cowboys sing always came when the cowboy was seeking diversion or recreation, rather than while he was working cattle.

What appears to be the first popular magazine article specifically about cowboy songs, "Cowboy Songs and Dance," was written by Grace B. Ward and published in the January 1903 issue of *Pearson's Magazine*. Ward included texts to "Sam Bass," "The Dying Cowboy," and "Black Jack Davy"; her discussion focused on singing around the campfire at night. The texts were incomplete, and her commentary provided nothing of value to aid in understanding the function and development of cowboy songs and singing.

In 1908, Sharlot M. Hall published an article, "Songs of the Old Cattle Trails," in the March issue of *Out West*; she wrote the article while in Dewey, Arizona, and provided complete texts for four songs collected in the area. Hall had an interesting opening verse for "The Cowboy's Lament":

> As I rode out to Latern in Barin
> As I rode out so early one day,
> 'Twas there I espied a handsome young cowboy
> All dressed in white linen and clothed for the grave.[19]

This verse is a mixture of Irish origin and cowboy setting, but the additional four verses and chorus are similar to the Maynard-traditional verses. In her narrative, Hall explained that "Tex" was singing the cattle to sleep with "Lorena" while the others were singing around the campfire. Apparently Sharlot Hall heard only the sad songs of the cowboys because she wrote, "There is inherent sadness in the music of all people who live close to the earth."[20]

The third popular magazine article to appear was written by Mrs. John A. Lomax. "Trail Songs of the Cow-Puncher" appeared in the January 1912 issue of *The Overland Monthly*, and, even though the work was her own, her songs and attitudes reflected the work and interpretations of her husband. The article was a concise, romanticized trip up the trail from Texas to Kansas, with a wide variety of songs to illustrate the work and relaxation along the way. Mrs. Lomax wrote that, "His [the cowboy's] songs are timed to the lope of his horse, or suited to the taste of his comrades he met about the chuck-wagon."[21] This was the first statement about the rhythm of a song being timed to the gait of a horse, a fact that is not true. According to Dallas Turner, Curley Fletcher believed that a good cowboy song had to be in ¾ or waltz rhythm, and, indeed, many of the most popular cowboy theme songs are in waltz time. It would require a three-legged horse to accomplish a ¾ gait, but the idea is an interpretation of cowboy singing that has been slow in dying.

Another romanticized description followed Mrs. Lomax's explanation about singing while night herding: "it was during such hours that the puncher learned to talk to his charges much as a chiding mother might quiet her restless child."[22] The rough cowboy would have laughed at the comparison, for he was more prone to curse than to chide. But the three early articles in popular magazines, written by collectors who were women, had an extremely romantic, sentimental description of the cowboys and the function of singing.

Dane Coolidge wrote "Cowboy Songs" for the November 1912 issue of *Sunset* and provided another viewpoint. Coolidge was an 1898 graduate of Stanford University, who had worked his way through school as a field collector of western fauna, and, in time, became a writer of western novels. His experience of collecting in remote areas and his literary flair led him to cowboy culture, and many of his summers were spent in Arizona. Thus, "Cowboy Songs" and Coolidge's collection of songs came from Arizona cowboys.

Coolidge implied that cowboys sang to pass the time and that "Casey Jones" was popular among cowboys. He claimed that there were at least two hundred verses, each fouler than the last, but instead of "Casey Jones," he chose to include in the article "Barbara Allen" as sung by a cowboy. Coolidge carried a camera with him, and in exchange for a photograph, he made each cowboy "write" the words of a song, often one that they would not sing for ladies. He believed that most of the humorous bawdy songs would be ignored or expunged by scholars for "some time to come."

Scholarly Journals

The first appearance of cowboy theme songs and singing in scholarly journals was in the *Journal of American Folklore (JAF)*. Annie Laurie Ellis of Uvalde, Texas, sent the words and musical notation to "Oh, Bury Me Not on the Lone Prairie." It was printed in the July-September 1901 issue, along with the instruction, "All notes should be slurred more or less to give the wailing effect." No history or interpretation accompanied the text.

G. F. Will indicated in the *JAF* that he had been trying to collect old cowboy songs in North Dakota, but faced the difficulty of finding many cowboys who knew an entire song, an early indication that cowboy singing was not as widespread as popularly believed. He put together three cowboy songs and a shanty, along with a concise explanatory statement and the names of his sources. When published in the April-June 1909 issue of *JAF*, his article, "Songs of Western Cowboys," became the first serious presentation of cowboy songs for scholarly consideration. The songs were a fragmented version of "Amanda, the Captive," an excellent version of "Home on the Range," and a five-verse variant of "The Dying Cowboy" or "The Cowboy's Lament," which had a strange opening. Instead of the narrator being at Tom Sherman's barroom or in Laredo, in Will's version he was riding "down to the theater." Will wrote that the songs were "shouted in saloons," sung "at the stag dances," "heard at the camp-fire," and "in quieting cattle at night."[23]

In the April-June 1912 issue of *JAF*, Charles Peabody had a longer version of "Amanda, the Captive" published under the title "A Texas Version of 'The White Captive,'" and he traced the development or lineage of the song. The following year, G. F. Will had three more cowboy songs and one shanty published, but although his informants were identified, no attempt was made to provide additional information about the songs. After that article, cowboy songs and studies were relegated to other scholarly and regional folk society publications; the *Journal of American Folklore* carried no more cowboy songs.

Also in 1913, Louise Pound published an article, "The Southwestern Cowboy Songs and the English and Scottish Popular Ballads," in *Modern Philology*. She used texts that John A. Lomax had collected to wage war against "the Harvard school" belief in communal composition of folk balladry (the belief that ballads were cooperatively composed by more than one person in group or communal settings). Pound's comparison of cowboy songs to English and Scottish ballads led her to believe cowboy songs to be poetically inferior, characterized by "rude and nearly formless style." She made an interesting observation that the older ballads concerned kings, queens, and other nobility and their lives, whereas cowboy ballads were not about bosses and ranchers, but rather about the cowboys and their lives. This observation was part of Pound's evidence to show individual creativity. She did lightly touch upon the belief that folk singers did not care about the origin of a song; that their concern was and is in liking and enjoying a song. The essay attracted much animosity toward Pound, and she continued to attract it during more than fifty years of active scholarly warfare with communalists.[24] While Pound did not contribute new texts within her essay, she did create a greater scholarly awareness of cowboy songs and later added texts from her collecting efforts to the corpus of cowboy balladry.

"The Rattle Snake King"

Other individuals who did not write for popular magazines or scholarly journals were also collecting cowboy texts. Owen Wister used fragments of cowboy songs to give dimension and credibility to his novels; Stewart Edward White used "My Love Is a Rider" or "Bucking Bronco" in *Arizona Night* (1907), which had appeared in 1904 in *McClure's Magazine*. But the first appearance of a "collection" of cowboy songs was in a strange paperback book published to sell snake oil.

Clark Stanley, "Better Known as the Rattle Snake King," bottled a cure-all patent medicine in Providence, Rhode Island—"Clark Stanley's Snake Oil Liniment"—and in 1897 published a thirty-nine-page booklet or pamphlet to promote his snake oil liniment. J. Frank Dobie wrote about the booklet as "one of the curiosities of cowboy literature," and stated that it contained the earliest collection of cowboy songs that he knew.[25] But the concept of curiosity does not begin to describe Stanley and his publication. The first printing of *The Life and Adventures of the American Cow-Boy* in 1897 contained only three poems about Texas and cowboys. The other information was a rather disjointed guide about being a cowboy, along with information about snakes and Stanley's medicine. It contained eleven pages, not numbered, that were a variety of advertisements for his snake oil: "Good for Man and Beast" and "The Strongest and Best Liniment Known for the Cure of All Pain and Lameness." A biographical sketch on page twenty-six advised that Stanley went on his first trail drive when he was fourteen. His short tale about "My Last Trip up the Trail" included an incident about singing to cattle after a stampede. A copy in Yale University's Beinecke Library has the same 1897 imprint, thirty-nine numbered pages, and two unnumbered before the advertisements; it also includes a section, "Cowboy Songs and Dances." That section was the article that Grace Ward had published in *Pearson's Magazine* in 1903. It appears that Stanley plagiarized Ward and that the Beinecke copy, even though dated 1897, was printed after 1903. The songs and dance calls and the text are from Ward word for word; however, Stanley removed a few paragraphs about the dance calls, and a few punctuation marks are different. Everything about cowboys in the book except this section has a Texas setting; the Ward article had a New Mexico setting and so did Stanley's.

A copy of the booklet in the Eugene C. Barker Texas History Center in Austin has no printing date; it contains identical material, but Stanley apparently "remembered" more important facts about cowboys and expanded the article to fifty-nine pages. The cowboy song information was not changed. Both the Beinecke Library copy and the Barker copy contain additional pages about Stanley's "Western Herbs" remedy, "Worm Medicine," "Herbaline Ointment," and "White Cactus Soap"—all of his products were "western" in origin and had tested curative powers. The Barker copy contains Stanley's story about how he and his cowboy friends, the Rough Riders, attended the inauguration of their old friend "Teddy" Roosevelt in 1907, and how they visited him afterward.

Apparently Stanley left the snake oil business after having been the Rattle Snake King for at least nine years and became "the American Cowboy." He published another booklet, *True Life in the Far West by the American Cowboy*. The cowboy song section was not changed, but Stanley expanded the booklet's total size to seventy-eight pages by inserting a guide to spinning ropes and by including more wild stories. All pages containing advertising of snake oil, western herbs, and other remedies were removed. The noted bookman Wright Howes remarked, "If the medicine this faker sold was as ineffective as his book the snakes died in vain." [26] It is probable that Stanley had never been a cowboy and that not only were the songs and dance calls plagiarized, but most of his text was also.

N. Howard "Jack" Thorp

The year that McCoy opened Abilene to the trail drives of the range cattle industry—1867—was the year that the man who became the first field collector of cowboy songs was born in New York City. Nathan Howard "Jack" Thorp not only collected cowboy songs but also was the first to publish a collection in book form. Thorp was educated at St. Paul's School in Concord, New Hampshire, but he spent his summers on his brother's ranch near Stanton, Nebraska. Wanting to become a cowboy, in 1886 he moved to New Mexico and started buying horses to sell in the East to be trained as polo ponies. It was a successful business, and Thorp learned the ways of the West and the techniques of cowboying.

Thorp became a singing cowboy who carried his banjo-mandolin with him as he rode from cow camp to cow camp. His collecting story and other stories were published posthumously in 1945 (copyright 1943) under the title *Pardner of the Wind*; the opening chapter "Banjo in the Cow Camps" (previously published in the August 1940, *Atlantic Monthly* in a slightly modified version) was Thorp's account of how he started collecting and where the interest led him. It remains one of the best, if not the best, essays about cowboy songs. It was a "young man's impulse" that directed Thorp toward collecting, and he recalled: "In the nineties, with the exception of about a dozen, cowboy songs were not generally known. The only ones I could find I gathered, a verse here and a verse there, on horseback trips that lasted months and took me hundreds of miles through half a dozen cow-country states, most of the time being spent in cow camps, at chuck wagons and line camps." [27]

It was in March 1889, as the trail-driving years were coming to a close, when Thorp decided to take his collecting trip. After a forty-five-mile ride hunting two stray horses, Thorp stayed the night in a cow camp and swapped songs with the cowboys. He was excited by the experience and decided to quit his job in order to find more songs. He rode toward Texas, carrying a notebook into which he "jotted the words to any cowboy song that he heard."

One of the first songs Thorp collected was "Sam Bass," which was popular among cowboys and has been mentioned time and again by

N. Howard "Jack" Thorp. (Guy Logsdon–Jack Thorp Collection.)

them in their printed memoirs; it was supposedly "written by John Denton of Gainesville, Texas, in 1879." Thorp's problem was that cowboys only knew one or two verses; therefore, he had to collect it from many sources before he could put eight verses together into a coherent ballad.[28] It was many years later before Thorp learned the full eleven-stanza ballad as standardized in subsequent printed collections. Other songs were put together the same way. Thorp expurgated and bowdlerized his material:

> Take into account that many of the songs had to be dry-cleaned for unprintable words before they went to press, and you get some notion of the chore a song collector had who was only a cowboy himself. . . . it wasn't always parlor talk . . . the entire range version of "The Top Hand" . . . was a scorcher in itself, and the words of the song would have burned the reader's eyeballs. . . . I expurgated and had to change even the title, and the song has appeared exactly as I rendered it in all books of cowboy songs published since.[29]

Thorp emphasized that cowboys seldom knew what tune they were using for a song, that they seldom had good voices, and that the songs were sung by one person, "never by a group." The function of singing was for fellowship and to break loneliness. He had views different than earlier observers about night-herd singing, but it must be remembered that he wrote about range-herding and not about trail-herding:

> It is generally thought that cowboys did a lot of singing around the herd at night to quiet them on the bed ground. I have been asked about this, and I'll say that I have stood my share of night watches in fifty years, and I seldom heard any singing of that kind. What you would hear as you passed your partner on guard, would be kind of low hum or whistle, and you wouldn't know what it was. Just some old hymn tune, like as not—something to kill time and not bad enough to make the herd want to get up and run.[30]

Thorp spent one year traveling approximately fifteen hundred miles —on horseback—collecting songs. His travels took him into Indian Territory, to Dallas, and as far south as San Antonio before returning to New Mexico. Some of those songs along with a few that he wrote, for Jack Thorp became a fine cowboy poet, appeared in his *Songs of the*

Cowboys—the first book of cowboy songs. In 1908, Thorp paid the News Print Shop in Estancia, New Mexico, 6 cents each to print two thousand copies of his small collection. When finished, it was a small fifty-page paperback book, covered in red, that contained twenty-three songs but no music. The now widely known "Little Joe, the Wrangler" was the lead song. Thorp also wrote other songs or poems, such as "Chopo," "The Pecos River Queen," "Whose Old Cow," and "Speckles," but he did not put his name on them as the author. How many actually entered tradition is not known, although a few appeared in later collections.

When other collectors and publishers started using the songs, Thorp wanted credit. In fact, in 1932, when Thorp learned that recordings of "Little Joe, the Wrangler" had been released, he hired the firm of Botts and Botts in Albuquerque to file a law suit against RCA Victor for failure to pay royalty to him. When the firm consulted copyright experts in New York City and Washington, D.C., about Thorp's suit, they all discouraged legal action. Grounds cited were that composers of other even more popular songs had often received no royalties, and that more than five years since the release of the recording had lapsed before Thorp tried to take legal action. He and his attorneys didn't abandon their attempt to sue until three years later, but at no time was there any question about Thorp being the songs' author.[31]

Thorp eventually had poems published in *Poetry* and regional journals; he published *Tales of the Chuckwagon* in 1926, some five years after *Songs of the Cowboys* was expanded and published in 1921. Not only was Thorp a poet, but he was also a teller of tales. J. Frank Dobie wrote to Neil Clark, Thorp's collaborator on *Pardner of the Wind*, that Thorp was the source for a number of stories that Dobie used in two or three of his books and that "All Jack needed was a good listener. He never seemed to run out and yet his stories always had pertinence and were based on character more than on anything else."[32] Dobie so appreciated Thorp that he dedicated Chapter 5, "Stompedes," in his book, *The Longhorns*, to him.

John A. Lomax

The year that Thorp published his first collection of songs was also the year that a young Texan took a cylinder recorder into the field to collect cowboy songs; it was the first known collecting of Anglo-folksongs with the aid of a recorder. John Avery Lomax, while a student at

Harvard University, was encouraged to collect cowboy songs actively, and to make the undertaking possible he was granted $500 as a Sheldon Fellow from Harvard University. He used his money to travel in the West with his recorder, seeking out cowboy songs, however many cowboys would not sing into the horn until they were well lubricated: "Not one song did I ever get from them except through the influence of generous amounts of whiskey, rye and straight from the bottle or jug."[33]

In 1910, two years after that initial collecting trip, Lomax saw his efforts published as *Cowboy Songs and Other Frontier Ballads* by Sturgis and Walton Company. It became the most widely circulated collection of cowboy songs ever published and exerted much influence on later generations of cowboy singers. And even though the claim was made that the songs were collected in the field, Lomax obtained many songs from printed sources and from correspondents who had learned of his interest through newspaper and magazine articles about the project.

As did Thorp, Lomax expurgated, bowdlerized, edited, and rewrote some of the songs. In the introduction to his 1938 edition, he quoted R. S. Scott, an old-time cowboy: "In the singing about camp, a cowboy would often cut loose with a song too vile to repeat; great cheers and hurrays would usually follow and there would be calls for more. After the climax in this class of songs had been reached, some puncher would strike up an old-time religious hymn, and that also would be cheered to the echo."[34]

Lomax did hear many of the bawdy songs, and also received a few through his correspondents. About an informant, Tom Hight, who was one of his best sources, Lomax wrote that, "If ever printed, many of Tom's songs could be circulated by express shipment and then not without danger."[35] However, he apparently did not record or copy many of the bawdy songs, although he did use Hight's version of "The Bull Whacker," a variant of "Root, Hog, or Die," after bowdlerizing it. The song's typescript in the Lomax Papers in the Eugene C. Barker Texas History Collection at the University of Texas reflects the changes. "Son-of-a-bitch" became "son-of-a-gun," but more severely cut were the lines, "She could fuck and she could suck," which were changed to "She could smile and she could chuckle"; "To slip it up her water works" was changed to "I'll carry her to my dugout." The rhyming couplet "quit" and "shit" became "slam" and "dam."[36]

One of Lomax's weaknesses was in not crediting his sources. This evoked Thorp's anger, for Lomax used songs from his book without

John A. Lomax. (Courtesy of the Barker Texas History Center, University of Texas at Austin.)

crediting Thorp. In 1916, Lomax expanded the collection, and a new edition was printed—again, Thorp received no credit.

Thorp, with ironic humor, used Lomax's 1916 edition as an aid in putting together his own expanded edition of *Songs of the Cowboys*, published by Houghton Mifflin in 1921. Thorp wrote comments on each of his songs such as "Chopo" ("My own, taken from my book") and "Top Hand" ("as expunged by me") in his copy of the Lomax book.[37] He wrote "Have" and numbered sixty-nine songs, many of which were used in his 1921 edition. However not all the songs that Thorp used in 1921 were identical to Lomax's versions, for Thorp made textual and title corrections—at least to Thorp they were corrections. For example, he considered "The Cowgirl" to be the same song as "Bucking Bronco." Thorp seemed to consider that once he expurgated, bowdlerized, and revised a song, it became his own; and he seemed to enjoy correcting Lomax, for he marked through "The Melancholy Cowboy" and wrote "See Page 365," which is "Old Time Cowboy" and was to him the correct title and version. Why Lomax included almost identical variants of songs without reference or explanation is unknown, but he did it twice—Thorp found both of them. All, in all, Lomax used at least nineteen songs from the Thorp collection, a few of which were identical to Thorp's 1908 book. Thorp had reason to be unhappy with Lomax and apparently felt justified in reversing the role.[38]

In the Thorp and Lomax books it is difficult to determine which songs were actually field collected and were songs sung by cowboys or poems recited by them. In 1921, in his collection of 101 songs Thorp included at least twenty-seven songs—or poems—that he wrote, most of which never entered oral tradition, and no music or melody lines accompanied the songs. Lomax's publisher included only a few melody lines, and Lomax definitely included material obtained from printed sources. Perhaps both men should have used "and Poems" in the titles of their books and should have emphasized the importance of printed sources.

In tracing the lineage of cowboy songs, one other Lomax book must be acknowledged; for the most part, it is ignored simply because it is an anthology of cowboy poems rather than cowboy song book. *Songs of the Cattle Trail and Cow Camp* was published by the Macmillan Company in 1919. In this publication, Lomax credited each poet when he knew a correct identity. In his foreword, while acknowledging that each poem had been in print, he did try to leave the impression that the poems were traveling through oral transmission, when only a handful were ever a part of cowboy traditions, to be either sung or recited.

Siringo, Finger, and Barnes

During the years when Thorp and Lomax were publishing their efforts, second-generation cowboys were writing poems that were quickly accepted in the existing cowboy culture. Curley Fletcher, Charles Badger Clark, Gail Gardner, and other previously mentioned poets were writing poems that their contemporaries absorbed and set to music, for example, "The Strawberry Roan" and "The Sierry Petes." Other collectors were also spurred into the excitement and pleasure of finding new variants and new songs. However, not all of the printed collections included new variants; instead, they noticeably resembled, or were identical to, the Lomax texts. One such publication was the small—forty-two pages—paperback booklet, *The Song Companion of a Lone Star Cowboy*, compiled by Charles A. Siringo and published in 1919, probably in Sante Fe, New Mexico. It contained fourteen songs, but no music, supposedly mentioned in his book *A Lone Star Cowboy*, published the same year. However in his book Siringo apparently forgot to mention singing and songs, other than "Sam Bass." He was, nevertheless, an important contributor to the literature of the range cattle industry; his book *A Texas Cow Boy*, published in 1885, is considered to be the first autobiography written by a working cowboy during the trail-drive era. But as in Siringo's other works, no mention is made of singing; apparently, he was not a singing cowboy until the Lomax collection appeared. Siringo's small song collection was printed in a format similar to the 1908 Thorp booklet and sold for 35 cents; it is almost as difficult to find as is Thorp's in the current rare book trade.

Charles J. Finger compiled a few songs that were published as a sixty-four-page paperback in 1923 by the Haldeman-Julius Company of Girard, Kansas, under the title *Sailor Chanties and Cowboy Songs*. Finger wrote a narrative about his experiences and informants. He claimed to have heard "Sam Bass" on March 1, 1897, in Texas, but his version is identical to Lomax's except for a few punctuation marks, which is true with each of Finger's cowboy songs. It is probable that he heard fragments and turned to Lomax for the longer, more complete texts. It is also possible that Finger's creative flair at story-telling provided much of the narrative that fit a song that he liked.

Finger expanded his collection into *Frontier Ballads*, which was published by Doubleday, Page in 1927. With impressive woodcuts for illustrations, it was an attractive book that included some melody lines. In fairness, Finger's version of "Harry Bale" was six lines longer (with four

Charles A. Siringo. (Guy Logsdon Collection.)

eight-line stanzas) than the Lomax text. So not all of the Finger texts were from Lomax. In preparing his later edition, Lomax eliminated the song and wrote on the manuscript text, "in Finger."

Along with Thorp's "Banjo in the Cow Camp," one of the most realistic approaches was written by an Arizona cowboy, Will C. Barnes. His observations and interpretations appeared in 1925 in the *Saturday Evening Post*:

> as to cowboy songs and the custom of singing to the cattle at night when on guard over the herd. . . . Far be it from me to discount the effect of music, no matter how crude or refined, upon a range cow's nerves. However, some thirty-odd years of cowboy life . . . have taught me to believe that the music had nothing to do with it. . . . which ran all the way from sacred hymns to some of the commonest doggerel imaginable. The simple fact is that no animals are more readily alarmed at night, when in a mass, than the average range cattle.[39]

Cattle would stampede if a horse shook itself, if a cowboy sneezed too loudly, and if any unnatural sound occurred. The "sweet" sounds of a cowboy, in his pastoral setting, singing to the cows had nothing to do with controlling cattle; in fact, most cowboys, if they sang, would have caused a stampede. If singing were essential to controlling cattle, only singers would have been hired for night herding, instead of having each cowboy take a turn. Evidence also exists that some cowboys played the fiddle during night herding; which is to say that they did what was necessary to stay awake and to break the loneliness of the dark. Their sounds—singing, humming, talking, fiddling—were familiar to the cattle and covered most of the sudden, unexpected sounds of the night. In fact, the presence of horses probably had more to do with controlling cattle than did the sounds of humans.

Barns stated that the singer and the songs were:

> those he picked up from all sorts of sources—mainly saloons, barber shops, cheap shows and others of his kind. In almost every outfit I ever worked with there was some one man who was the troubadour of the bunch. He generally had a clear musical voice, a lively imagination and a very retentive memory. Several I can recall when given a worthwhile suggestion could make up almost unlimited yards of doggerel to fit almost any subject or incident.

Some writers on this subject have claimed to find a deep religious feeling in many of these songs of the round-up camps, but ninety per cent of such songs show a decided lack of any religious element.

Some of the very best so-called cowboy poetry in existence has been written by college men who knew little or nothing of the real life and work of the ranges.[40]

Barnes was correct about the proliferation of "western" poetry, but most of the poem-songs that entered oral tradition before the 1930s were written by men who were cowboys or who at least had a close relationship to the occupation, for example, O'Malley, Fletcher, and Gardner. Barnes ended his article with a description of the first generation of range cowboys somewhat akin to that written by McCoy—"uneducated," "rollicky and devilish," and their language was "disreputable and low-down."

Sires and German

In 1928, C. C. Birchard and Company published a twenty-nine-song collection, *Songs of the Open Range*, as compiled and edited by Ina Sires. Full piano accompaniments were provided for each text, and although she acknowledged the use of both the Thorp and Lomax collections, Sires included some of the songs and texts that she had collected. Born in west Texas and a graduate of Baylor University, she was genuinely a collector of cowboy songs, but she also romanticized of the cowboy. Sires traveled as a lecturer-singer who presented her dramatic program, "The Cowboy as the Builder of the West," illustrated by songs of the cowboys. Part of her romantic interpretation was similar to that in her "Collector's Note": "In these songs, born of the saddle, are the greyness of the prairies, the wail of the Texas norther, the loneliness of the coyote, and a rhythm that fits into the gait of the cowboy's pony. Not all these ballads are beautiful; but all are sincere and reflect as accurately as a mirror, the life of the cowboy."[41]

The short narrative that accompanied each song reflected much of Sires's romantic interpretation of them. Her songs may have been timed to the gait of a horse, but it is hard to sing cowboy songs to the rhythm of a trot, lope, and gallop, much less to a full run. Again, it is a concept of cowboy singing that has been hard in dying.

In 1929, George B. German, following Thorp's format, included some

The Cowboy

of

The Chaparral, Mesquite and Bunch Grass
Country.   How He Lived and Did His
Part as the Pioneer and Builder
of the Great West

LECTURE AND SONGS

Given in Costume By

Miss Ina Sires

The Cowboy

as

The Builder of
The West

is a humorous, interesting, instructive lecture,
full of laughs, full of real history.   You cannot spend a more delightful evening than
to hear Miss Sires talk, sing the songs that
kept the herd quiet, that expressed the faith,
love and joy of the real cowboy in his big
out-of-doors.

As a novel, interesting attraction, Miss
Sires' lecture cannot be duplicated.   It is
new, delightfully entertaining.   Write for
dates, cost, etc.   As a main attraction for
your church, lodge or other local entertainment, you are assured of a big success.

The Cowboy's Favorite Songs, compiled by Miss
Sires and introduced in her lecture, are as typical
a part of the folk lore of the West as the negro melodies are a part of the folk lore of the South.

Miss Ina Sires

WRITER AND LECTURER

Ina Sires lecture pamphlet. (Guy Logsdon Collection.)

of his own poems along with traditional songs in *Cowboy Campfire Ballads*, which credits German's printed sources in the foreward. In 1932, he expanded his collection with the assistance of his wife. Again, most of the songs were taken from Lomax, to whom a general statement of credit was give. During the 1920s German worked on ranches in the Wickenburg, Arizona, area, where he became acquainted with Romaine Lowdermilk, a popular Arizona cowboy singer who introduced German to cowboy songs and taught him to love them. In 1928, back in Yankton, South Dakota, German was given his own radio show, more by accident than design, and he sang cowboy songs over the air. His collections were published for his radio audience and helped spread cowboy songs in the northern Great Plains.[42]

The 1920s saw an increased interest, but certainly not an overwhelming one, in cowboy songs among Texans. The Texas Folklore Society was growing and they published an *Annual*. Although Texas scholars interested in folklore and folk song had grown beyond one —John A. Lomax—they must have been intimidated by his publications; only a few scattered articles about cowboy songs were published in the *Annual*. Those articles were not much more than extensions of the themes established by Lomax; nonetheless, Walter Prescott Webb, J. Frank Dobie, and J. Evetts Haley each became acclaimed scholars of the Plains and the range-cattle industry, used folk sources to add depth to their works, and used cowboy songs in a peripheral manner. Dobie became the best known of the group for his use of legends and folk tales.

The Romance Spreads in Popular Media

A catalyst in the romanticized cowboy myth was the impact that Hollywood was having on the nation and the world. William S. Hart and Tom Mix were household words, and their portrayal of cowboys and the cowboy moral ethic were a far cry from the cowboy McCoy described. Hart at least attempted to dress in authentic clothing, but although he did not portray a singing cowboy, his producers used the romantic concept. In his silent movie *Tumbleweeds*, which had words flashed on the screen, a group of "jolly" cowboys were seen riding at a trot and singing together—probably in harmony.

Another factor in the growing acceptance and popularity of cowboy singing during the 1920s was the impact of the proliferation of radio stations and receiving sets. Radio stations were desperate for live talent, and a variety of "cowboy" singers helped alleviate the problem. One early station west of the Mississippi River was KFRU—"Kind Friends Remember Us"—in Bristow, Oklahoma; it went on the air in January 1925 and later became KVOO in Tulsa. One of the original live programs to emanate from Bristow was that of Otto Gray and his Oklahoma Cowboys. Within a short time after their first broadcast, which was heard as far away as Boston, they became one of the most popular radio and stage shows in the nation. No country or hillbilly show in Nashville at that time enjoyed such popularity. Dressed in cowboy clothes, singing cowboy songs, and using cowboy tools (ropes and snake whips), Gray and the Oklahoma Cowboys entertained the entire nation, young and old, from coast to coast for ten years. They helped perpetuate a singing cowboy image, as well as stimulate a change toward the popularization of cowboy clothes.[43]

At the same time, the recording industry started capitalizing on the growing interest in cowboy songs. There were enough songs using the theme of cowboy life to leave the impression that there were long-standing lists of such traditional songs, when, in fact, the songs were often fairly new material. Singers of cowboy songs and cowboy musicians such as Carl T. Sprague, Eck Robertson, Jules Vern Allen, John I. White, and many more were recorded; the public could take the records home and learn the songs from them. Next to the Lomax texts, the recording industry played the largest role in standardizing cowboy song texts, although most of the recording cowboys used Lomax texts.

An interesting and perplexing question about folk song transmission is demonstrated by the D. K. Wilgus Folksong Collection, "Cowboy Songs," in the library at Western Kentucky University and in the Western Kentucky Archives at the University of California, Los Angeles. Many of the texts are similar to southern mountain singers' early recordings of cowboy songs. Did the recordings spread cowboy songs in the South, and, if so, where and why did the southern singers learn the songs? Is it possible that the cowboys who came from the South took their songs back with them when they visited or moved back home? Whatever the answer, it is secondary to the fact of the widespread popularity of cowboy songs in the South.

The rising influence of western novels also helped create the growing cowboy myth. Owen Wister, Andy Adams, and Emerson Hough were joined by B. M. Bowers, Clarence Mulford—the creator of Hopalong Cassidy—and many more novelists. The most widely read was Zane

Grey; his romantic presentation of western character and his flair for physical description of the natural setting actually inspired untold thousands in the East to move to, or at least visit, the West. Yet, Grey did not use cowboy songs and singing in his novels. Only a few novelists, as previously mentioned, did use songs in their narratives, but as the concept of the cowboy changed, the new songs about cowboys—composed for public consumption—took the characteristics of the romantic novelists. There was a growing market both nationally and internationally for the mythical cowboy, and the 1930s became the peak period for marketing the romanticized cowboy.

John I. White, a native of Washington, D.C., had developed an early interest in cowboy songs that was intensified when he heard real cowboy music while on a visit to Arizona in 1924. He auditioned as a singer of cowboy songs for NBC radio in New York City in 1926, landed a radio show, and became known as "The Lonesome Cowboy." White earned a show as a regular over WOR, and in 1929, along with the station's musical director, George Shackley, compiled a cowboy song folio that contained twenty songs. Four songs were poems from western poets E. A. Brininstool and James Barton Adams that were set to music. Lomax texts of a few standard popular cowboy songs were also included, and White used songs that he had learned while in Arizona and when traveling other trails. The collection was a major departure from the dominance of Lomax texts and, published as *The Lonesome Cowboy: Songs of the Plains and Hills*, it signaled the beginning of a decade of cowboy song folios. White ultimately recorded twenty songs for the American Record Company and was heard for six years on the original *Death Valley Days* radio show. His impact on cowboy songs was secondary to his research into the origin of the songs, however, for no scholar has put as much effort into the research as he.[44]

Margaret Larkin lived and collected in New Mexico; in 1931, her compilation of songs, *Singing Cowboy: A Book of Western Songs*, was published by Alfred Knopf. As did Ina Sires, Larkin lectured and sang cowboy songs across the nation. In her book she identified sources, places, and when possible, time of collection. Her comments about each song were far more extensive and explanatory than any other collector had written, yet she, too, laced them with romanticism. In her introduction, she wrote that cowboy songs were not work songs and that if a song happened to fit the gait of the horse, it was a "happy accident"—the concept was "more romantic than logical."[45] Larkin also stressed that the

importance and function of singing varied according to the individual—
some cowboys sang and some did not. In her song notes, however, she
wrote that a song "lopes" and that "The cowboys on night herding duty
keep up a constant clucking, whistling, crooning and singing to 'drown
the wild sound' and quiet the cattle, as well as to keep themselves from
dozing in the saddle. Any song might be sung for night herding if it has a
lonesome sounding tune that can travel as slowly as a walking horse." [46]

One of the colorful characters in cowboy songs and poems was Jack
H. "Powder River" Lee, who, along with his wife Kitty, was a cowboy
entertainer in the twenties and thirties. The Lees told stories and sang
about cowboys, and left the impression that "Powder River" Jack was
a genuine, old-time cowboy. He also claimed to be the author of some
traditional songs such as Gail Gardner's "Tying Knots in the Devil's Tail."
No matter what he claimed—from being in Buffalo Bill's Wild West Show
to being the friend of five different presidents and on and on and on—
Lee was an entertaining singer. His first book *Powder River Jack and
Kitty Lee's Cowboy Song Book*, was privately printed in 1926. In 1936 he
re-printed it and published three more volumes, but there was repeti-
tion within each. Even allowing for his propensity for elaboration and
exaggeration, Lee did know many songs; Glenn Ohrlin credits "Powder
River" Jack as the source for many of his songs, and Dallas "Nevada
Slim" Turner also praises Lee.

Even a Broadway play in New York City helped spread cowboy songs
to a growing audience. Oklahoma-born playwright Lynn Riggs used cowboy and other folk songs in his play *Green Grow the Lilacs* (on which
the classic *Oklahoma* was based). Cowboy songs were used in the play
itself, a Theatre Guild production in the 1930–31 season, and during
interludes of singing between scenes. In 1932, the Samuel French Company published sixteen songs in an eighteen-page booklet as a supplement to their printed text of the play, a venture intended to be an aid
for both professional and amateur productions. Margaret Larkin's song
texts were used, along with songs from Everett Cheetham and Tex Ritter.
The play was, in fact, the springboard for Tex Ritter's singing career.
Riggs was wise enough to select texts that were natural to his singers
and did not impose Lomax texts on them. The audiences responded well
to the uniqueness of the production, which enjoyed a lengthy run on
Broadway.

In keeping with the dissemination of the cowboy culture as well as
songs, the radio and recording cowboy singer Jules Verne Allen com-

Jack H. "Powder River" Lee (right), with an unidentified cowboy, March 6, 1943. (Photo by DeVere Helfrich, National Cowboy Hall of Fame Collection.)

piled *Cowboy Lore*, published by the Naylor Company in 1933. The text offered thirty-six songs with music combined with a hodge-podge of information about cowboy life and cattle brands; most of the song texts were Lomax's. Although Allen was a Texan who had probable cowboy experience, the tone of the book was obvious through his oversimplified and, once again, romantic statement about cowboy songs: "Most all cowboy songs originated around the chuck wagon after the happenings of some event of vital importance such as one of the boys being killed in a stampede."[47]

Allen was an important contributor to the cowboy image through his radio shows in Dallas and Los Angeles as "Longhorn Luke and His Cowboys" and as "Shiftless" in San Antonio. A Longhorn Luke song folio or booklet was issued; however, I have not seen a copy.

Cheap paperback cowboy song books and/or folios were widely available when Kenneth S. Clark compiled *The Cowboy Sings* in 1932. By 1940, he had compiled three additional cowboy song books: *The Happy Cowboy Sings and Plays Songs of Pioneer Days* (1934), *Songs for the Rodeo* (1937), and *Buckaroo Ballads, the Golden West in Songs and Pictures* (1940). Clark combined traditional songs taken from other collections with contemporary Tin Pan Alley cowboy songs, which made a curious mixture; he also set poems by cowboy poets to music. Each new song book contained songs from his previous books, but the interested consumer did not care. A song's beauty, theme, and appeal were what mattered, which was exactly the same attitude that the trail herd cowboy and succeeding generations of real cowboys had. The general widespread interest in cowboy songs was reflected in an increased publication of songs in sheet music format, but even more indicative of growing popularity was the inclusion of a cowboy song in the 1934 Ziegfeld Follies.

Billy Hill and the Sons of the Pioneers

One of the most interesting stories—not completely unrelated to the cowboy traditions—about songwriters and illegal use of their songs is that of Billy Hill. Born William Joseph Hill in 1899 in the Roxbury section of Boston, Billy Hill traveled west in 1916 and worked as a cowboy and dance hall piano player along with other jobs as he drifted. He wrote songs and sold each for a few dollars; it is not known if any songs written during those days were actually cowboy-theme songs. Hill, inspired

"The End of a Cowboy's Day" is a typical 1930s romanticized, posed photograph on a ranch near Pitchfork, Wyoming, November 20, 1932. (Photo by Charles Belden; courtesy of the Denver Public Library, Western History Department.)

to be a professional songwriter, moved to New York City in the early throes of the Great Depression. But songwriting competition was stiff, and it was a difficult time for a man with a pregnant wife. In despair, Hill started to sell a new song, "The Last Round-Up," for $25, when the president of ASCAP heard of his problem and advanced him enough money to survive until he could sell the song at a fair price. Although composed in 1933, "The Last Round-Up" and an earlier Hill song, "Wagon Wheels," became hits in the 1934 Ziegfeld Follies. This success provided enough financial security for him to concentrate his efforts toward composing songs, which include "Empty Saddles," "In the Chapel in the Moonlight," "Cabin in the Pines," "Call of the Canyon," and "The Old Spinning Wheel." Hill died in 1940, leaving a small, but important, group of western songs; "Empty Saddles" is still sung by a few traditional cowboy singers. He played a strong hand in making cowboy-type songs popular in the 1930s, and in 1936 testified before the House of Representatives' Committee on Patents, Revision of Copyright Laws' hearings about composers' problems. Hill's emotional story helped sway Congress to tighten regulations in favor of composers.

Parallel to Hill's career was the organization of the Sons of the Pioneers. In late 1933, when they started performing, the original group was the Pioneer Trio: Bob Nolan, Tim Spencer, and Leonard Slye (better known as Roy Rogers). The Pioneer Trio had practiced long hours to develop a tight harmony, and with Billy Hill's song, "The Last Round-Up," worked into a strong, impressive sound, they wrangled their own radio show over KFWB in Hollywood.[48] That song and arrangement, in effect, pushed them out of the "home corral" onto a singing trail that created a new popular concept of cowboy songs. The group solidified the romanticized group singing sound of the range. But before the Sons of the Pioneers became a household name in the West, Hugh and Karl Farr, Lloyd Perryman, and Pat Brady were added, and Roy Rogers left in 1937 to become a singing cowboy star. In 1934, shortly after the first new member arrived—and the group was no longer a trio—a radio announcer introduced them as the "Sons of the Pioneers," which became their legendary western music name.

The group's early cowboy and pioneer selections other than Hill's songs did not include traditional cowboy songs; instead, they were the compositions of Bob Nolan and Tim Spencer, with Nolan composing the greater number of hits for them. Such composition was in keeping with the development of traditional songs, for it is common, when westerners make music, for someone to ask for "Cool Water" or "Tumbling Tumbleweeds." Only time and tradition will determine if those two songs will survive in oral tradition, but Nolan's "Sky Ball Paint" already has entered cowboy tradition. The outlaw or tough horse that always throws its rider, or is conquered by its rider, has long been a popular cowboy theme. "Sky Ball Paint" is sung by singers who do not know who composed it or when—it's just another old song to them.

Pete Seeger and Arlo Guthrie often perform Nolan's "Way Out There," and Hank Williams used Nolan's "Happy Cowboy" as his theme song. The singing and writing of the Sons of the Pioneers and the ultimate inclusion of traditional cowboy songs into their repertoire on stage, on recordings, and especially in the B-grade western movies, inspired many groups to copy them and made them the epitome of western singing. A dude ranch without a Sons sing-a-long group is not a complete dude ranch. Yet, the real cowboy continued his traditional sounds and songs, absorbing from the Sons only those songs that captured his imagination. The Sons merely enjoyed working a stage that had been already set by romanticizers.

Gene Autry

Although the 1930s provided the greatest spurt of cowboy myth and music development, the major thrust started in 1929 when Gene Autry cut his first records for American Record Corporation, which produced records for chain stores such as Sears, Roebuck and Company. Thus, Autry's records were promoted in the Sears catalog and reached the agriculture and rural audience, and he became a regular member of the Chicago-based WLS "Barn Dance."[49] That successful relationship led to a small role in 1934 in the Ken Maynard movie *In Old Santa Fe*; Autry was well received and because Hollywood needed a new type of western, Republic Studios created the "horse opera" for him—the original singing cowboy. But Autry was not really the "first"; Ken Maynard had already tried singing in his movies, and even Bob Steele and John Wayne (voiced over, not actually singing himself) had tried unsuccessfully.

In realistic retrospect, Gene Autry was the original successful singing cowboy; he had been billed for at least five years as "The Oklahoma Yodeling Cowboy." But he did not sing cowboy songs; instead, he recorded and sang hillbilly songs and songs that he and friends composed. In his second song folio, *Gene Autry's Famous Cowboy Songs and*

Gene Autry at an unidentified rodeo during the 1940s. (Photo by R. R. Doubleday, National Cowboy Hall of Fame Collection.)

Mountain Ballads (1934) he included his own composition "There's an Empty Cot in the Bunk House Tonight," which has become a favorite of many traditional cowboy singers who do not know that Autry wrote it.

Following Autry's horse opera success were Roy Rogers, Dick Foran, Tex Ritter, Jimmy Wakely, Eddie Dean, Rex Allen, and others. They all helped shape a popular image of cowboy singers and songs, and occasionally an original song would have the quality that appealed to the real cowboy and would become a part of the cowboy's repertoire.

During the 1930s, two very important booklets were published. John I. White, "The Lonesome Cowboy," had developed through his interest in cowboy songs a friendship with the great cowboy poet D. J. O'Malley. In 1934, White published in an eighteen-page booklet, including a biographical sketch, nine of O'Malley's best poems, two of which had already been favored by cowboy singers. The booklet was titled in a straightforward manner: *D. J. O'Malley "Cowboy Poet."*

The following year a cowboy poet who has become a legend among Arizona folklorists and cowboys, Gail I. Gardner, published his own works—again a small booklet—under the title *Orejana Bull for Cowboys Only.* The lead poem was "The Sierry Petes" (or, "Tying the Knots in the Devil's Tail"), his poem of 1918 that had required only a short time to enter the cowboys' tradition. This booklet has now gone into its seventh edition, and in each there were changes and additions.

Buck Jones

The mid-to-late 1930s saw a proliferation of non-singing cowboy movie stars having song folios published under their names; perhaps in response to the new Saturday matinee competition from the horse operas, but in all probability a commercial response to the cowboy craze. The most interesting was *Buck Jones Rangers-Cowboys Collection* published in 1935; Jones, in order to stimulate popularity, had a nationwide club—the Buck Jones Rangers Club of America. Virtually every community in the nation had at least one member, and the club had an official song, "The Buck Jones Rangers," which was the lead song in the folio. In the foreword, to authenticate the folio, was written, "the authors and composers have endeavored to present a concise and practical collection of cowboy and ranger lore that will meet the requirements of every Buck Jones Ranger." Buck Jones gave his official endorsement with the admonition, "A few minutes' study and practice each day will make each ranger proficient in the arts of roping, story-telling, harmonica playing, and skillful in imitation upon the piano . . . can visualize the nights we spent singing them as we sat around the campfire." The publication carried the official and personal endorsement of "Your pal, Buck Jones," although most of the fifteen cowboy songs were from Lomax. Also in the booklet were "Bugle Instructions," "How to Play the Harmonica," "Photographs," "How to Tell a Story of the West," "Buck Jones Rangers' Pledge," "Piano Tricks and Imitations," "Rope Spinning," "Range Expressions," and "Arm Chevrons." How could any parent object to Buck Jones and his movies?

Jones was not the only star to issue song folios, even Tom Mix, who authorized many means of capitalizing on his popularity, was the subject of the 1935 *Tom Mix Western Songs*. The songs were all of the Tin Pan Alley type, and no traditional songs were included. No doubt Mix endorsed a publishing house project without knowing what songs were to be published. It was the practice of companies such as M. M. Cole in Chicago to hire songwriters to crank out songs for a set fee. When a star agreed to a song folio contract, the company would pull songs from their files, or they might have a "stock" book ready to publish with the title and photographs waiting to be inserted when a star signed the contract.

Dane Coolidge, naturalist and novelist, included cowboy lore in his years of collecting and writing, as indicated in his 1912 article. From his collecting experiences he wrote three books about cowboys he had known: *Texas Cowboys* (1937), *Arizona Cowboys* (1938), and *Old California Cowboys* (1939), all published by E. P. Dutton. In *Texas Cowboys*, Coolidge devoted two chapters to songs he had collected, but his Texas cowboys were men he knew in Arizona, who were from Texas. The song texts were written for him by the cowboys, although it is probable that Coolidge edited them for spelling and punctuation. It is also probable that his cowboys were influenced by Lomax texts. Coolidge's contribution to cowboy lore deserves more serious study and consideration.

In May and November 1937, two small mimeographed pamphlets titled *Cowboy Songs* were issued by the Federal Writers' Project in Nebraska as part of their Nebraska Folklore Pamphlet series. No informants, place names, or dates were included, and the texts were basically word-for-word, verse-for-verse Lomax texts. Although the songs were probably in current oral tradition in Nebraska, no evidence was submitted to prove it. Although it is assumed that project workers heard the songs, such publications leave open the possibility that an editor or compiler merely chose titles from Lomax that evoked a recall of once having heard the song. Of course, the collecting of folk material in Nebraska and by Federal Writers' Projects workers in other states was often genuine field work; how many other songs, specifically cowboy songs, reside in the archives of the Federal Writers' Project has not been documented, and the frequency of editorial substitution of complete and poetically acceptable texts for actual field collected texts is unknown.

During the Great Depression, people found entertainment and relief through cowboy songs and singing cowboys, but the entire cowboy image and myth also reached new heights. Cowboy reminiscences were abundant, however only a few within the large body of published memoirs mentioned cowboy singing. One that did and that seldom has been quoted was an article by Colonel John Alley, "Memories of Roundup Days," published in *The Sooner Magazine* in January 1934. Alley was involved in the removal of all cattle from the Cherokee Outlet during the fall of 1890. Even though he worked a relatively short time among cowboys, he heard singing that made an impression on his young memory. He makes no mention of singing to cattle, instead, he refers to the content of songs in contrast to those he heard in the thirties. The vulgar songs had been put aside and the "better ones" had been "censored." Obviously, Alley's short stay in Oklahoma provided an ample sampling of the bawdy element in cowboy singing.

From the 1930s to the 1960s

Every possible variety of cowboy song and song book was published in the 1930s; the decade marked the apex of cowboy song popularity. Toward the end of the decade, John A. Lomax, with the assistance of his son, Alan, complied and edited a new edition of the popular and influential *Cowboy Songs*. It was time for changes and additions, for John A. Lomax had become the preeminent collector of folk songs in the nation, if not the world. His son Alan had joined him in his work. As a team they had two books already on the market that had been well received by the American public, *American Ballads and Folk Songs* and *Negro Folk Songs as Sung by Leadbelly*. The Lomaxes had developed national recognition through their collecting efforts, and John A. Lomax had served as honorary consultant and curator of the Archive of American Folk Song in the Library of Congress since 1934. Alan Lomax was employed as an assistant curator in 1937. Because of the Lomaxes' prominence, many interested citizens thought that they organized that division within the Library of Congress; however, Robert W. Gordon was responsible for its organization and its foundation collection.

Gordon was an academician totally devoted to collecting and researching American folk songs. His devotion to folk song collecting and his methods, such as writing a monthly column in the pop magazine *Adventure* from 1923 to 1927, evoked contempt from his colleagues in the English Department at the University of California, Berkeley; this criticism combined with departmental politics resulted in his dismissal in 1924. As an unemployed scholar, Gordon became a full-time collector of folk songs by using his own funds and by occasionally getting a writing contract and small grants. One contract for a series of articles was with the *New York Times Magazine* in 1925, and the January 22, 1928, article dealt with cowboy songs.[50] Although it provided limited insights to individual songs and to the functions of the songs, at least the texts were fresh, although heavily influenced by Lomax texts. As a result of Gordon's tenacious dedication, in 1928 funds were made available through the Library of Congress for him to establish the Archive of American Folk Song (now the Archive of Folk Culture). He collected and cataloged material until the funds ran out in 1932.

Two years later, Lomax assumed his honorary position as curator. Gordon had left approximately eight thousand song texts, along with songsters (small song books), manuscripts, recordings, and finding guides. Included in the manuscripts were letters and songs that Gordon had received in response to his *Adventure* column, from which he organized a file of bawdy songs that had been randomly sent by men from across the country.[51] That file, "The Inferno Collection," has seldom been used by scholars. While the Lomaxes had much material that they had already collected, the Gordon collection provided a strong foundation for building the greater archives. It is not known how many, if any, of the Gordon texts may have been used when *Cowboy Songs* was restructured a few years later.

The revised and enlarged edition of *Cowboy Songs and Other Frontier Ballads* was published by the Macmillan Company in 1938 and continued to be the popular cowboy song collection. In the new edition there were 200 songs, compared to 152 in the 1916 edition, of which 33 song texts had been omitted and replaced by new material. In response to scholarly criticism, the Lomaxes expanded their annotations and source information, but the information still fell far short of being complete or even adequate.[52] Questions were compounded, not resolved, about which songs actually were collected from oral tradition, which were from printed sources or received by mail, and which songs were actually alive in tradition. However, cowboys and the book-buying public still accepted Lomax and the new edition as the final authority on cowboy songs. For many more years it remained a solid seller and went through many printings, the latest in 1986. It was the last significant cowboy song book to be published for twenty-eight years. Even the cowboy craze generated by Hopalong Cassidy (William Boyd) and Gene Autry in the early days of television did not rekindle the popular cowboy song interest experienced during the 1930s.

A curious anomaly took shape in the 1930s as country musicians slowly acquired the trappings, particularly the clothing, of cowboys. By the 1940s, a pattern for dress and songs about cowboys existed that is still copied in the 1980s. The cowboy continues to be a popular country song character and theme, and many cowboy song folios and country song folios contained and still include songs composed for recording and radio and television stars, not for or by cowboys.

John A. Lomax contributed another major source of information when in 1947, Macmillan published his autobiography, *Adventures of a Ballad Hunter*. He wrote an interesting, readable account of his travels and adventures in searching for individuals who could sing or play folk songs. Lomax's disappointments were as exciting as his successes, but in the chapter, "Hunting Cowboy Songs," the same romanticized images and interpretations were repeated as were found in his previous collections and articles, however elaboration and embellishment made his autobiography more interesting. These concepts and romantizations were perpetuated by Morton Kamins in *Persimmon Hill* (1984), published by the National Cowboy Hall of Fame. Kamins, a Los Angeles-based freelance writer with a journalistic approach, rewrote, in his article "John A. Lomax, the Ballad Hunter," information gleaned from the Lomax autobiography. However, Kamins took liberty with the text, for he wrote that Lomax as a child heard cowboys singing the "Night-Herding Song"— an experience Lomax never claimed. Instead, Lomax specifically told that the song was sent to him by a former student, Harry Stephens, who wrote it long after his student days with Lomax. The romanticizers write on and on and on.

It is necessary to mention the essay that well may have been John A.

Lomax's best about cowboys. Published posthumously in 1967 in book format by the Encino Press, *Cow Camps and Cattle Herds* was written in 1945 at the request of Stith Thompson for a proposed anthology of regional folklore. Lomax was seventy-eight when he mailed his contribution to Thompson, but the anthology was never published. The essay was returned to the family after the death of John Lomax in early 1948 and lay dormant for nearly twenty years. Because it was printed in a limited edition, it is still difficult to obtain. It was, however, an attempt by Lomax to condense his lifetime of interest in cowboy culture into a few pages, and he did it well in what is more than an essay. Lomax, a poet at heart, put into his writing the years of folk song collecting that had given him a greater understanding of cowboy songs and the process of oral transmission. Although he retained his somewhat romanticized interpretation—with occasional reference to songs too rank to be printed or sung in mixed company—the essay was an eloquent condensation of cowboy life. He held tenaciously, but with slight modification, to his position of group composition—or at least alteration, and to songs being controlled by the gait of a horse. He remained true—as did his cowboys—to his beliefs; perhaps his romantic concepts were ingrained as a result of growing up in an age of sentimental, romantic expression and the fact that he was not a cowboy himself.

Another significant work appeared in 1966, when Austin E. and Alta S. Fife's edited edition of the 1908 *Songs of the Cowboys* by Thorp was published by Clarkson N. Potter. At that time, it was the finest scholarly work in cowboy song research, and it remains an example of thoroughness. The Fifes used variants, made commentary, provided informational notes, included a lexicon of western words, and, equally as important, a melody line and musical variants were given for each song. As a result of this volume and earlier published articles about western songs, the Fifes became the country's preeminent cowboy song collectors and scholars. The Thorp edition was followed in 1969 by *Cowboy and Western Songs*, also published by Clarkson N. Potter. The Fifes used two hundred songs to illustrate the cowboys' experience as stated through song, grouping the songs into fourteen distinct subjects. The subjects were diverse but specifically cowboy related, for example "Red Men and White," "Treacherous Women," "Swing Your Partner," and "The Last Roundup." The texts and melody lines came from a variety of collections as well as the Fifes' own and from printed sources, but as with Lomax it was not made clear if all songs were actually from oral tradition. It is doubtful that they were; a poem such as "At a Cowboy Dance" was exactly as James Barton Adams published it in 1889. Although the Fifes made no claim that all selections were from oral tradition, it would have been of great value if the informant, date, and place—not just the collector—had been identified.

An interesting study by the Fifes was published in 1970 by the Utah State University Press: *Heaven on Horseback: Revivalist Songs and Verse in the Cowboy Idiom*. The authors focused on the texts in which the cowboy idiom expressed "religious and transcendental ideas," but, again, not all texts were from oral tradition and not necessarily written by real cowboys, obviously the complete opposite of the material presented in this book. The Fifes followed the Lomax footsteps when in 1970 the American West Publishing Company issued their compilation of songs and poems, *Ballads of the Great West*, wherein they used a few ballads with no music, along with much cowboy poetry from printed sources. It was an anthology of poetry, not an oral tradition study.

The Period of Renewed Interest

Two large volumes were published back to back almost simultaneously with the Fife publication, an indication of renewed interest in cowboy songs. Both volumes were gleaned primarily from printed sources and contribute nothing to the study of orally transmitted song; their strength lies in the compilers' commentaries and bibliographical efforts. Both volumes include western songs from a variety of occupations—not just cowboying—as well as songs from gold rush days to the present. In 1967, the Macmillan Company published *Songs of the Great American West*, compiled and edited by Irwin Silber. The following year the University of California Press published *Songs of the American West*, compiled and edited by Richard E. Lingenfelter, Richard A. Dwyer, and David Cohen.

In 1971, the University of Illinois Press initiated the "Music in American Life" series and published two important cowboy volumes. *The Hell-Bound Train: A Cowboy Songbook* (1973) contained a hundred songs as collected and sung by Glenn Ohrlin, who learned his songs from other cowboys; and some of his selections appeared for the first time in printed form. Ohrlin contributed excellent rodeo lore and songs that had been ignored previously and proved that songs continue to enter oral tradition. His commentary about each song is valuable, as is Harlan Daniels's biblio-discography for each song.

Two years later, the same press released *Git Along, Little Dogies*, John I. White's collection of essays about various cowboy poets and songs. The book represented White's research dating back to the late 1920s and is the most valuable book written for tracing and understanding the origin of many traditional cowboy songs.

An unusual approach to cowboy songs was written by Katie Lee, an Arizonian who, at that time, had collected and sung cowboy songs for more than twenty years. Published by the Northland Press in 1976, *Ten Thousand Goddam Cattle* was a collection of traditional songs mixed with more than fifty compositions by Lee and her friends. The songs were interwoven into the narrative to form a history of the cowboy as seen and interpreted by Lee. It was a mixture of realism and romanticism, and unique.

A few additional volumes for children or for popular consumption were published in the sixties and seventies by different commercial firms, but none added any new information about origins, utility, style, or structure of cowboy songs and singing. The standard Lomax texts were used for clever or, at least attractive, packaging for quick and often low-cost sales. But in 1981, the University Presses of Florida published an oversized, profusely illustrated volume compiled and edited Jim Bob Tinsley, *He Was Singin' This Song*.

Tinsley started collecting cowboy songs in the 1930s when he was a radio performer; he readily admitted to having learned a few songs from sheet music and early recordings, whereas others were pulled from books. However, he did learn from, or at least recorded, traditional cowboy singers in his collecting travels, although the source of most texts was not identified. Therefore, it is not known if the songs are or were in oral tradition or if they represent his aesthetic tastes. Tinsley states that the Norman Luboff Choir arrangements of some of the songs are the best ever.[53] In contrast, the songs in this collection are gleaned from the earthy sound and strength of traditional singers. Nevertheless, the Tinsley book contains extensive commentary about each song, wherein lies its value and strength. Tinsley's research into origins, as well as his placement of the song into its historical context, are well done.

In 1983, the University of Texas Press published the reminiscences of William A. Owens, *Tell Me a Story, Sing Me a Song . . .* ; in the chapter "Cowboy Laments," Owens wrote of his memory of a few cowboy songs. In the late 1930s, he received meager funds (but at least some money) from the University of Texas to collect folk songs. His background was that of a northeast Texas farm boy—not that of a west Texas ranch youth—who grew up hearing and learning folk songs. To his credit, he writes that his family sang only three or four cowboy songs. Most of his songs before to his subsidized collecting trip were standard southern folk songs, along with sentimental popular songs as they eased into oral tradition. Owen's first collection of songs (the result of his doctoral dissertation in 1941) was a Texas Folklore Society publication in 1950 —*Texas Folk Songs* in which no chapter was devoted to songs about cowboys, even though a few songs sung by cowboys were included. No doubt, Owen's farm background and the almost oppressive influence of Lomax prevented him from including a cowboy chapter in his earlier book. But by 1983, the pressure had been reduced, and cowboy songs were given a separate chapter. Owens did write, however, that his best sources for cowboy songs were J. Frank Dobie, Roy Bedichek, and Walter Prescott Webb, so his sources were not traditional, everyday working cowboys, but rather carriers of romanticized cowboy lore. Nevertheless, Owens's narrative is enjoyable reading even though no new insights or conceptualizations about cowboy songs and singing are provided.

Although not specifically a cowboy book, the 1983 annual publication of the Texas Folklore Society, *Singin' Texas* by Francis Edward Abernethy, is a regional song book in which cowboy and western songs are reproduced. The songs—many are cowboy songs—were collected either by Abernethy or by his friends, but unfortunately, in order to get the best text possible, they were gleaned from printed sources. No date, no place, and very few informants are listed; however Abernathy has an excellent writing style, so the flowing commentary is entertaining and enjoyable although it is not a representative field collection of folk song. A true, honest, accurate fragment of a song with pertinent information is far superior to another reprint of a Lomax text, which makes Glenn Ohrlin's collection the best in many years. Abernethy did include "When You and I Were Young Maggie," which has often been cited in early cowboy memoirs as a range cowboy favorite, in the cowboy section.

Thorp and Lomax stand as individual leaders from the herd of collectors and editors; others have merely followed. The differences between the two were both honest and significant—they were both educated, but Lomax earned academic degrees and was a teacher. They were both collectors, but Lomax eventually devoted his life to collecting all types of American folk songs, whereas Thorp lived as a cowboy, a storyteller, and a poet. Both men would have been encouraged by and enthusiastic about the attention directed to cowboy culture in the 1980s.

The American Folklife Center

The American Folklife Center, established by Congress in 1976 as a division of the Library of Congress, sponsored during 1978–80 an extensive, in-depth study about traditional ranch and cowboy life in Paradise Valley, Nevada. In 1980–81, an exhibit gleaned from the project was displayed in the National Museum of American History in Washington, D.C. Howard W. Marshall and Richard E. Ahlborn wrote a summary of the project and documentation, as well as an exhibition catalog, *Buckaroos in Paradise: Cowboy Life in Northern Nevada*, published by the Library of Congress in 1980. According to Marshall and Ahlborn, cowboy songs and singing were not in abundance, and they make no mention of cowboys singing at work. Instead, they felt that oral traditions of singing, poetry recitation, and storytelling functioned for recreational purposes, and many songs and poems, such as "The Castration of the Strawberry Roan," were usually relegated to situations in which strong drink lubricated the mind and reduced inhibitions. The exhibit documented cowboy traditions influenced more by the California-Hispanic cultures than by the Texas-Hispanic cattle industry.

The "Buckaroo" exhibition was followed by "The American Cowboy Exhibition" in the Library of Congress from March 26, 1983 to October 2, 1983. It and related activities attracted new interest in the cowboy myth. The American Folklife Center assembled an impressive array of exhibit items to portray the American cowboy, both real and imaginary; cowboy songs and singers from real cowboy life, as contrasted with the Hollywood image, were amply represented. Lonn Taylor and Ingrid Maar assembled an excellent array of essays and illustrations that made the catalog *The American Cowboy* one of the most interesting cowboy items to be published in the 1980s. A symposium, "Songs and Music of the American Cowboy: From the Trail Drive to the Silver Screen," was presented at the Library of Congress on July 21, 1983. Cowboy singers, musicians, and scholars presented their reflections on, and interpretations of, cowboy songs.

Almost simultaneous with the American Folklife Center exhibition activities, the National Council for the Traditional Arts, with the support of the National Endowment for the Arts, Folk Arts Program, and other arts councils, organized a national tour of cowboys—"The Cowboy Tour." The participants, cowboys from Louisiana to Montana to Hawaii, provided their audiences with songs, poetry, fiddle music, and stories. An audio cassette, "The Cowboy Tour," was produced from their concerts.

While the exhibitions and tour were introducing cowboy culture to new audiences, plans were being made for a "Cowboy Poetry Gathering," a meeting of cowboy poets organized by western state folklorists and interested friends. The Institute of the American West, headquartered in Salt Lake City, was the organizational sponsor, and Hal Cannon was the director. From January 31, 1985 to February 2, 1985, cowboy poets gathered in Elko, Nevada, to read and recite their poems and to sing their songs along with a few of the traditional songs and poems. The purpose of the Gathering was to give recognition to a tradition as old as that of singing and to the tradition from which the songs emanated —the tradition of writing and reciting poetry. Old-time singers often do not know, or cannot hear, the difference between singing and speaking; it is the rhythm and rhyme of the words that create music—their poems are songs, or their songs are poems. Imagery is the essence of their performance. The Gathering showcased reciters and poets, literally hundreds of cowboys and cowgirls from most western states participated. The event's success demanded that it become an annual event, and Hal Cannon compiled old and new poems and songs into an attractive collection, *Cowboy Poetry: A Gathering* (1985).

It is impossible even to speculate about the possibility of even one poem or song becoming loved enough to enter the traditional repertoire, but it can be predicted that the cowboy tradition will continue for many generations. And it was obvious at the Gathering that an appreciation of the humor that is expressed through bawdy songs and poems and their performance will continue.

One of the most recent collections is Don Edwards's *Songs of the Cowboys*, published in 1986. Edwards, a cowboy romantic, admires the work of Jack Thorp and has written a tribute, "The Ballad Hunter," to him. His collection is an interesting combination of traditional songs mixed with new material and Hollywood songs. Edwards includes comments about the songs, and his approach is one singer's honest discussion of what he enjoys singing.

By no means has every book and article that mentions cowboy songs been discussed in the preceding; such an attempt would require a single volume bibliography. Instead, I have included those texts that I believe to be the most important for the study of cowboy songs.

Bawdy Songs

Cowboys both wrote and sang songs that ranged from the suggestive to the obscene; a fact attested to by Thorp, Lomax, Coolidge, Barnes, Wister, and others who actually lived, worked, and/or collected among cowboys. But cowboys are not the only occupation to do so. In fact, be it songs, limericks, jokes, or other forms of orally transmitted lore, the bawdy and the obscene have been and are very much a part of all occupations and all levels of society. It is not to be directly or indirectly implied, however, that all cowboys, or that all humans, indulge in transmitting or even listening to the bawdy and obscene. Many people are genuinely offended even by mild cursing, and by the word *sex,* many are morally indignant about explicit words. But the massive quantity of "dirty" jokes alone indicates that a high percentage of our society participates to some degree in transmitting the bawdy. From both primitive and sophisticated literate, there has been and still is a humor that comes from sexual and scatological experience and knowledge. The cowboy merely found and finds humor where those before him found it.

To indicate that all the bawdy songs in this collection are humorous is misleading, even though the original intent was humor. They may have been humorous in the setting in which they were transmitted, for example, stag dances, bars, bunk houses, and cow camps, but when seen in print, isolated from the setting, some lose much humor and appear to be crude and vulgar. It was clearly stated by those from whom they were collected, as well as by the writers mentioned previously, that bawdy songs were not sung to cattle; instead, hymns were often sung to cattle at night.

For a variety of reasons, the primary one of which has been publishers' refusals, other collectors have been reluctant to include bawdy material in their published field collections. Until recent years this reluctance has not been limited to songs, but has included all genres of folklife—speech, proverbs, riddles, tales, and jokes. Song, however, has been the last folk genre to break the barrier and to be published as collected. Perhaps song is still subconsciously associated with religious emotion. Nevertheless, collectors have traditionally removed the bawdy from song collections.

In "Bowdlerization and Expurgation; Academic and Folk," Kenneth Goldstein makes a reasonable distinction between bowdlerizing and expunging and the degrees of both. Bowdlerization refers "to censorship by commission—the intentional alteration or modification of any item of sexual folklore by substituting or exchanging one or more words, phrases, verses, or an entire item, for another"; expurgation refers "to censorship by omission—the intentional deletion of all or part of any erotic or obscene item of folklore."[54] Although Thorp referred to "expunging" songs, he and Lomax and many other collectors and scholars actually bowdlerized the songs by rewriting them. Only in a few songs such as "The Old Chisholm Trail" were verses actually expunged. It was in the process of publishing the collections that extensive expurgation was employed; collectors removed most sexual and bawdy material and bowdlerized a small portion.

Perhaps the greatest example of expurgating a collection is found in the published works of Vance Randolph. No other collector has recorded a region as thoroughly and successfully as Randolph did the Ozark folk culture. His published works about the Ozarks are numerous, and his four-volume *Ozark Folksongs* is the finest of all regional folk song collections. But when publication by the State Historical Society of Missouri was begun in 1946, approximately two hundred bawdy songs were expunged by the publisher, and the collection became only a partial reflection of folk song in the Ozarks.

Randolph made no value judgements; he collected any and all verbal lore that he could, and much of his valuable material remains unpublished in archival manuscripts. Copies of his manuscripts were deposited at the Library of Congress and the Kinsey Institute for Research in Sex, Gender, and Reproduction at Indiana University. He categorized the collection into "Unprintable Songs from the Ozarks," "Unprintable Ozark Folk-Beliefs," "Obscenity in Ozark Riddles," "Latriniana, or Folk Epigraphy from the Ozarks," "Ribaldry at Ozark Dances," "Vulgar Lore from Ozark Children," and "Bawdy Elements in the Ozark Speech." His collection of folk tales, *Pissing in the Snow and Other Ozark Folktales*, was published, showing academic publishing courage, by the University of Illinois Press in 1976.

In her introduction to *Pissing in the Snow*, Rayna Green traces the slow development of academic publication of bawdy and obscene lore as well as the scholar's reluctance to collect or to accept such material as a part of human experience. She stresses that Randolph had wanted the obscene lore to be included in the appropriate printed collection as a part of a genre instead of being isolated out of context. Green expanded her study of folklore and bawdry into the essay, "Folk Is a Four-letter Word: Dealing with Traditional **** in Fieldwork, Analysis, and Presentation," which was published in Richard Dorson's *Handbook of American Folklore* in 1983.

Other collections such as the previously mentioned Gordon "Inferno" in the Library of Congress include a smaller amount of material that Gordon labeled "California Inferno" and a selection of miscellaneous songs—primarily soldier songs—from a variety of sources labeled "Bawdy Songs." Another unpublished collection was gathered by Kenneth Larson between 1920 to 1952 while he was a public school teacher in Idaho; he originally intended to use it as a master's thesis, but eventually deposited typescripts of "Barnyard Folklore of Southeastern Idaho" in appropriate folk archival collections. In 1972, he reorganized his material under the title "Countryside Folklore: Songs and Ballads of Bygone Times." Larson included material that Gershon Legman, the leading collector of obscene lore, had sent him.

Although it is not known why Larson did not use his collection for a thesis, it might be assumed that his adviser would not accept it. Academicians were, and some still are, of the persuasion that the study of folk song had no place for bawdry. That conservative attitude started to recede in 1952 when Horace P. Beck, Jr., submitted his dissertation, "Down-East Ballads and Songs," to his committee at the University of Pennsylvania. He included as his last chapter eleven bawdy songs that he collected in Maine, with the rationale that not to include the bawdy songs of loggers and sailors would paint an untrue picture of the men in the occupations, an argument that also applies to the cowboy occupation. Another collection that contained bawdy songs and was used as a thesis study was "Annotated Field Collection of Songs from the American College Student Oral Tradition" as submitted by Richard A. Reuss at Indiana University in 1965.

Not all of the traditional songs of the student community are bawdy, but the Reuss study reflected a vast body of ribald songs. Fraternity life in particular has long been a conduit through which bawdy lore has traveled. I have long heard of numerous mimeographed and photocopied song books circulated by fraternity members, but had been unable to obtain copies. In the spring of 1987, however, the *Shitty Songs of Sigma Nu* was sent to me by a friend. In keeping with the tradition, the booklet contains no information about when or where it was produced. There must be hundreds of these collections that, when published, probably involve changing only the front cover to indicate the identity of the specific fraternity or campus organization.

In an academic library unknown to me somewhere on the West Coast is the typescript, "Apples of Eden: A Private Collection of American Folk-Lore. Gathered from cowboys, college boys, and latino americanos by a liberal who does not believe that these choice morsels should be thrown out of American Literature because of their vigorous and unconventional language. After all, a manure pile by any other name would smell no better! And even a manure pile has its values." A few years ago the manuscript was surreptitiously acquired from the library by an unknown person who loaned it to a friend of mine, who, knowing of my interest, loaned it to me. I made a copy before it was returned, and I hope it was redeposited in its original home.

Perhaps the most widespread printed collection that has been a campus favorite for many years is *Immortalia*, "An Anthology of American Ballads, Sailors' Songs, Cowboy Songs, College Songs, Parodies, Limericks, and Other Humorous Verses and Doggerel Now for the First Time Brought Together in Book Form by a Gentlemen About Town." It was published anonymously in 1927, but it has been attributed to T. R. Smith [George Macy], who also edited *Poetica Erotica*—a collection of erotic "amatory" verse—the same year. In this country, *Immortalia* has been the most influential and most widely published and circulated collection of bawdry; even though it was not all song, almost all collections of printed bawdy songs since then have some texts that are identical to those in it. How many times it has been reprinted is not known, but I have inspected printings from 1958, 1960, and 1971. The 1971 printing by Hart Publishing even included melody lines, when known, to the songs. There is at least one typescript of the 1927 printing, a result of some industrious typist who obviously borrowed a printed copy. It is impossible to speculate about the book's many methods of reproduction and about how many copies have circulated.

In *Immortalia*, there was heavy emphasis on limericks. The limericks combined with the other texts indicate that the songs and lore came from a sophisticated, educated level of society. Poems or doggerel attributed to James Joyce and D. H. Lawrence are included. The book does not contain the crude or coarse content and style of occupational bawdy lore that has been field-collected. *Immortalia* and many later printed bawdy collections have more double entendre songs than normally are found in folk culture. The bawdy cowboy songs in my collection, for example, use explicit language; sophisticated subtlety is seldom seen.

In addition to *Immortalia*, numerous collections of songs that soldiers learned in military—specifically those of World War I veterans—were published both in the United States and England. John Jacob Niles and friends edited *The Songs My Mother Never Taught Me* (1929) and *Singing Soldiers* (1927), wherein the songs were both expurgated and bowdlerized into sterile texts. The same was true for Frank Shay's *My Pious Friends and Drunken Companions* (1927). In England in 1917, Frederick Thomas Nettleingham compiled at least two volumes of *Tommy's Tunes; The Long Trail* (1965), compiled by John Brophy and Eric Partridge, was equally innocuous. Only the veterans knew what was missing or what had been replaced. The same was true for the volumes produced after World War II. Alteration of texts even extended into hobo songs when George Milburn's *The Hobo's Hornbook* was published in 1930.

After the Vietnam War, along with changing societal attitudes about published bawdry, at least two uncensored volumes of military songs were published. Anthony Hopkins, a veteran of Canadian military action in World War II, compiled *Songs from the Front and Rear: Canadian Servicemen's Songs of the Second World War*, published by Hurtig Publishers in Edmonton, Alberta (1979). The publishers stated on the copyright page that their intent was to "reproduce songs in their authentic wartime form wherever possible notwithstanding the language contained therein." C. W. "Bill" Getz, a retired United States Air Force officer, readily admits to spending much time in Officers' Club bars collecting approximately one thousand songs sung by airmen from World War I through the Vietnam War. He compiled them into two volumes titled *The Wild Blue Yonder: Songs of the Air Force* and published by The Redwood Press in Burlingame, California. The first volume, published in 1981, contains six hundred and sixty-two non-bawdy songs. A letter of endorsement by General J. H. "Jimmy" Doolittle makes it a collection acceptable for the coffee table of any Air Force veteran; however the second volume, published in 1986 and labeled "Stag Bar Edition," contains nearly four hundred songs, poems, and toasts of which approximately one-half are bawdy. No doubt this volume is an under-the-coffee-table book. Unfortunately, neither volume contains melody lines, but no longer will military chroniclers need to allude to military bawdry.

Untouched bawdy songs circulated among the military through oral transmission, by typescript, or by some form of manual duplication, but not through published books. There were numerous collections of this type, which ranged from a few to many pages. Getz includes an impressive list of such publications in his two volumes. As with the fraternity collections, I have heard about these manuscripts but have not seen them and so have made no attempt to include a special bibliographical section.

The folk revival of the 1950s and 1960s coincided with reduced restrictions on publishing. The growing interest in folk songs in the urban areas also created a market for bawdy folk songs on records and in print. In the mid-1950s, the Audio Fidelity label featured Oscar Brand singing a multi-volume series, *Bawdy Songs and Backroom Ballads*, and in 1960, Brand edited a selection of the songs published under the same title by the Dorchester Press. Coinciding with Brand's recordings, Electra Records released a multi-volume series titled *When Dalliance Was in Flower and Maidens Lost Their Heads* sung by Ed McCurdy. Brand's material was a cross-section of occupations, geographic origins, and time, whereas McCurdy's songs were predominantly older English and Scottish ballads with some nontraditional songs included. Both phonograph album series and Brand's book were for sophisticated audiences who wanted a hint of sexually bawdy lyrics. The truly bawdy songs were bowdlerized and expurgated into mere whispers compared to the original words, and a heavy double entendre content pervaded. Brand did devote his sixth record album to *Bawdy Western Songs*, a few of which have never been mentioned in any cowboy literature or cowboy song books. Reversing the trend of cleansing songs, Brand wrote suggestive lyrics for some folk songs that previously had not been associated with bawdy lyrics. But both series and Brand's book marked the beginning of publishing bawdy song collections in this country.

Ed Cray, under the pseudonym E. R. Linton, compiled (without tampering with the words) *The Dirty Song Book* (1965), published by Medco Books in Los Angles. It was the first commercial attempt that I know of to publish erotic songs, but obviously the market was limited and many book stores did not stock it. Cray revised and enlarged the collection and added scholarly notes and annotations along with the song histories—when known—and a bibliography. The songs were genuine, uncensored traditional songs. The collection was expanded and published as *The Erotic Muse* by Oak Publications in 1969 and remains as the only scholarly study of bawdy-erotic songs to be published in this country. Other printed collections appear to be more for titillating than for educating.

A collection compiled and collected at the University of Illinois and edited by Harry Babad, *Roll Me Over*, was also published by Oak Publications in 1972. The content was influenced by Brand and to a lesser extent by McCurdy's recordings; however the "dirty" words were reinserted. The annotations were short and inadequate, and as with Brand, it is doubtful that all of the songs were traditional. In fact, it was the editor's intention to publish a dirty song book for singers; at least honesty in purpose was stated, in contrast to Craig McGregor's *Bawdy Ballads and Sexy Songs*, also published in 1972. This collection was for commercial purposes only and contained no melody line and nothing new in content.

Ten years later, Jerry Silverman, known for his "folk" instruments, how-to guides, and stage performances of folk music, compiled *The Dirty Song Book*, published by Stein and Day. Again, the claim was made that the songs were traditional, but no sources were cited and no attempt was made to supply any information other than a few clever reasons—none were needed—for publishing the book. Melody lines were included with guitar chords resulting in a how-to-sing-dirty-songs book.

Bawdy Songs in Other English-Speaking Countries

Bawdy songs were not only being published in the United States, but in England and Australia as well. As with their counterparts, the compilers used both old and relatively new songs, depending on the stated purposes of the collections. The most comprehensive of the Australian collections, *The Best Bawdry*, was compiled by Don Laycock and published in 1983 by Angus and Robertson. This collection represents bawdy material collected in Australia, the United States, and New Guinea. While in the United States, Laycock, whose collecting has spanned more than twenty-five years, was recorded in an informal session by Joe Hickerson for the Archive of Folk Culture.

Other Australian collections are Bill Wannan's *Robust Ribald and Rude Verse in Australia*, published in 1972 by Lansdowne Press, and Ron Edward's *Australian Bawdy Ballads*, published in 1973 by the Rams Skull Press. Edwards's included comments, sources, and dates and is an excellent collection. An anonymously edited and published collection appeared in 1962 under the title *Snatches and Lays* and was reprinted by Sun Books (1973) with credit given to the editors Sebastian Hogbotel and Simon ffuckes—both pseudonyms.

In England and Scotland, collectors and publishers confronted bawdy songs with equal timidity and intimidation coupled with prior restraint fears. Bishop Percy's *Reliques of Ancient English Poetry* was published in 1765 as a three-volume collection without the bawdy songs. A fourth manuscript folio lay suppressed and dormant until 1868, when Frederick J. Furnivall edited and published it as *Loose and Humorous Songs from Bishop Percy's Folio Manuscript.* This privately printed volume was limited in quantity and remained difficult to obtain until it was reprinted in 1963 by Folklore Associates and Herbert Jenkins. John Greenway wrote an introduction that documented the background of the folio as well as the anthropologist's interpretation of bawdry and censorship.

Thomas D'Urfey's 1720 edition of *Wit and Mirth, or Pills to Purge Melancholy* contained songs written by him and is well documented in various folk and literature sources. In 1967, S. A. J. Bradley edited a selection, *Sixty Ribald Songs from Pills to Purge Melancholy*, published by Frederick A. Praeger. Bradley's introduction provides a concise background of the book's lineage and of bawdry in England.

In the introduction to the reprint of John Stephens Farmer's *Merry Songs and Ballads*, Gershon Legman wrote that it "is by far the most valuable collection in English of unexpurgated folksongs and ballads, and of uncastrated art and folk poetry." Farmer compiled his five-volume collection, apparently as a method to raise funds to finance other projects, which are all well documented by Legman. The volumes, *Merry Songs and Ballads Prior to the Year A. D. 1800*, were privately published in 1897. Reprinted by Cooper Square Publishers in 1964 with Legman's introduction, they remain the foundation upon which a printed bawdy collection should be built.

Robert Burns is equally important in bawdry scholarship. He collected and wrote bawdy songs that were printed in *The Merry Muses of Caledonia.* The book's publishing history, darkened by the cloud of censorship and prurient attitudes, remains questionable; however, James Barke and Sydney Goodsir Smith edited and analyzed a new edition published in England in 1959 and published in this country in 1964 by G. P. Putnam's Sons. Their essays, along with an essay by J. DeLancey Ferguson, investigated all aspects of Burns's suppressed poems, bawdry in society, and the background of *Merry Muses.* Gerson Legman also devoted a lengthy section about Burns and *Merry Muses* in *The Horn Book.*

In 1957, Vivian De Sola Pinto and Allan Edwin Rodway included

Burns's songs in their anthology, *The Common Muse: An Anthology of Popular British Ballad Poetry XVth–XXth Century*.

Folk song field collections in England include those that were gleaned by Cecil James Sharp, Sabine Baring-Gould, H. E. D. Hammond, and George B. Gardiner. James Reeves edited the suppressed songs from those collections into two books. *The Idiom of the People*, published in 1958 by Heinemann, was composed of bawdy songs from the Sharp manuscripts; *The Everlasting Circle* (1960), also published by Heinemann, was composed of bawdy songs selected from the manuscripts of the other three scholars.

Peggy Seeger and Ewan MacColl compiled *The Singing Island* published by Mills Music in 1960 and edited a larger selection in *Travellers' Songs from England and Ireland* published in 1977 by the University of Tennessee Press. Both collections include bawdy songs.

Frank Purslow edited three books of bawdy or double entendre songs: *The Wanton Seed* (1969); *The Constant Lovers* (1972); and *The Foggy Dew* (1974), all published by E. F. D. S. Publications. And Roy Palmer included a few bawdy items in *Everyman's Book of British Ballads*, published by J. M. Dent and Sons in 1980.

However, the most impressive collection from England was published in 1975 by Schirmer Books. Peter Kennedy edited three hundred and sixty songs into a large volume titled *Folksongs of Britain and Ireland*. Kennedy was a producer and field collector in the 1950s for the weekly BBC radio program, "As I Roved Out," a program of authentic folk music. He compiled and edited their collecting efforts into a scholarly documented and annotated collection that included currently sung bawdy songs; it is an accurate reflection of traditional songs and singers. It is what Vance Randolph wanted to do with his Ozark collections— integrate the bawdy into the body of the printed collection as naturally as traditional singers carry the songs.

The English, Scottish, and Irish bawdy songs in print (at least in the collections I have seen) are different from my bawdy collection; very few are as explicit as those I have collected. The Australian songs lie somewhere between the two extremes. The songs from the British Isles do not seem to reflect the wild roughness of language found in many cowboy songs.

The inclusion of bawdry has been slowly, but steadily, increasing in printed field collections, thus reflecting a truer image of folk traditions and of a singer's repertoire. Other notable collections include

Edith Fowke's *Traditional Singers and Songs from Ontario* (1965) and Stan Hugill's *Shanties from the Seven Seas* (1966) and *Songs of the Seas* (1977). The bawdy songs that each collector included were moderate in degree of sexual content; they were not coarse, but at least enough of the bawdy was included to indicate that the collections were unexpurgated.

There have been two other scholarly studies and collections in this country that have encouraged, through example, the publication of oral traditions as collected, not bowdlerized and expurgated. Both present black oral traditions with obscene and bawdy content. The first was Roger Abrahams's *Deep Down in the Jungle*, published by Folklore Associates in 1964, a collection from the Philadelphia black community. The second study was Bruce Jackson's *"Get Your Ass in the Water and Swim Like Me,"* published by Harvard University Press in 1974. Jackson collected toasts, or narrative poems, from many black informants in a wide geographical area, and many contained obscene and bawdy material. Rounder Records issued an album (Rounder 2014) under the same title, on which fifteen of the toasts were recited.

Gershon Legman

Gershon Legman, who has lived in France for approximately the past forty-five years, has devoted his life to erotic folklore. His detailed, meticulous scholarship and personal evaluation and opinions of bawdry have placed him in a unique sphere of intellectual competency. He is a true individualist of whom Bruce Jackson once wrote: "Few American scholars would admit that Legman knows more about erotica than anyone else. That is because he has for many years with great skill, wit, scholarship and occasional perverse glee attacked most of their sacred cows and revealed them to be dry and motheaten skins." [55]

In *Love and Death: A Study in Censorship* (1949), Legman took the position that sadistic violence is more obscene and offensive than sexual activity. His rationale for his belief is far more complex than such a simplified condensation implies, but it is a theme that reappears consistently in his works. He always supplies facts before theorizing, but his theories are built on a strong Freudian psychoanalytic base, a point at which he perhaps loses some who read his scholarly works. But no one can deny Legman's indefatigable collecting efforts and his meticulous bibliographic skills. To attempt to simplify his study of bawdy songs would be futile, but in order to work seriously in almost all genres of folklore—for most if not all will have bawdy elements—it is imperative to study *The Horn Book: Studies in Erotic Folklore and Bibliography*, published by University Books in 1964. Because bawdy songs are intended to be humorous, Legman's two-volume psychoanalytic study of dirty jokes is essential: *Rationale of the Dirty Joke: An Analysis of Sexual Humour* (Grove Press, 1968), and *No Laughing Matter* (Breaking Point, 1975). Both volumes have been reprinted by Indiana University Press. Legman's first major study about sexual humor was *The Limerick: 1700 Examples, with Notes, Variants and Index* (Les Hautes Ètudes, 1953). It, too, has been reprinted many times and is a classic study. His announced but yet unpublished book of unexpurgated folk songs should be appropriate for future folk song studies.

In *Rationale of the Dirty Joke*, Legman analyzed obscene jokes in terms that apply to humor in obscene or bawdy songs. He feels that the obscene element of humor is an attempt to make the irrational rational and is an expression of conscious or subconscious fears:

> The ordinary dirty joke (or limerick, or ballad) engages directly and apparently therefore pleasureably with taboo themes: sex, scatology, incest, and the sexual mocking of authority-figures, such as parents, teachers, policemen, royalty, nobility (Englishmen, millionaires, and movie-stars), clergymen, and gods. The telling of dirty jokes, like the whispering of bawdy words to strange women in the street or by telephone, or the chalking of genital monosyllables on walls, serves in its simplest form— as shown by Freud—as a sort of vocal and inescapable sexual relationship with other persons of the desired sex. It is for this reason that listeners not wanting such relationships will agree to listen to dirty jokes only with the proviso '. . . If they're *clever*'; 'Clever' means that all taboo words and graphic descriptions will be avoided in the telling, thus allowing the listener either to accept, or (by not laughing or 'not understanding') to refuse to accept, the intimacy of any particular *double entendre*. Jokes not conforming to this rule are the opposite of clever: they are 'stupid.' That is to say, they are unavoidably clear, and lacking in direction—verbal rape, as opposed to verbal seduction.
>
> There is, however, an entirely different function that the retailing of obscenities performs. For this function, the grosser the vocabulary and the more horrible and excruciating the actual content of the joke or poem, the better it seems to serve. The

purpose here is to absorb and control, even to slough off, by means of jocular presentation and laughter, the great anxiety that both teller and listener feel in connection with certain culturally determined themes. The really fearful themes, in our society, are, above all: venereal disease, homosexuality, and castration.[56]

Another question that remains partially unanswered is that of who writes bawdy songs. In addition to Robert Burns, other known writers of bawdry include such respected literary figures as Mark Twain, Eugene Fields, and Rudyard Kipling. And in the 1930s, the songwriter Joe Davis wrote many parodies and original songs for fun and profit; he supplied night club performers with bawdy songs, but it is doubtful that any entered oral tradition.

Among cowboy writers, the best known contributor was Curly Fletcher. His "Strawberry Roan" is one of the most popular cowboy ballads and has been adapted into several other songs, one of which is "The Castration of the Strawberry Roan."[57] He also wrote the long bawdy monologue that is for recitation, "The Open Book," as well as "The Wild Buckaroo." Fletcher saved the parodists the effort of parodying his songs by doing it himself. But although some authors are known, the identity of most writers of bawdry as with most folk songs has been lost.

A misconception about bawdry is that such songs are sung only by and for men. In fact, women sing and probably write the songs; the problem of documentation lies in the reticence of female informants to sing them to collectors. Aunt Molly Jackson, for example, recited bawdy toasts for Alan Lomax in 1939 that are in the Library of Congress. Because her brother, Jim Garland, knew bawdy songs, it is probable that she and their sister, Sarah Gunning, also learned a few. Another traditional folk singer who sings bawdy material is Sara Cleveland of Brant Lake, New York. Collectors are more likely to hear double entendre than coarse songs, but by no means are women less prone to sing the coarse songs. In fact, Dallas "Nevada Slim" Turner learned many "plumb dirty cowboy ballads" from his mother, who collected bawdy songs and even wrote a few.[58] There were also a few other female singers who did sing rougher songs for the Library of Congress field collectors.

Rayna Green has been collecting the bawdy lore of women and in an excellent essay, "Magnolias Grow in Dirt: The Bawdy Lore of Southern Women" (*Southern Exposure*, 1977) has documented the female appetite for bawdry. In *One Potato, Two Potato . . . : The Secret Education of*

American Children, (W. W. Norton and Company, 1976), Mary Knapp and Herbert Knapp included bawdy material collected from children. By including the bawdry they became pioneer scholars in publishing a complete approach to childlore studies, and their study shows that bawdy lore is and always has been popular among children as well as among their elders.

Phonograph Records

Recordings of bawdy songs are difficult to find even though they are numerous. The commercial efforts of Brand and McCurdy are possibly available from used and rare record dealers, but they were not pressed in great quantities by the record companies. Party records that might include traditional bawdy songs are equally difficult to find. However, two excellent long-play recordings of traditional singers have been issued. In 1960, Mack McCormick privately pressed an album *The Unexpurgated Folk Songs of Men* (Raglan R-51), the result of a 1959 song-swapping session of a group of men in Texas. Songs and recitations were included, but although recorded in Texas, no cowboy theme songs are included. It is, however, the first album of traditional bawdy songs recorded in a natural setting with nonprofessional singers. Twenty years later another bawdy folk record was issued. Rounder Records released *Just Something My Uncle Told Me: Blaggardy Folk Songs from the Southern States* (Rounder 0141) in 1981, featuring seven singers performing songs, recitations, and toasts. It is an excellent sampling of bawdry; but the concept of "southern" is misleading, for some of the singers, all male, are from the Southwest, and the songs sung by Glenn Ohrlin are cowboy songs, specifically those of Curly Fletcher. The record is limited to rural singers, yet bawdry is one tradition that transcends all levels of society, regions, sexes, ages, and educational backgrounds.

During the 1920s and 1930s when the recording industry was in its formative years and music was not an industry, the record companies issued most of their nonclassical records for regional appeal, not for national or worldwide sales. Hillbilly was primarily southern country music, and it was not unusual for western songs and singers to be listed as cowboy or folk. Recordings of blues singers, country blues singers, black jazz, and black swing bands were generically referred to as "race records." It is well known and documented that blues lyrics often were heavily laden with sexual content or overtones. Yet the sexual content of hillbilly music has largely been ignored, when, in fact, there were many double entendre and suggestive songs. There were many recordings in all of the categories that were not released because of the sexual content or imagery.

In recent years, Stash Records and Jass Records have issued long-play albums that contain many of the sex songs of the twenties and thirties sung by legendary musicians such as Jelly Roll Morton, Bessie Smith, the Light Crust Doughboys, Cliff Edwards (the voice of Jiminy Cricket), a Gene Autry imitator, Jimmie Rodgers, Sophie Tucker, and many more. A few of the albums are: *Copulating Rhytmn*, volumes one and two (Jass 3 and 5); *Copulatin' Blues*, volumes one and two (Stash ST-101 and ST-122); *Streetwalking Blues* (Stash ST-117); and *Banned* (Living Era AJA 5030). Song titles are often double entendre: "What's It?," "I'm Going to Give It to Mary with Love," "Take Out that Thing," "Pussy, Pussy, Pussy," "It's Too Big Papa," "It Feels So Good," "She Squeezed My Lemon," "I'll Keep Sittin' on It (If I Can't Sell It)," "Please Warm My Wiener," and "What's That Smells Like Fish?" There was and is a strong market for songs with sexual implication and content.

Recordings of a few bawdy songs are in the Archive of Folk Culture in the Library of Congress, but considering the popularity of bawdy it is a surprisingly small amount in comparison to the quantity of songs. Traditional singers were and are not prone to record the obscene; they do not want it to be widely known that they know such songs. It is possibly an extension of guilt about sex and obscenity that pervades in our society; the sad reality of the guilt is that many songs have been lost, but a least a few singers of bawdry have been willing to deposit their voices and knowledge into our national treasury of song. It is also possible that the singers know that they possess musical treasures and do not want to lose control of them, which would diminish individual attention and importance.

As my collecting and writing have progressed and as I have visited with friends about this collection, additional variants and songs have been brought to my attention. This constant activity indicates that bawdy songs may very well be the most popular and durable of all traditional songs among all occupations—not just cowboys.

NOTES

1. J. Frank Dobie, "Ballads and Songs of the Frontier Folk," *Texas and Southwestern Lore* (Austin: Texas Folklore Society, 1927), p. 143.

2. For a concise account of this era of trail driving see Ralph P. Bieber's introduction to the reprint of Joseph G. McCoy's *Historic Sketches of the Cattle Trade of the West and Southwest* (Kansas City, Mo.: Ramsey, Millett, and Hudson, 1874, repr. Glendale, Calif: Arthur H. Clark, 1940), pp. 17–68.
3. McCoy, *Historic Sketches of the Cattle Trade*, pp. 50–53.
4. Ibid., p. 101.
5. Ibid., pp. 137–41.
6. Ibid., p. 10.
7. Ibid., p. 205.
8. James W. Freeman, ed., *Prose and Poetry of the Live Stock Industry of the United States* (Kansas City, Mo.: National Live Stock Association, 1905), p. 508.
9. McCoy, *Historic Sketches of the Cattle Trade*, p. 206.
10. Freeman, *Prose and Poetry of the Live Stock Industry*, pp. 550–51.
11. Ibid., p. 612.
12. Ibid., pp. 561–62.
13. James Cox, *Historical and Biographical Record of the Cattle Industry and the Cattlemen of Texas and Adjacent Territory* (St. Louis: Woodward and Tiernan Printing, 1895), pp. 172–73.
14. Cox, *Historical and Biographical Record*, p. 174.
15. Ibid., p. 54.
16. Reginald Aldridge, *Life on a Ranch: Ranch Notes in Kansas, Colorado, the Indian Territory, and Northern Texas* (New York: D. Appleton, 1884), p. 62.
17. Louis C. Bradford, "Among the Cowboys," *Lippincott's Magazine* (June 1881): 589.
18. Elmo Scott Watson, "Colorado Spring Man Claims Authorship of Famous Old Cowboy Ballad," *Colorado Springs Sunday Gazette and Telegraph*, January 27, 1924, n.p.
19. Sharlot M. Hall, "Songs of the Old Cattle Trails," *Out West* 28 (1908):217.
20. Hall, "Songs of the Old Cattle Trails," p. 221.
21. Mrs. John A. Lomax, "Trail Songs of the Cowpuncher," *The Overland Monthly* 59 (1912):28.
22. Lomax. "Trail Songs," p. 28.
23. G. F. Will, "Songs of Western Cowboys," *Journal of American Folklore* 22 (1909):256.
24. For an excellent discussion and analysis of Pound and the ballad origin issue, see D. K. Wilgus, *Anglo-American Folksong Scholarship since 1898* (New Brunswick: Rutgers University Press, 1959).
25. J. Frank Dobie, *Guide to Life and Literature of the Southwest* (Dallas: Southern Methodist University Press, 1952), p. 120.
26. Wright Howes, *U. S. Iana (1650–1950)* (New York: R. R. Bowker, 1962), p. 553.
27. N. Howard (Jack) Thorp, *Pardner of the Wind* (Caldwell, Idaho: Caxton Printers, 1945), p. 22.

28. Thorp, *Pardner of the Wind*, pp. 28–29.

29. Ibid., pp. 41–42.

30. Ibid., pp. 29–30.

31. In December 1979, I acquired from Neil Clark his files about Jack Thorp and *Pardner of the Wind*. Included were correspondence and business records, clippings, the manuscript, and Clark's personal copy of the book. Before this, through the outstanding services of the Jenkins Company of Austin, Texas, I had acquired Thorp's gift copy of his 1908 and 1921 editions that had been given to Clark. I also obtained Thorp's copy of the 1916 edition of Lomax's *Cowboy Songs and Other Frontier Ballads*.

32. Dobie to Clark, February 11, 1941, Thorp-Clark Collection in Guy Logsdon Collection, Tulsa, Oklahoma.

33. John A. Lomax, *Adventures of a Ballad Hunter* (New York: Macmillan, 1947), p. 41.

34. John A. Lomax and Alan Lomax, *Cowboy Songs and Other Frontier Ballads*, rev. and enlarged. (New York: Macmillan, 1938), pp. xvi–xvii.

35. Lomax and Lomax, *Cowboy Songs*, p. xviii.

36. The problems of Lomax's expurgating and bowdlerizing, along with his methods of collecting and presentation of folk songs, have been addressed thoroughly by D. K. Wilgus in the *Anglo- American Folk Song Scholarship since 1898*.

37. In the collection of Guy Logsdon.

38. Again, D. K. Wilgus contrasts the two in his book, and in 1969 in *Western Folklore*, John O. West in his article, "Jack Throp and John Lomax: Oral or Written Transmissions?" added additional evidence to the charge that Lomax used Thorp texts.

39. Will C. Barnes, "The Cowboy and His Songs," *Saturday Evening Post*, June 27, 1925, p. 14.

40. Barnes, "The Cowboy and His Songs."

41. Ina Sires, *Songs of the Open Range* (Boston: C. C. Birchard, 1928), n.p. "collector's note."

42. More information on German is found in Glenn Ohrlin's *The Hell-Bound Train* (Urbana: University of Illinois Press, 1973).

43. Glenn Shirley, "Daddy of the Cowboy Bands," *Oklahoma Today* 9 (Fall 1959):6–8.

44. John I. White, *Git Along, Little Dogies* (Urbana: University of Illinois Press, 1975), pp. 1–15. This chapter provides information about White's career and research.

45. Margaret Larkin, *Singing Cowboy: A Book of Western Songs* (New York: Alfred A. Knopf, 1931), p. xi.

46. Larkin, *Singing Cowboy*, p. 9.

47. Jules Verne Allen, *Cowboy Lore* (San Antonio: Naylor Printing, 1933), p. 20.

48. Ken Griffis, *Hear My Song: The Story of the Celebrated Sons of the Pioneers* (Los Angeles: The John Edwards Memorial Foundation, 1974), p. 13.

49. Gene Autry, *Back in the Saddle Again* (New York: Doubleday, 1978), pp. 14–17.

50. Reprinted in Robert Winslow Gordon, *Folk-Songs of America* (New York: National Service Bureau, 1938), pp. 101–09.

51. A concise coverage of Gordon's career was written by Debora G. Kodish, "'A National Project with Many Workers' Robert Winslow Gordon and the Archive of American Folk Song," *The Quarterly Journal of the Library of Congress* 35 (1978):218–33; Kodish expanded her study to book length in *Good Friends and Bad Enemies* (Urbana: University of Illinois Press, 1986).

52. Wilgus, *Anglo-American Folksong Scholarship since 1898*, pp. 158–60. See also, Norman Cohen's discussion of "Cole Younger" in *Long Steel Rail* (Urbana: University of Illinois Press, 1981), pp. 117–21.

53. Jim Bob Tinsley, *He Was Singin' This Song* (Orlando: University Presses of Florida), p. xiii.

54. Kenneth S. Goldstein, "Bowdlerization and Expurgation: Academic and Folk," *Journal of American Folklore* 80 (1967):375.

55. Bruce Jackson, "Legman: The King of X700," *Maledicta* 1 (Winter 1977): 111; also see, John McLeish, "A Bibliography of F. Legman," *Maledicta* 1 (Winter 1977):127–38.

56. Gershon Legman, *Rationale of the Dirty Joke* (New York: Grove Press, 1968), pp. 13–14.

57. For an annotated listing, see Austin E. Fife, "The Strawberry Roan and His Progeny," *JEMF Quarterly* 8 (1972):149–65.

58. Dallas Turner to Judith McCulloh, June 6, 1976.

GLOSSARY

For the following definitions, I refer frequently to Fay E. Ward's *The Cowboy at Work* and Ramon F. Adams's *Western Words: A Dictionary of the American West.* Ward's is the most valuable book available for information about cowboys, their work, and their tools. Other references are Russel H. Beatie's *Saddles* and Lee M. Rice and Glenn R. Vernam's *They Saddled the West.* Another book not cited but recommended is Joe Mora's *Trail Dust and Saddle Leather.* The words in capital letters are defined elsewhere in the Glossary.

Arroyo. A creek; Spanish word, meaning rivulet. In the Southwest, it is a narrow gully or gorge cut into soft earth, usually by heavy rains or flash floods.

Auger. A tool for boring holes; often used as a euphemism for the penis.

Augur. To talk; boastful talking; also used as a cowboy term for his boss. (See: Adams, p. 10.)

Bit. A metal bar that fits into a horse's mouth; when a headstall and reins are attached to it, they form a bridle. The bit is a common device for training and controlling a horse; some cowboys use a hackamore (rope halter with reins) instead of a bridle. (See: Ward, pp. 187–92; Adams, p. 20.)

Branding. The practice of burning a mark of identity on the hide of an animal, a mark of ownership. Each rancher registers his or her brand and the location of the brand (right or left shoulder, right or left hip, etc.) in the county and state where the animals are run, and the brand becomes the legal deed of ownership. Thieves carry a RUNNING IRON, used illegally to alter or change a brand. A few old, tough range animals might carry many different brands on their hides, indicating a variety of owners. Additional marks of ownership are made with a knife, see CROPPED HIS EARS. (See: Ward, pp. 59–60; Adams, pp. 32–33.)

Bronc, or **Bronco.** A wild, untamed horse.

Bronco Steer. A crazy, wild, castrated bovine creature.

Buckaroo. A cowboy; used in northern, Rocky Mountain, and western ranges; not often heard in the Southwest. Probably a corruption of the Spanish *vaquero* or *boyero*.

Bunch Quitter. A horse that habitually leaves the REMUDA and heads for home or other unknown places. In reference to cowboys, the term is a nice way of stating that a man is unreliable, undependable, has no sense of loyalty, and is probably cowardly.

Catclaw, or **Devilsclaw.** Spiny scrub brush, or small tree, that grows in thickets in the arid regions of the Southwest and West. The sharp spines are like a cat's claw, tear clothing and flesh, and can penetrate thick CHAPS. Hated by all cowboys who have to work in it. Species of *Acacia greggii*.

Catgut. Cowboys' term for a rope, usually made from rawhide.

Cayuse. A term for a wild, scrubby horse; named for Cayuse Indians who were great horsemen; now term is used by northern cowboys to refer to any horse.

Center-Fire Saddle, California Saddle, or **Single-Rigged Saddle.** A saddle with the rigging ring placed in the center of the TREE, has one CINCH; the center position of the cinch allows the saddle to rock on a bucking horse; popular with DALLY-WELTA men and on the the West Coast. (See: Ward, pp. 209–10; Adams, p. 51; Beatie, pp. 67–78.)

Chaps, or **Chaparejos.** Spanish word for leather breeches; shortened by the American cowboy to *chaps* (pronounced *shaps*); the working cowboys' leg protection, or armour, against thorny brush, cactuses, animal bits, etc. In northern states, angora chaps were also used to help keep the legs warm and dry. (See: Ward, pp. 225–28; Adams, pp. 60–61.)

Cholla Cactus. From the Spanish *cholla,* meaning "head-shaped"; approximately twenty species of the genus *Opuntia* are found in the Southwest; they have cylindrical joints, and the crown of branches and joints often forms the shape of a human head. They are considered to be the most dangerous of all cactuses.

Cinch, or **Cincha.** The Spanish *cincha* means "girth." It is a wide band, usually woven horsehair or mohair, that goes under a horse's belly to hold the saddle in place. Cinches vary according to the type of saddle being used. (See: Ward, pp. 216–19; Adams, p. 67.)

Cocinero. Cowboys' name for the cook; Spanish for a male cook. For the range cook's role, see "cookie" in Adams (pp. 73–74).

Cow. Generic term for all cattle, regardless of sex or age.

Cropped His Ears. This is a method, along with BRANDING, of marking a cow to show ownership. An ear is cut in a pattern that is usually registered along with the rancher's mark or brand. *Crop* also means to cut off one-half of the ear.

Dalley Welters, Dally-Welta, Dally. From the Spanish phrase *dar la vuelta,* meaning "to take a turn with the rope"; cowboys shortened it to dally-welta and dally. A dally is a half-hitch or turn of the ROPE around the saddle HORN after the cowboy's catch is made; this allows the cowboy to work the rope or to let it go in case of an emergency—the opposite of TYING HARD AND FAST to the saddle horn. It is not unusual for dally men to lose a thumb or fingers by letting one get between the rope and the saddle horn, or letting his thumb point down instead of up. Dallying a rope is easier on stock being roped and the roping horse than is tying hard and fast, and it usually requires a longer rope. (See: Ward, pp. 154–84; Adams, p. 88.)

Dogies. A commonly used term for a calf, but more specifically for a scrubby calf suffering from malnutrition. Controversy surrounding the origin of "dogie" is explained by Adams (p. 96). During the Great Depression in the Southwest, the term *okie* became popular for the *dogie.*

Double-Rigged Saddle, Double Barrel, Double Fire, or **Rim Fire.** SADDLES of this type have two CINCHES, or the saddle is double-cinched on the horse. It was the most popular saddle among the old-time trail-drive cowboys. (See: Ward, pp. 193–95; Beatie, 67–78.)

Epizootic. Cowboys' term for equine influenza, also known as distemper; symptoms are respiratory problems, inflammation of mucous membranes, and other systemic problems.

Flue. A passageway in a chimney to carry smoke and flame to outer air; euphemism for the vulva.

Fork. The front part of the SADDLETREE on which the HORN is mounted. The shape or design of the fork and horn is determined by the intended use of the SADDLE by the cowboy, for example roping, riding, etc. (See: Ward, pp. 193–205; Beatie, 97–102.)

Frijole Chomper. In the Southwest, *frijole* is a dried bean, usually a pinto bean; a Mexican dried bean. A frijole chomper is one who eats many dried, or pinto, beans; a derogatory term for Mexicans.

Frog Walkin'. Short hops made by a horse while trying to throw its rider.

Garcia Gut-Hooks. SPURS made by G. S. Garcia in Elko, Nevada; he established his shop in 1896 and became famous for SADDLES, SILVER TRIMMING, BITS, and spurs. Garcia was and is a highly respected name on cowboy GEAR; the Garcia Bit & Spur Company is now owned and operated as a part of the J. M. Capriola Company in Elko.

Gear. A cowboy term used collectively for clothing and moveable personal equipment and belongs.

Glanders. A highly contagious disease of horses, mules, and asses, that can be transmitted to other animals, including humans, but not to bovine creatures. It is a form of venereal disease among horses; symptoms include nodules and ulcers that discharge thin, yellowish material and can scab over, the nostrils discharge whitish, sticky material tinged with blood, and the animals manifested high temperature and general debility. In cowboys, glanders usually ran its course and terminated fatally.

Gunsel. A tenderfoot, or a stupid person. (See: Adams, p. 136.)

Gut Shot. Slang for a wound in the stomach or intestines; while it is not always fatal, it is feared as the most painful wound as well as a slow way to die.

Hamley. A SADDLE made by Hamley & Company in Pendleton, Oregon. In 1890, two brothers, Henry and John J. Hamley, established Hamley & Company in Kendrick, Idaho. Following the death of Henry and a disastrous fire, John J. moved the company in 1904 to Pendleton, where it has continuously produced Hamley saddles. (See: Rice and Vernam, pp. 112–20; Ward, pp. 208–9.)

Honda. The eye or eyelet on the loop end of a rope through which the main line is passed to form a loop for roping. It usually is spliced into the main line and is covered with leather to protect it from wear and tear. A honda can be formed by a knot, or it can be a metal ring—neither is popular among working cowboys. (See: Ward, pp. 157–59; Adams, p. 151.)

Hondoo. Euphemism for the vulva derived from HONDA.

Horn, or Saddle Horn. The technical term is *pommel,* but is not often used by working cowboys. The horn is the knob at the front of the SADDLE essential for roping. The TYING HARD AND FAST roper ties his catch rope to the horn; the DALLY roper does not tie to the horn, but wraps the rope around it and allows the ROPE to slide or become free if necessary. The horn was originally made of wood, but various metals became popular; it is bolted to the FORK; the design of the horn varies according to intended usage and preference. (See: Ward, pp. 202, 211–15; Beatie, p. 103–7.)

Kack. A cowboy term for a saddle: a *Texas kack* is a Texas saddle.

Lariat. Americanization of *la reata;* usually it refers to a ROPE made of horsehair, but occasionally refers to hemp and rawhide ropes.

Lasso. Spanish *lazo reata,* meaning *snare rope,* is from Portuguese *laco* or snare; lasso is the Americanized term meaning a long ROPE. It is not a popular word among most cowboys, but cowboys along the Pacific Coast do use it. Usually when it is used, particularly as a verb, it signifies TENDERFOOT. (See: Ward, p. 155; Adams, p. 173.)

Maguey. A Mexican-made ROPE, from the fiber of the maguey plant; good for calf roping and trick roping. It is a light rope sometimes used by DALLY men. (See: Ward, p. 157; Adams, p. 188.)

Malpais. Spanish *mal pais* meaning bad country. In the Southwest, it is badlands, rough country underlain by dark basaltic lava.

Norther. A northerly wind; a driving gale that moves down the Plains region into the Southwest causing a rapid and extreme drop in temperature. Usually it brings moisture in the form of snow and is referred to as a blizzard by people not connected with agriculture.

Off-Ox. A teamster's term; when a team of horses, mules, or oxen is driven, the teamster walks on the left or *near* side, or rides the left or *near* animal; the animal (ox) on the right or *off* side is the off-animal (off-ox). Horses, mules,and oxen are mounted from the left; to ride the off-animal would require getting between the two and risk probable injury. It was a tradition that passengers entered a vehicle from the left, *near*, side.

O K Spurs. August Buermann of Newark, New Jersey, manufactured a wide variety of spurs for all types of horsemanship. Approximately eight designs were O K spurs; most carried an "O K" stamped in the metal.

Quirley. Cowboy word for a cigarette.

Quirt. A short handle riding whip that is made from many different designs. (See: Ward, pp. 263–69.)

Reata, or **Riata.** From the Spanish, *la reata,* meaning *the rope,* also *rope to tie horses in single file.* Cowboys usually use it in reference to a plaited or a braided rawhide or leather ROPE. It is not designed to be used for TYING HARD AND FAST to a saddlehorn. (See: Ward, pp. 154–55; Adams, p. 246.)

Red Eye. Common term for whiskey.

Remuda. On roundup, each working cowboy needs six or seven horses assigned for his use; a half-day of hard work wears horses down. Thus, a cowboy uses two horses each day and gives them three days' rest. When all horses are herded together, the herd is called the remuda. It is a southwestern term; in northern states the herd is usually called the *cavvy* or *saddle band.* (See: Ward, pp. 33–41; Adams, p. 7.)

Rig, or **Riggin'.** These words have various meanings; they may refer to a type or style of SADDLE, or to various parts of the saddle. Usually riggin' refers to CINCHES and the manner in which they are attached to the saddle; rig and riggin' are used as slang for saddle as well as for anything that has been made or is being constructed. (See: Ward, p. 194; Beatie, p. 360.)

Rope. The word *rope* is seldom used for the cowboys' working tool; instead, they call it LARIAT, REATA, SEAGO, MAGUEY, CATGUT, and many other names. Rope is used as a verb: he roped a bear; and it is used as an adjective: rope corral, roping horse, rope-shy, rope tricks, etc. (See: Ward, pp. 154–84; Adams, pp. 256–58.)

Roundup. To gather the cattle in a central location for branding and/or for harvesting the crop. Traditionally, there are two roundups: the spring roundup is to brand, castrate, and doctor and the fall roundup is to brand, castrate, and doctor those missed in the spring and to ship the crop to market. On large ranches in rough country, roundup can last from a few weeks to four months; it is the time when most cowboy work is done. (See: Ward, pp. 19–41; Adams, pp. 259–60.)

Running Iron. A BRANDING iron that looks like a straight poker with the end curved; a good running iron artist can change a brand without leaving visible evidence. In some areas the possession of a running iron was and is automatic admission of being a rustler. (See: Ward, p. 63; Adams, p. 261.)

Sack-Up Your Saddle. The practice of putting a SADDLE in a grain sack and checking it to be shipped by train or other conveyance to a specified destination; *sacked his saddle* became an expression to say that a cowboy died and is on his way to the home range or ranch house in the sky.

Saddles. From the time when man domesticated the horse to be ridden, devices to make the ride and work more comfortable and safer have been invented; saddles evolved through thousands of years and necessities. The western saddle developed as the cattle industry grew in this country, but while evolving from a general style and construction, the types of Western saddles are as varied as the regions and saddle makers. Western saddles are designed for specific purposes: roping saddles, saddles for breaking horses, rodeo saddles, leisure riding and show saddles, etc. The saddle is a cowboy's essential tool; without a good saddle a cowboy and a cow horse are not much good. (See: Beatie; Rice and Vernam; Ward, pp. 193–05.)

Sam Stack Tree, or **Sam Stagg Tree.** In song, *Sam Stagg* became *Sam Stack;* Sam Stagg was a SADDLE maker (probably in Texas) about whom little is known; his identity remains a mystery, but his method of RIGGIN' a saddle is known among cowboys and saddle makers. He used one piece of leather looped around the SADDLE HORN and down each side to the front riggin'. It was his method of making a saddle tree that made his name legendary. He developed a saddle horn and FORK in one piece of steel—a steel fork. He made a tree with a half wooden fork; the steel fork was riveted to the tree and formed a half metal and half wood fork. It gave way to improved horns and trees, for it would work loose from the tree after being used for heavy roping. (See: Ward: pp. 194–95, 206–8; Beatie, pp. 71–72.)

Seago. A loosely twisted hemp rope; from the Spanish *la soga.*

Set-Fasts. Cowboy slang for SADDLE sores, or sores rubbed on a horse's back through improper saddling and care.

Silver Trimmed Rig. A SADDLE with silver ornaments attached for decoration and showmanship. Very few or no silver ornaments are found on a working saddle.

Stag. A male unaccompanied by a female, often used as a term for bachelor or temporarily unmarried cowboys. Also, a male animal castrated after maturity.

Spurs. Essential equipment worn on each boot for the control of a cowboy's horse. When used properly, they are signals for turning and starting as well as a source of encouragement for the horse to do what it may not want to do. (See: Ward, pp. 229–33; Adams, pp. 297–98.)

Steer. A castrated bovine creature. Bull calves that show the formation of being

good for breeding are spared the cutting knife; all other bull calves are castrated. Their testicles are a delicacy on the cowboys' table and are known as
calf fries, mountain oysters, and other equally descriptive cowboy gourmet
terms.

Suckling. A calf that has not been weaned; when it is old enough to wean, it is
called a *weaner.*

Swallow Forked. An ear mark to show ownership. With a knife, the ear is split
halfway down the middle lengthwise, followed by two divergent cuts in the
middle of the ear that form a forty–five degree angle. The ear looks like a *Y*
has been cut down it. (See: Ward. pp. 68–74; Adams, p. 313.)

Taps, or **Tapaderas.** A pointed piece of leather that covers all sides of a stirrup
except the back (toe fenders); taps are used to protect the feet, as CHAPS
protect the legs, from brush, thorns, and bad weather. Their weight helps
hold a cowboy's feet down when a horse bucks. (See: Ward, pp. 220–24.)

Tenderfoot. Cowboys' term for a new, inexperienced, uninitiated person on the
range; implies that the person possesses an obvious degree of ignorance
about cowboy work and customs. Originally, a tenderfoot was an imported
cow.

Tree, or **Saddle Tree.** The frame on which a SADDLE is made, called a *tree* because components originally came from a tree; a saddletree has a HORN,
bars, FORK, and cantle that are screwed, glued, and bolted together, covered
with wet rawhide. When the rawhide drys, the tree is a rigid, durable frame.
A saddle is no better than its frame, and saddle makers develop their repu-
tation on the design and construction of their trees. However, not many of
today's saddle makers construct their trees; they get them from companies
that specialize in making them. They do, however, use their own method
of wrapping the rawhide. Trees can be custom made to fit a horse and the
rider. (See: Beatie, pp. 93–111; Ward, p. 193–206.)

Twister. Shortened form of *bronc twister,* or a cowboy who breaks horses as a
steady business; a hazardous trade. Also, a Southwest term for a tornado.

Tying Hard and Fast. The Texas sytle of roping; the catch rope is tied securely
to the SADDLE HORN so it will not slip off. When roped, the animal will be held
under all circumstances except when the ROPE breaks or the SADDLE is jerked
off. This style requires a strong LARIANT, usually shorter than used by DALLY
men; it is harder on horses, saddles, cattle, and cowboys. The Texas style
is to jerk or "pop" the animal down, but when the horse goes down instead,
the cowboy is usually injured. However, dally men lose more thumbs. (See:
Ward, pp. 154–84.)

Vaquero. A common term in the Southwest for a cowboy, but usually used for
a Mexican cowboy.

Wethers. Castrated sheep.

Wrangler, or **Horse Wrangler.** The man or boy who took care of the horses; he kept the horses together (herded them) and ready for work. It was the lowest level of work in the cow camp and was work assigned to beginners, such as "Little Joe, the Wrangler." (See: Adams, p. 353.)

Yearling. A one-year-old calf or colt.

BIBLIOGRAPHY

Unpublished References: Manuscripts and Field Collections:

"Apples of Eden: A Private Collection of American Folklore. Gathered from cowboys, college boys, and latino americanos by a liberal who does not believe that these choice morsels should be thrown out of American Literature because of their vigorous and unconventional language. After all, a manure pile by any other name would smell no better! And even a manure pile has its values." Typescript, no additional information available.

Archive of Folk Culture, Library of Congress, Washington, D.C., dates back to July 1, 1928, when the Library of Congress established the Archive of American Folk-Song as a unit within its Music Division. In 1976, Congress established the American Folklife Center, and the Archive became a division of the Center; the name has been changed to the Archive of Folk Culture. The citation code for field-collected songs had been LC-AFS (Archive of Folk Song); in order to avoid confusion *AFS* was retained. The Archive houses extensive subject files that contain information about hundreds of folk songs and related topics, including a "Bawdy Songs" folder.

Arizona Friends of Folklore. This collection was gathered under the direction of Keith and Kathryn Cunningham, Northern Arizona University, Flagstaff. It contains a wide variety of traditional genres including songs.

Bean, Charles W. "An Index of Folksongs Contained in Theses and Dissertations in The Library of Congress, Washington D.C." Master's thesis, Loughborough University of Technology, Loughborough, Leicestershire, England.

Beck, Horace Palmer, Jr. "Down-East Ballads and Songs." Ph.D. diss., University of Pennsylvania, 1952.

Culwell, Gene Allen. "The English Language Songs in the Ben Gray Lumpkin Collection of Colorado Folklore." Ph.D. diss. University of Colorado.

Fife, Austin E. "Anthology of Folk Literature of Soldiers of the Pacific Theater" in Bawdy Songs folder, Archive of Folk Culture, Library of Congress, Washington, D.C.

Fife Folklore Archives, Merrill Library, Utah State University, Logan. This archival collection compiled by Austin E. and Alta S. Fife is composed of forty-one bound volumes of texts, music, and commentary and two subject collections—the Fife Mormon Collection (FMC) and the Fife American Collection (FAC); I refer only to their field-collected entries. See also: Walker, Barbara.

Gelber, Mark. "Traditional Ballads of Colorado." Master's thesis, University of Colorado, 1963.

Gordon, Robert W. The Gordon "Inferno" collection is composed of bawdy texts received in response to the *Adventure* magazine column "Old Songs That Men Have Sung," edited by Gordon from 1923–27; there are also "California Inferno" texts collected by Gordon in 1922–23 along with "Davids Mss," texts written down by R. M. Davids, Cross X Ranch, Woodmere, Florida, in approximately 1924, and sent to Gordon in 1929.

Hickerson-Hitchcock. Joe Hickerson, on October 19–20, 1963, recorded a variety of singers in an informal song session; the primary informant was Jim Hitchcock. This collection (LC-AFS 17022) is in the Archive of Folk Culture, Library of Congress, Washington, D.C.

Hickerson-Laycock. Joe Hickerson recorded bawdy songs as sung by Don Laycock; this collection (LC-AFS 17023–24) is in the Archive of Folk Culture, Library of Congress, Washington, D.C. See: Laycock. *The Best Bawdry*.

"Immortalia. An Anthology of American ballads, sailor's songs, cowboy songs, college songs, parodies, limericks, and other humorous verses and doggerel now for the first time brought together in book form by a Gentleman About Town." Attributed to T. R. Smith [George Macy]. Typescript copy of the 1927 printing; I do not know if the pagination is identical to the printed copy.

Larson, Kenneth. "Barnyard Folklore of Southeastern Idaho." Collected between 1920 and 1952, Salt Lake City, Utah, November 11, 1952; mimeographed copy bound under the title "The Folklore Trade." Copy in Archive of Folk Culture, Library of Congress, Washington, D.C.

Larson, Kenneth. "Countryside Folklore: Songs and Ballads of Bygone Times." Collected during 1930–33 in Idaho and reorganized September 5, 1972, Salt Lake City, Utah. Mimeograph copy in the Archive of Folk Culture, Library of Congress, Washington, D.C.

Larson, Kenneth. "Songs of Eastern Idaho." Graduate paper for American Folklore, University of Utah, November 30, 1950. Copy in Archive of Folk Culture, Library of Congress, Washington, D.C.

LC-AFS. See: Archive of Folk Culture.

LC–Subject File. See: Archive of Folk Culture.

Legman, Gershon. "Typical Specimens of Vulgar Folklore: From the Collection of Gershon Legman," typed by Kenneth Larson, November 28, 1952; mimeographed copy bound with Kenneth Larson's "Barnyard Folklore . . ." under the title "The Folklore Trade." Archive of Folk Culture, Library of Congress, Washington, D.C.

Lincoln, Martha Louise. "The Cherokee Outlet and Its Music." Master's thesis, University of Southern California, 1949.

Logsdon, Guy. Taped interviews and songs, correspondence, commercial recordings, and printed material. The collection includes a N. Howard "Jack" Thorp–Neil Clark collection; a John A. Lomax vertical file; taped interviews with Riley Neal, Lewis R. Pyle, Baxter Black, Bill Long, Dallas Turner, and others; correspondence with John I. White, Glenn Ohrlin, Dallas Turner, Riley Neal, Archie Green, Stephen Makara, Jim Bramlett, and others. Also, I have copies of the correspondence of Dallas Turner to Judith McCulloh; copies of the "Cowboy Songs" in the D. K. Wilgus–Western Kentucky Folklore Archives; and a copy of the Todd-Sonkin Collection.

Lomax, John A. Manuscripts and papers, Eugene C. Barker Texas History Center, University of Texas, Austin.

Lomax, John A. Vertical File. See: Logsdon Collection.

Makara, Stephen. "Oh! That Strawberry Roan!"; this manuscript is a lengthy unpublished article about Curley Fletcher in the Archive of Folk Culture, Subject File.

Owens, William A. "Texas Folk Songs." Ph.D. diss., State University of Iowa, 1941.

Plumb, Margaret L. "Folksongs of Wyoming." Ph.D. diss. in Education, University of Wyoming, 1965.

Randolph, Vance. Manuscripts, "Unprintable Songs from the Ozarks." Copy in Performing Arts Division, Library of Congress, Washington, D.C. The collection also includes "Bawdy Elements in the Ozark Speech," "Vulgar Lore from Ozark Children," "Ribaldry at Ozark Dances," "Latriniana, or Folk Epigraphy from the Ozarks," "Obscenity in Ozark Riddles," "Pissing in the Snow," and "Unprintable Ozark Folk-Beliefs."

Reuss, Richard A. "An Annotated Field Collection of Songs from the American College Student Oral Tradition." Master's thesis, Indiana University, 1965.

Scroggins, Sterling. "Cowboy Songs." Master's thesis, University of Colorado, 1976.

Shitty Songs of Sigma Nu. Mimeographed collection, copy in Guy Logsdon Collection.

Todd-Sonkin Collection. In 1940–41, Charles Todd and Robert Sonkin recorded songs and other verbal lore in migrant camps in California; their collection is in the Archive of Folk Culture, Library of Congress, Washington, D.C. The sound recordings are listed among recordings; in my references the Todd-

Sonkin citations refer to the typescript "Catalogue of Recordings." There are also "Field Notes" and "Song Texts" available as reference tools in using the collection.

Utz, Ruth Adele. "Trails and Trail Drivers of Texas." Master's thesis, Southwest Texas State Teachers College, 1938.

Walker, Barbara. "A Folksong and Ballad Index to the Fife Mormon and Fife American Collections." Master's thesis, Utah State University, 1986.

Wilgus, D. K. Western Kentucky Folklore Archives. This is a collection of field-collected songs, and copies are available at the University of California at Los Angeles as well as at Western Kentucky University, Bowling Green.

Published References: These printed references are books and articles that were valuable for my research, although not all are cited in my text.

Aarne, Antti. *The Types of the Folktale.* Translated and enlarged by Stith Thompson. FF Communications no. 184. Helsinki: Academia Scientiarum Fennica, 1964.

Abernethy, Francis Edward. *Singin' Texas.* Dallas: E-Heart Press, 1983.

Abbott, Edward Charles. *We Pointed Them North.* New York: Farrar and Rinehart, 1939.

Abrahams, Roger D. *Deep Down in the Jungle.* Hatboro, Pa.: Folklore Associates, 1964.

Adams, Ramon F. *The Old-Time Cowhand.* New York: Macmillan, 1961.

Adams, Ramon F. "Singin' Cowboy." *Southwest Review* 31 (1946):170–73.

Adams, Ramon F. *Western Words: A Dictionary of the American West.* New ed. rev. and enlarged. Norman: University of Oklahoma Press, 1968.

Agay, Denes. *Best Loved Songs of the American People.* Garden City, N.Y.: Doubleday, 1975.

Alderson, William L. " 'The Days of '49,' Reprise." *Northwest Folklore* 1 (1965):5–10.

Aldridge, Reginald. *Life on a Ranch: Ranch Notes in Kansas, Colorado, the Indian Territory, and Northern Texas.* New York: D. Appleton, 1884.

Allan, Francis D. *Allan's Lone Star Ballads: A Collection of Southern Patriotic Songs, Made During Confederate Times.* Galveston: J. D. Sawyer, 1874.

Allen, Jules Verne. *Cowboy Lore.* San Antonio: Naylor, 1933.

Alley, John. "Memories of Roundup Days." Norman: University of Oklahoma Association, 1934 (originally published in the *Sooner Magazine,* January 1934).

American Cowboy Songs. New York: Robbins Music, 1936.

The Arkansas Traveller's Songster. New York: Dick and Fitzgerald, 1864.

Armstrong, Ruth W. "Voice of the Southwest." *Arizona Highways,* July 1953, pp. 30–33.

Asch, Moses, and Irwin Silber, eds. *900 Miles: The Ballads, Blues and Folk Songs of Cisco Houston*. New York: Oak Publications, 1965.

Autry, Gene. *Back in the Saddle Again*. Garden City, N.Y.: Doubleday, 1978.

(Autry). *Gene Autry's Famous Cowboy Songs and Mountain Ballads: Book No. 2*. Chicago: M. M. Cole Publishing, 1934.

Babad, Harry, ed. *Roll Me Over*. New York: Oak Publications, 1972.

Back in the Saddle. Milwaukee: Hal Leonard Publishing, 1982.

Baker, Ronald L. "Lady Lil and Pisspot Pete." *Journal of American Folklore* 100 (1987):191–99.

Barnes, Will C. "The Cowboy and His Songs." *Saturday Evening Post*, June 27, 1925, pp. 14–15, 122, 125, 128.

Barnes, Will C. *Tales from the X-Bar Horse Camp*. Chicago: The Breeders' Gazette, 1920.

Barsness, John. "The Dying Cowboy Song." *Western American Literature* 2 (1967): 50–57.

Beatie, Russel H. *Saddles*. Norman: University of Oklahoma Press, 1981.

Beadle's Dime Song Book: A Collection of New and Popular, Comic and Sentimental Songs, no. 1. New York: Irwin P. Beadle, 1859.

Belden, H. M., ed. *Ballads and Songs Collected by the Missouri Folk-Lore Society*. Columbia: University of Missouri, 1940.

Benton, Jesse James. *Cow by the Tail*. Boston: Houghton Mifflin, 1943.

Black, Baxter. *Buckaroo History*. Brighton, Colo.: Coyote Cowboy Co., 1985.

Black, Baxter. *The Cowboy and His Dog or "Go Git in the Pickup!"*. Brighton, Colo.: Coyote Cowboy Co., 1980.

Black, Baxter. *Coyote Cowboy Poetry*. Brighton, Colo.: Coyote Cowboy Co., 1986.

Black, Baxter. *"Doc, While You're Here . . ."*. Brighton, Colo.: Coyote Cowboy Co., 1984.

Black, Baxter. *On the Edge of Common Sense*. Brighton, Colo.: Coyote Cowboy Co., 1983.

Black, Baxter. *A Rider, a Roper and a Heck 'uva Windmill Man*. Brighton, Colo.: Coyote Cowboy Co., 1982.

Bluestein, Gene. "The Lomaxes' New Canon of American Folksong." *Texas Quarterly* 5 (1962):49–59.

Boni, Margaret Bradford. *The Fireside Book of Folk Songs*. New York: Simon and Schuster, 1947.

Botkin, B. A., ed. *A Treasury of American Folklore*. New York: Crown Publishers, 1944.

Botkin, B. A., ed. *A Treasury of Western Folklore*. New York: Crown Publishers, 1951.

Botkin, J. T. "Concerning a Day When Cowboys Were Cowboys." *Collections of the Kansas State Historical Society* 16 (1923–25):493–96.

Bradford, Louis C. "Among the Cowboys." *Lippincott's Magazine*, June 1881, pp. 565–71.

Bradley, S. A. J., ed. *Sixty Ribald Songs from Pills to Purge Melancholy*. New York: Fredrick A. Praeger, 1968.

Bramlett, Jim. *The Original Strawberry Roan*. N.p.: Published by the author, 1987.

Bramlett, Jim. *Ride for the High Points: The Real Story of Will James*. Missoula, Mont.: Mountain Press Publishing, 1987.

Brand, Oscar, comp. *Bawdy Songs and Backroom Ballads*. New York: Dorchester Press, 1960.

Brand, Oscar, ed. *Folk Songs for Fun*. New York: Hollis Music, 1961.

Brand, Oscar. "Hear de Ding Dong Ring . . . ." *Rogue*, October 1960, p. 23.

Brophy, John, and Eric Partridge. *The Long Trail*. London: Andre Deutsch, 1965.

(Brown). *The Frank C. Brown Collection of North Carolina Folklore*. Vols. 1 and 2 edited by Henry M. Belden and Arthur Palmer Hudson, Durham: Duke University Press, 1952. Vol. 4 edited by Jan Philip Schinhan, Durham: Duke University Press, 1957.

Brumley, Albert E., ed. *Book of Log Cabin Songs*. Powell, Mo.: Stamps-Baxter Music and Printing, 1944.

Brumley, Albert E. *Songs of the Pioneers: A Collection of Songs and Ballads of the Romantic Past*. Powell, Mo.: Albert E. Brumley and Sons, 1970.

Brunnings, Florence E. *Folk Song Index: A Comprehensive Guide to the Florence E. Brunnings Collection*. New York: Garland Publishing, 1981.

Burns, Robert. *The Merry Muses of Caledonia*. Edited by James Barke and Sydney Goodsir Smith. New York: G. P. Putman's Sons, 1964.

Burt, Olive Woolley. *American Murder Ballads*. New York: Oxford University Press, 1958.

Burton, Thomas G., and Ambrose N. Manning. *The East Tennessee State University Collection of Folklore: Folksongs*. 2d ed. Johnson City, Tenn.: The Research Advisory Council of East Tennessee State University, 1970.

Burton, Thomas G., and Ambrose N. Manning. *The East Tennessee State University Collection of Folklore: Folksongs II*. Johnson City, Tenn.: The Research Advisory Council of East Tennessee State University, 1969.

Caldo, Joseph J. "Cowboy Life as Reflected in Cowboy Songs." *Western Folklore* 6 (1947):335–40.

Cannon, Hal, ed. *Cowboy Poetry: A Gathering*. Salt Lake City: Peregrine Smith Books, 1985.

Cheney, Thomas E. *Mormon Songs from the Rocky Mountains*. Austin: University of Texas Press, 1968.

Children's Cowboy Songs. New York: Treasure Chest Publications, 1946.

Chittenden, William Lawrence. *Ranch Verses*. New York: G. P. Putman's Sons, 1893.

Christy, E. Byron, comp. *Charley Fox's Ethiopian Songster*. New York: Frederic A. Brady, 1858.

Clark, Kenneth S., ed. *Buckaroo Ballads, the Golden West in Songs and Pictures*. New York: Paull-Pioneer Music, 1940.

Clark, Kenneth S., ed. *The Cowboy Sings*. New York: Paull-Pioneer Music, 1932.

Clark, Kenneth S., ed. *The Happy Cowboy Sings and Plays Songs of Pioneer Days*. New York: Paull-Pioneer Music, 1934.

Clark, Kenneth S., ed. *Songs for the Rodeo*. New York: Paull-Pioneer Music, 1937.

Clayton, Lawrence. "Elements of Realism in the Songs of the Cowboy." In *American Renaissance and American West*, edited by Christopher S. Durer et al. Laramie: University of Wyoming, 1982.

Cleary, Don. *Wilf Carter Discography*. Privately printed, no date.

Clifford, John. "Range Ballads." *Kansas Historical Quarterly* 21 (1955):588–97.

Coffin, Tristram Potter. *The British Traditional Ballad in North America*, with a supplement by Roger deV. Renwick. Austin: University of Texas Press, 1977.

Cohen, Norm. *Long Steel Rail*. Music edited by David Cohen. Urbana: University of Illinois Press, 1981.

Cohen, Norman. "Tin Pan Alley's Contribution to Folk Music." *Western Folklore* 29 (1970):9–20.

Colcord, Joanna C. *Songs of American Sailormen*. New York: Oak Publications, 1964.

Coolidge, Dane. *Arizona Cowboys*. New York: E. P. Dutton, 1938.

Coolidge, Dane. "Cowboy Songs." *Sunset*, November 1912, pp. 503–10.

Coolidge, Dane. *Old California Cowboys*. New York: E. P. Dutton, 1939.

Coolidge, Dane. *Texas Cowboys*. New York: E. P. Dutton, 1937.

Cowboy Poetry Gathering, January 31, 1984, Elko, Nev. This is the tabloid program published each year for the annual Gathering.

Cowboy Songs. Chicago: Belmont Music, 1937.

Cox, James. *Historical and Biographical Record of the Cattle Industry and the Cattlemen of Texas and Adjacent Territory*. St. Louis: Woodward and Tiernan Printing, 1895.

Cox, John Harrington, ed. *Folk-Songs of the South*. Cambridge: Harvard University Press, 1925.

Craddock, John R. "Songs the Cowboys Sing." *Texas and Southwestern Lore* 6 (1927):184–92 (publication of the Texas Folk Lore Society).

Crawford, Captain Jack. *The Poet Scout: A Book of Song and Story*. New York: Funk and Wagnalls, 1886.

Cray, Edward [E. R. Linton]. *The Dirty Song Book*. Los Angeles: Medco Books, 1965.

Cray, Edward, comp. *The Erotic Muse*. New York: Oak Publications, 1969.

Croy, Homer. *Corn Country*. New York: Duell, Sloan and Pearce, 1947.

Curtiss, Lou. *The Original Record Finder*, no. 146. San Diego, Calif.: Rare Records, n.d.

Davis, Joe. *Joe Davis' Songs of the Roaming Ranger*. New York: Joe Davis, 1935. Reprinted as *Tip Top Songs of the Roaming Ranger*. New York: Tip Top Publishing, 1935.

de Charms, Desiree, and Paul F. Breed. *Songs in Collections: An Index*. Detroit: Information Service, 1966.

Deems, Deborah, and William Nowlan. *Supplementary Listing of Recorded Songs in the English Language in the Library of Congress Archive of Folk Song through Recording No. AFS 4332 (October, 1940)*. Washington, D.C.: Archive of Folk Song, Library of Congress, 1977.

DeVore, Paul T. "Saloon Entrepreneurs of Russell's Art and the Pilgrimage of One Collection." *Montana: The Magazine of Western History*, Autumn 1977, pp. 34–53.

De Witt, Hugh. *Bawdy Barrack-room Ballads*. London: Tandem, 1970.

Dobie, J. Frank. "Ballads & Songs of the Frontier Folks." *Texas and Southwestern Lore* 6 (1927):121–83 (publication of the Texas Folk Lore Society).

Dobie, J. Frank. "The Cowboy and His Songs." *The Texas Review* 5 (1920):163–69.

Dobie, J. Frank. "Cowboy Songs." *The Country Gentlemen*, January 10, 1925, p. 9. Reprinted under the title "Why Cowboys Sing," in *The Saturday Evening Post Saga of the American West*. Indianapolis: Curtis Publishing, 1980.

Dobie, J. Frank. *Guide to Life and Literature of the Southwest*. Dallas: Southern Methodist University Press, 1952.

Dobie, J. Frank. "More Ballads and Songs of the Frontier Folk." *Foller de Drinkin' Gou'd* 7 (1928): 155–80 (publication of the Texas Folk Lore Society).

Dobie, J. Frank. *The Mustangs*. Boston: Little, Brown, 1952.

Dobie, J. Frank. *Some Part of Myself*. Boston: Little, Brown, 1952.

Dobie, J. Frank. "The Tempo of the Range." *Western Folklore* 26 (1967):177–81.

Dolph, Edward Arthur. *"Sound Off!" Soldier Songs from the Revolution to World War II*. New York: Farrar and Rinehart, 1942.

Dorson, Richard M., ed. *Handbook of American Folklore*. Bloomington: Indiana University Press, 1983.

D'Urfey, Thomas, ed. *Wit and Mirth; or, Pills to Purge Melancholy; Being a Collection of the Best Merry Ballads and Songs, Old and New*. 6 vols. London: Printed for J. Tonson, 1719–20.

Dwyer, Richard A., and Richard Lingenfelter, eds. *The Songs of the Gold Rush*. Berkeley: University of California Press, 1965.

Edwards, Don. *Songs of the Cowboys*. Weatherford, Tex.: Sevenshoux Publishing, 1986.

Edwards, Ron. *Australian Bawdy Ballads*. Holloway Beach Calif.: Rams Skull Press, 1973.

Edwards, Ron. *Australian Folk Songs*. Holloways Beach, Queensland, Australia: Rams Skull Press, 1972.

Eliot, T. S. *The Cocktail Party*. London: Faber and Faber, 1950.

Ellis, Annie Laurie. "Oh, Bury Me Not on the Lone Prairie." *Journal of American Folklore* 14 (1901):186.

Emrich, Duncan. *Folklore on the American Land*. Boston: Little, Brown, 1972.

Emrich, Duncan. *It's an Old Wild West Custom*. New York: Vanguard Press, 1949.

Emurian, Ernest D. *The Sweetheart of the Civil War*. Natick, Mass.: W. A. Wilde, 1962.

Ewen, David, ed. *American Popular Songs from the Revolutionary War to the Present*. New York: Random House, 1966.

Farmer, John S. *Merry Songs and Ballads prior to the Year A.D. 1800*. 5 vols. London: Privately printed for subscribers only, 1897. Reprinted with an introduction by Gerson Legman, New York: Cooper Square Publishers, 1964.

Felton, Harold W. *Cowboy Jamboree: Western Songs & Lore*. New York: Alfred A. Knopf, 1951.

Fife, Austin E. "California Joe." *Western Folklore* 22 (1973):49–51.

Fife, Austin E. "The Strawberry Roan and His Progeny." *JEMF Quarterly* 8 (1972): 149–65.

Fife, Austin E., and Alta S. Fife, eds. *Ballads of the Great West*. Palo Alto: American West Publishing, 1970.

Fife, Austin E., and Alta S. Fife, eds. *Cowboy and Western Songs*. New York: Clarkson N. Potter, 1969.

Fife, Austin E., and Alta S. Fife. *Heaven on Horseback: Revivalist Songs and Verse in the Cowboy Idiom*. Logan: Utah State University Press, 1970.

Fife, Austin E., and Alta S. Fife. "Spurs and Saddlebags." *The American West*, September 1970, pp. 44–47.

Finger, Charles J. *Frontier Ballads*. Garden City, N.Y.: Doubleday, Page, 1927.

Finger, Charles J. *Sailor Chanties and Cowboy Songs*. Girard, Kan.: E. Haldeman-Julius, 1923.

Fletcher, Curley W. *Ballads of the Badlands*. Los Angeles: Frontier Publishing, 1932.

Fletcher, Curley W. *Rhymes of the Round-Up*. San Francisco: Privately printed, 1917.

Fletcher, Curley W., ed. *Silverado: Nevada's Annual Souvenir Magazine for 1946*. Carson City, Nev.: Kit Carson Post, Veterans of Foreign Wars, 1946.

Fletcher, Curley W. *Songs of the Sage*. Los Angeles: Frontier Publishing, 1931. Reprinted with a preface by Hal Cannon, Salt Lake City: Gibbs M. Smith, 1986.

Fowke, Edith. "American Cowboy and Western Pioneer Songs in Canada." *Western Folklore* 21 (1962):247–56.

Fowke, Edith. "Bawdy Ballads in Print, Record and Tradition." *Sing and String*, Summer 1963, pp. 3–9.

Fowke, Edith. "A Sampling of Bawdy Ballads from Ontario." In *Folklore and Society: Essays in Honor of Benj. A. Botkin*, edited by Bruce Jackson. Hatboro, Pa.: Folklore Associates, 1966.

Fowke, Edith, ed. *Sea Songs and Ballads from Nineteenth-Century Nova Scotia*. New York: Folklorica, 1981.

Fowke, Edith. *Traditional Singers and Songs from Ontario*. Hatboro, Pa.: Folklore Associates, 1965.

Freeman, James W., ed. *Prose and Poetry of the Live Stock Industry of the United States*. Kansas City, Mo.: National Live Stock Association, 1905.

Fremont, Robert A., ed. *Favorite Songs of the Nineties*. New York: Dover Publications, 1973.

Frey, Hugo, ed. *American Cowboy Songs*. Enlarged ed. New York: Robbins Music, 1936.

Furlong, Charles Wellington. *Let 'er Buck*. New York: G. P. Putnam's Sons, 1921.

Furnivall, Frederick J. *Bishop Percy's Folio Manuscript, Loose and Humorous Songs*. London: Printed by and for the author, 1868. Reprinted with an introduction by John Greenway as *Loose and Humorous Songs from Bishop Percy's Folio Manuscript*. Hatboro, Pa.: Folklore Associates, 1963.

Gainer, Patrick W. *Folk Songs from the West Virginia Hills*. Grantsville, W.Va.: Seneca Books, 1975.

Gaines, Newton. "Some Characteristics of Cowboy Songs." *Foller de Drinkin' Gou'd* 7 (1928):145–54 (publication of the Texas Folk Lore Society).

Gardner, Gail I. *Orejana Bull for Cowboys Only*. Phoenix: Messenger Printing, 1935, 1950. Reprint: 5th printing, Prescott, Az.: privately printed, 1976. 7th printing, Prescott, Az.: Sharlot Hall Museum Press, 1987.

Gardner, Gail I. "The Sierry Petes (or, Tying the Knots in the Devil's Tail)." *Sing Out!*, August-September 1967, pp. 7–9.

German, George. *Cowboy Campfire Ballads*. Yankton, S.D.: Privately printed, 1929. 2d ed., 1932.

Getz, C. W. "Bill," ed. *The Wild Blue Yonder: Songs of the Air Force*. San Mateo, Calif.: Redwood Press, 1981.

Getz, C. W. "Bill," ed. *The Wild Blue Yonder: Songs of the Air Force*. Stag Bar Edition, vol. 2. Burlingame, Calif.: Redwood Press, 1986.

Gillis, Everett A. "Literary Origin of Some Western Ballads." *Western Folklore* 13 (1954):101–6.

Glass, Paul, and Louis C. Singer. *Songs of the West*. New York: Grossett and Dunlap, 1966.

Glassmacher, W. J., ed. *Sing 'Em Cowboy Sing 'Em*. New York: Amsco Music Sales, 1934.

Goldstein, Kenneth S. "Bowdlerization and Expurgation: Academic and Folk." *Journal of American Folklore* 80 (1967):374–86.

Goldstein, Kenneth. S., ed. *Harry Jackson: The Cowboy, His Songs, Ballads & Brag Talk*. Liner notes for Folkways Records FH 5723.

Goodier, Sunny. "California Joe." *Western Folklore* 30 (1971): 133–37.

Gordon, Robert W. *Folk-Songs of America*. New York: National Service Bureau, 1938.

Gough, L. (Lysius). *Western Travels and Other Rhymes*. Dallas: A. D. Aldridge, 1886. Title page reproduced in Lysius Gough's *Spur Jingles and Saddle Songs*, Amarillo, Tex.: Russell Stationery, 1935.

Gray, Roland Palmer, ed. *Songs and Ballads of the Maine Lumberjacks*. Cambridge: Harvard University Press, 1925.

Green, Archie. "Commercial Music Graphics: Twenty-three." *JEMF Quarterly* 8 (1972):196–202.

Green, Archie. "Dobie's Cowboy Friends." *JEMF Quarterly* 12 (1976): 21–29.

Green, Archie. "Hillbilly Music: Source and Symbol." *Journal of American Folklore* 78 (1965):204–28.

Green, Archie. "The Library of Congress's Cowboy Exhibit." *JEMF Quarterly* 19 (1983):85–102.

Green, Archie. "Midnight and Other Cowboys." *JEMF Quarterly* 11 (1975):137–52.

Green, Ben K. *The Color of Horses*. Flagstaff, Az.: Northland Press, 1974.

Green, Douglas B. "The Singing Cowboy: An American Dream." *Journal of Country Music*, May 1978, pp. 4–61.

Green, Rayna. "Folk Is a Four-Letter Word: Dealing with Traditional **** in Fieldwork, Analysis, and Presentation." In *Handbook of American Folklore*, edited by Richard M. Dorson. Bloomington: Indiana University Press, 1983.

Green, Rayna. Introduction to *Pissing in the Snow and Other Ozark Folktales* by Vance Randolph. Urbana: University of Illinois Press, 1976.

Green, Rayna. "Magnolias Grow in Dirt: The Bawdy Lore of Southern Women." *Southern Exposure* 4 (1977):29–33.

Griffis, Ken. *Hear My Song: The Story of the Celebrated Sons of the Pioneers*. Los Angeles: John Edwards Memorial Foundation, 1974.

Griffis, Ken. "The Ken Maynard Story." *JEMF Quarterly* 9 (1973): 67–69.

Haley, J. Evetts. *Charles Goodnight: Cowman & Plainsman*. Norman: University of Oklahoma Press, [1936], 1949.

Haley, J. Evetts. "Cowboy Songs Again." *Texas and Southwestern Lore* 6 (1927): 198–204 (publication of the Texas Folklore Society).

Haley, J. Evetts. *The XIT Ranch of Texas*. New ed. Norman: University of Oklahoma Press, 1953.

Hall, Sharlot M. "Old Range Days an New in Arizona." *Out West*, March 1908, 181–204.

Hall Sharlot M. "Songs of the Old Cattle Trails." *Out West*, March 1907, pp. 216–21.

Hart, Harold H., ed. *The Complete Immortalia*. 4 vols. New York: Hart Publishing, 1971.

Healy, James N., ed. *The Second Book of Irish Ballads*. 3d ed. Cork, Ireland: The Mercier Press, 1968.

Heaps, Willard A., and W. Porter Heaps. *The Singing Sixties: The Spirit of Civil War Days Drawn from the Music of the Times*. Norman: University of Oklahoma Press, 1960.

Henderson, Alice Corbin. "Cowboy Songs and Ballads." *Poetry* 10 (1917):225–59.

Herdon, Jerry A. " 'Blood on the Saddle': An Anonymous Folk Ballad?" *Journal of American Folklore* 88 (1975):300–4.

Hill, Billy. *Billy Hill's American Home Songs*. New York: Shapiro, Bernstein, 1934.

Hobo News. Two Hundred Popular Cowboy Songs, Mountain Ballads of Radio, State and Screen. No publishing information. See: Otis O. Rogers, entry with the same title. They are different, however, in that the pagination varies, and the *Hobo News* collection has a smaller format but carries more songs. The cover is the same on each publication.

Hoffmann, Frank. *Analytical Survey of Anglo-American Traditional Erotica*. Bowling Green, Ohio: Bowling Green University Popular Press, 1973.

Hogbotel, Sebastian, and Simon ffuckes [pseud.]. *Snatches & Lays: Songs Miss Lilly White Should Never Have Taught Us*. Melbourne: Sun Books, 1973; I have not seen the original 1962 printing.

Hood, Isabel, and Mary Allen. *The American Treasury of 1004 Folk Songs*, vol. 1. New York: Charles Hansen, 1977.

Hopkins, Anthony. *Songs from the Front & Rear: Canadian Servicemen's Songs of the Second World War*. Edmonton, Alberta: Hurtig Publishers, 1979.

Horstman, Dorothy. *Sing Your Heart Out, Country Boy*. New York: E. P. Dutton, 1975.

Howes, Wright. *U. S. Iana (1650–1950)*. New York: R. R. Bowker, 1962.

Hubbard, Lester A. *Ballads & Songs from Utah*. Salt Lake City: University of Utah Press, 1961.

Hugill, Stan. *Shanties from the Seven Seas*. New York: E. P. Dutton, 1966.

Hugill, Stan. *Songs of the Seas*. New York: McGraw-Hill, 1977.

Hull, Myra E. "Cowboy Ballads." *Kansas Historical Quarterly* 8 (1939):35–60.

Hunter, John Marvin, ed. *The Trail Drivers of Texas*, 2 vols. San Antonio: Jackson Printing, 1920–23.

Huntington, Gale. *Songs the Whalemen Sang*. Barre, Mass.: Barre Publishers, 1964.

Immortalia (1927). See "Immortalia" in "Unpublished Sources."

Immortalia. "An Anthology of American Ballads, Sailors' Songs, Cowboy Songs, College Songs, Parodies, Limericks, and other Humorous Verses and Doggerel Now for the First Time Brought Together in Book Form by a Gentleman about Town." Attributed to T. R. Smith [George Macy]. Privately printed, 1960.

Ives, Burl. *The Burl Ives Song Book*. New York: Ballantine Books, 1953.

Jackson, Bruce, ed. *Folklore and Society: Essays in Honor of Benj. A. Botkin*. Hatboro, Pa.: Folklore Associates, 1966.

Jackson, Bruce. *"Get Your Ass in the Water and Swim Like Me."* Cambridge: Harvard University Press, 1974.

Jackson, Bruce. "Legman: The King of X700." *Maledicta* 1 (1977): 110–24.

Jackson, Richard. *Popular Songs of Nineteenth-Century America*. New York: Dover Publications, 1976.

Jaques, Mary J. *Texan Ranch Life*. London: Horace Cox, 1894.

Johnson, Helen K. *Our Familiar Songs and Those Who Made Them*, 4 vols. New York: Holt, 1881.

Jones, Buck. *Buck Jones Rangers-Cowboys Collection*. New York: Amsco Music Sales, 1935.

Jones, Buck. *Songs of the Western Trails*. Chicago: Chart Music Publishing House, 1940.

Jones, F. O., ed. *A Handbook of American Music and Musicians*. Canaserga, N.Y.: F. O. Jones, 1886.

Joyner, Charles W. *Folk Song in South Carolina*. Columbia: University of South Carolina Press, 1971.

Kamins, Morton. "John A. Lomax, the Ballad Hunter." *Persimmion Hill*, Summer 1984, pp. 18–29.

Kennedy, Peter. *Folksongs of Britain and Ireland*. New York: Schirmer Books, 1975.

Kirchway, Freda. "The Birth of a Ballad." *Century Magazine*, May 1925, pp. 21–25.

Klickman, F. Henri, and Sterling Sherwin. *Songs of the Saddle*. New York: Sam Fox Publishing, 1933.

Knapp, Mary, and Herbert Knapp. *One Potato, Two Potato . . . . The Secret Education of American Children*. New York: W. W. Norton, 1976.

Kodish, Debora. *Good Friends and Bad Enemies: Robert Winslow Gordon and the Study of American Folksong*. Urbana: University of Illinois Press, 1986.

Kodish, Debora G. " 'A National Project with Many Workers': Robert Winslow Gordon and the Archive of American Folk Song." *Quarterly Journal of the Library of Congress* 35 (1978):218–33.

Koon, William Henry. "The Songs of Ken Maynard." *JEMF Quarterly* 9 (1973):70–77.

Koon, William, and Carol Collins. "Jules Verne Allen, 'The Original Singing Cowboy.' " *Old Time Music*, no. 10, pp. 17–19.

Larkin, Margaret. *Singing Cowboy: A Book of Western Songs*. New York: Alfred A. Knopf, 1931. Reprinted, New York: Oak Publications, 1963; the pagination does not correspond with the original.

Laws, G. Malcolm, Jr. *American Balladry from British Broadsides*. Philadelphia: American Folklore Society, 1957.

Laws, G. Malcolm, Jr. *Native American Balladry*. 2d ed. rev. Philadelphia: American Folklore Society, 1964.

Laycock, Don, comp. *The Best Bawdry*. London: Angus and Robertson Publishers, 1982.

Lee, Jack H. *Powder-River Jack and Kitty Lee's Cowboy Song Book*. Butte, Mont.: McKee Printing, 1936. I have not seen the original song book published in 1926.

Lee, Jack H. *Powder River, Let 'er Buck*. 2d ed. Boston: Christopher Publishing House, 1930.

Lee, Jack H. *The Stampede and Other Tales of the Far West*. Greensburg, Pa.: Standardized Press, c. 1941.

Lee, Jack H. *West of Powder River*. New York: Huntington Press, 1933.

Lee, Katie. "Songs the Cowboys Taught Me." *Arizona Highways*, February 1960, pp. 34–39.

Lee, Katie. *Ten Thousand Goddam Cattle: A History of the American Cowboy in Song, Story and Verse*. Flagstaff, Az.: Northland Press, 1976.

Legman, Gershon. "Bawdy Monologues and Rhymed Recitations." *Southern Folklore Quarterly* 40 (March/June 1976):59–123.

Legman, Gershon. "The Bawdy Song . . . in Fact and in Print." *Explorations* 7 (1957): 139–56.

Legman, Gershon. *The Horn Book: Studies in Erotic Folklore and Bibliography*. New Hyde Park, N.Y.: University Books, 1964.

Legman, Gershon. *The Limerick: 1700 Examples, with Notes, Variants and Index*. Paris: Les Hautes Etudes, 1953. Reprinted, New York: Bell Publishing, 1974.

Legman, Gershon. *Love & Death: A Study in Censorship*. New York: Breaking Point, 1949.

Legmon, Gershon. *Rationale of the Dirty Joke: An Analysis of Sexual Humor*. First series. New York: Grove Press, 1968. Second series: *No Laughing Matter*. Wharton, N. J.: Breaking Point, 1975. Both volumes were reprinted under the title *Rationale of the Dirty Joke: An Analysis of Sexual Humor* by the Indiana University Press in 1982.

Legman, Gershon. "A Word for It?" *Maledicta* 1 (1977):9–18.

Levy, Lester S. *Flashes of Merriment: A Century of Humorous Songs in America*. Norman: University of Oklahoma Press, 1971.

Licht, Michael. "America's Harp." *Folklife Center News*, July-September 1984, pp. 6–9.

Lingenfelter, Richard E., Richard A. Dwyer, and David Cohen, comps. *Songs of the American West*. Berkeley: University of California Press, 1968.

"Little Joe the Wrangler." *Sing Out!*, October-November 1960, pp. 24–25.

Logsdon, Guy. "Songs of the Cowboys." *True West*, February 1983, pp. 18–21.

Logsdon, Guy. Introduction to reprint edition of *Songs of the Cowboys* by N. Howard "Jack" Thorp. Lincoln: University of Nebraska Press, 1984.

Lomax, Alan. *Check-list of Recorded Songs in the English Language in the Archive of American Folk Song to July, 1940*. Washington, D.C.: Music Division, Library of Congress, 1942.

Lomax, Alan. *The Folk Songs of North America*. Garden City, N.Y.: Doubleday, 1960.

Lomax, John A. *Adventures of a Ballad Hunter*. New York: Macmillan, 1947.

Lomax, John A. *Cowboy Songs and Other Frontier Ballads*. New York: Sturgis and Walton, 1910.

Lomax, John A. *Cowboy Songs and Other Frontier Ballads*. New York: Sturgis and Walton, 1916. Reprint: New York: Macmillan, 1920.

Lomax, John A. "Cowboy Songs of the Mexican Border." *Sewanee Review* 19 (1911):1–18.

Lomax, John A. *Cow Camps & Cattle Herds*. Austin: Encino Press, 1967.

Lomax, John A. "Half-Million Dollar Song, Origin of 'Home on the Range.' " *Southwest Review* 32 (1945):1–8.

Lomax, John A. *Home on the Range*. Introduction by John H. Jenkins. Austin: Jenkins, 1986.

Lomax, John A. "Some Types of American Folk-Song." *Journal of American Folk-Lore* 28 (1915):1–17.

Lomax, John A. *Songs of the Cattle Trail and Cow Camp*. New York: Macmillan, 1919.

Lomax, John A., and Alan Lomax, comps. *American Ballads and Folk Songs*. New York: Macmillan, 1934.

Lomax, John A., and Alan Lomax. *Cowboy Songs and Other Frontier Ballads*. Rev. and enlarged. New York: Macmillan, 1938. Reprinted with an introduction by Alan Lomax and Joshua Berrett, New York: Macmillan, 1986.

Lomax, John A., and Alan Lomax. *Folk Song: U.S.A.* New York: Duell, Sloan and Pearce, 1947.

Lomax, John A., and Alan Lomax. *Negro Folk Songs as Sung by Leadbelly*. New York: Macmillan, 1936.

Lomax, Mrs. John A. "Trail Songs of the Cow-Puncher." *Overland Monthly*, January 1912, pp. 24–29.

Lowenstein, Wendy J. *Shocking, Shocking, Shocking: The Improper Play Rhymes of Australian Children*. Prahran, Victoria, Australia: Fish and Chip Press: 1974.

Lummis, Charles F. "The Days of 'Forty-Nine." *Out West* 13 (1903): 202–5.

Luther, Frank. *Americans and Their Songs*. New York: Harper and Brothers, 1942.

MacColl, Ewan, and Peggy Seeger. *Travellers' Songs from England and Scotland*. Knoxville: University of Tennessee Press, 1977.

Malone, Bill C. *Country Music, U.S.A.* Rev. ed. Austin: University of Texas Press, 1985.

Mare, Frank A. "Recordings of the Authentic Cowboys." *Old Time Music*, no. 8, pp. 20–22.

Marshall, Howard W., and Richard E. Ahlborn. *Buckaroos in Paradise: Cowboy Life in Northern Nevada.* Washington, D.C.: Library of Congress, 1980.

McCarthy, Tony, comp. *Bawdy British Folk Songs.* London: Wolfe Publishing, 1972.

McConathy, Osbourne, John W. Beattie, and Russell V. Morgan. *Music Highways and Byways.* New York: Silver Burdett, 1936.

McCoy, Joseph G. *Historic Sketches of the Cattle Trade of the West and Southwest.* Kansas City, Mo.: Ramsey, Millett and Hudson, 1874. Reprinted, edited by Ralph P. Bieber. Glendale, Calif.: Arthur H. Clark, 1940.

McGregor, Craig. *Bawdy Ballads and Sexy Songs.* New York: Belmont/Tower Books, 1972.

McLeish, John. "A Bibliography of G. Legman." *Maledicta* 4 (1980): 127–38.

McNeil, W. K., comp. and ed. *Southern Folk Ballads*, vol. 1. Little Rock, Ark.: August House, 1987.

Meade, Guthrie T., Jr. "The Sea Crab." *Midwest Folklore* 8 (1958): 91–100.

Mechem, Kirke. "Home on the Range." *Kansas Historical Quarterly* 17 (1949):313–39.

Meredith, John, and Hugh Anderson. *Folk Songs of Australia and the Men and Women Who Sang Them.* Sydney: Ure Smith, 1967.

Meridity, John. "Bawdy Bush Ballads." *Meanjin* 17 (1958):379–86.

Milburn, George. *The Hobo's Hornbook.* New York: Ives Washburn, 1930.

Milner, Joe E., and Earle R. Forrest. *California Joe, Noted Scout and Indian Fighter.* Caldwell, Idaho: Caxton Printers, 1935.

(Mix). *Tom Mix Western Songs.* Chicago: M. M. Cole Publishing, 1935.

Monaghan, Jay, ed. *The Book of the American West.* New York: Julian Messner, 1963.

Moon, Dolly M. *My Very First Book of Cowboy Songs.* New York: Dover Publications, 1982.

Moore, Ethel, and Chauncey O. Moore. *Ballads and Folk Songs of the Southwest.* Norman: University of Oklahoma Press, 1964.

Mora, Joe. *Trail Dust and Saddle Leather.* New York: Charles Scribner's Sons, 1946.

Morgan, Harry. *More Rugby Songs.* London: Sphere Books, 1968.

Nebraska Folklore: Cowboy Songs. Nebraska Folklore Pamphlets, pamphlets 1 and 11. Lincoln: Federal Writers' Project in Nebraska, 1937.

Nettleingham, Frederick Thomas. *More Tommy's Tunes.* London: Erskine Macdonald, 1918.

Nettleingham, F. T. *Tommy's Tunes: A Comprehensive Collection of Soldiers'*

Songs, Marching Melodies, Rude Rhymes, and Popular Parodies, Composed, Collected, and Arranged on Active Service with the B.E.F. London: Erskine Macdonald, 1917.

Niles, John J. *Singing Soldiers.* New York: Charles Scribner's Sons, 1927.

Niles, John J., Douglas S. Moore, and A. A. Wallgren. *The Songs My Mother Never Taught Me.* New York: Macaulay, 1929.

Nimmo, Joseph. "The American Cowboy." *Harper's New Monthly Magazine,* November 1886, pp. 880–84.

Nolan, Bob. *Bob Nolan's Folio of Original Cowboy Classics.* Portland: American Music, 1939.

Nolan, Paul T. *John Wallace Crawford.* Boston: Twayne, 1981.

Ohrlin, Glenn. "Glenn Ohrlin: Cowboy Singer." *Sing Out!,* May 1965, pp. 40–44.

Ohrlin, Glenn. *The Hell-Bound Train: A Cowboy Songbook.* Urbana: University of Illinois Press, 1973.

O'Malley, D. J., and John I. White. *D. J. O'Malley "Cowboy Poet."* EauClaire, Wis.: Published by the author, 1934. Reprinted, Helena: Folklife Project, 1986.

Owens, William A. *Tell Me a Story, Sing Me a Song . . . .* Austin: University of Texas Press, 1983.

Owens, William A. *Texas Folk Songs* 23 (1950) (publication of the Texas Folk Lore Society). Reprint: 2d ed., rev. Dallas: Southern Methodist University Press, 1976.

Page, Martin, ed. *Kiss Me Goodnight, Sergeant Major: The Songs and Ballads of World War II.* London: Hart-Davis, MacGibbon, 1973.

Palmer, Edgar A., ed. *G. I. Songs: Written, Composed and/or Collected by the Men in the Service.* New York: Sheridan House, 1944.

Palmer, Roy, ed. *Everyman's Book of British Ballads.* London: J. M. Dent and Sons, 1980.

Peabody, Charles. "A Texas Version of 'The White Captive.' " *Journal of American Folklore* 25 (1912):169–70.

Percy, Thomas. *Reliques of Ancient English Poetry: Consisting of Old Heroic Ballads, Songs, and Other Pieces of Our Earlier Poets (Chiefly of the Lyric Kind),* 3 vols. London: J. Dodsley, 1765.

Pinto, Vivian De Sola, and Alan Edwin Rodway, eds. *The Common Muse.* London: Chatto and Windus, 1957.

Pound, Louise. *American Ballads and Songs.* New York: Charles Scribner's Sons, [1922] 1972.

Pound, Louise. "American Folksong, Origins, Texts and Modes of Diffusion." *Southern Folklore Quarterly* 17 (1953):114–21.

Pound, Louise. "The Pedigree of a 'Western' Song." *Modern Language Notes* 29 (1914):30–31.

Pound, Louise. *Poetic Origins and the Ballad.* New York: Russell and Russell, [1921, 1948] 1962.

Pound, Louise. "Some Texts of Western Songs." *Southern Folklore Quarterly* 3 (1939):25–31.

Pound, Louise. "The Southwestern Cowboy Songs and the English and Scottish Popular Ballads." *Modern Philology* 11 (1913):195–207.

Pound, Louise. "Traditional Ballads in Nebraska." *Journal of American Folklore* 26 (1913):351–66.

"Powder River Jack: Famous Western Character Fifty Years Ago." *The Ranchman*, April 1967, pp. 30–31; May 1967, pp. 17–18.

Purslow, Frank, ed. *The Constant Lovers*. London: E.F.D.S. Publications, 1972.

Purslow, Frank. *The Foggy Dew*. London: E.F.D.S. Publications, 1974.

Purslow, Frank, ed. *The Wanton Seed*. London: E.F.D.S. Publications, 1969.

Randolph, Vance. *Ozark Folklore: A Bibliography*. Bloomington: Indiana University Research Center, 1972.

Randolph, Vance. *Ozark Folksongs*. 4 vols. Columbia: The State Historical Society of Missouri, 1946–50. Reprinted with an introduction by W. K. McNeil. Columbia: University of Missouri Press, 1980.

Randolph, Vance. *Ozark Folksongs*. Edited and abridged by Norm Cohen. Urbana: University of Illinois Press, 1982.

Randolph, Vance. *Pissing in the Snow and Other Ozark Folktales*. Urbana: University of Illinois Press, 1976.

Ratcliffe, Sam D. "The American Cowboy: A Note on the Development of a Musical Image." *JEMF Quarterly* 20 (1984):2–7.

Rattray, Bill. "The Cartwright Brothers' Story." *Old Time Music*, no. 9, pp. 10–14.

Reed, Allen C. "Creakin' Leather, Stan Jones—Music Man from Arizona." *Arizona Highways*, October 1957, pp. 28–32.

Reeves, James. *The Everlasting Circle*. London: Heinemann, 1960.

Reeves, James. *The Idiom of the People*. London: Heinemann, 1958.

Reprints from Sing Out! The Folk Song Magazine. New York: Oak Publications, no. 1, 1962; no. 7, 1964.

Rhodes, Eugene Manlove. *Stepsons of Light*. New York: Houghton Mifflin, 1921. Reprinted, Norman: University of Oklahoma Press, 1969.

Rice, Lee M., and Glenn R. Vernam. *They Saddled the West*. Cambridge, Md.: Cornell Maritime Press, 1975.

Ridings, Sam P. *The Chisholm Trail*. Guthrie, Okla.: Co-operative Publishing, 1936.

Riggs, Lynn. *Cowboy Songs, Folk Songs, and Ballads from Green Grow the Lilacs*. New York: Samuel French, 1932.

Rios, John F. "Dogie Doggerels and Lugubrious Lyrics." *Arizona Highways*, April 1955, pp. 4–7.

Roberts, Leonard. *Sang Branch Settlers: Folksongs and Tales of a Kentucky Mountain Family*. Austin: University of Texas Press, 1974.

Rogers, Otis O., ed. *Cowboy Songs of Ranch and Range*. New ed. New York: Otis O. Rogers, n.d.

Rogers, Otis O., ed. *Two Hundred Popular Cowboy Songs, Mountain Ballads of Radio Stage and Screen*. New York: Otis O. Rogers, n.d.

Rollins, Philip Ashton. *The Cowboy*. New York: Charles Scribner's Sons, 1926.

Rosenberg, Bruce A. *The Folksongs of Virginia: A Checklist of the WPA Holdings in the Alderman Library University of Virginia*. Charlottesville: University Press of Virginia, 1969.

Rothel, David. *The Singing Cowboys*. New York: A. S. Barnes, 1978.

Russell, Charles M. *Trails Plowed Under*. Garden City, N.Y.: Doubleday, Page, 1927.

Russell, Tony. *Blacks, Whites, and Blues*. New York: Stein and Day, 1970.

Sackett, Samuel John. *Cowboys and the Songs They Sang*. New York: William R. Scott, 1967.

Sandburg, Carl. *The American Songbag*. New York: Harcourt, Brace, 1927.

Schroeder, Rebecca B. "Unprintable Songs from the Ozarks: Forgotten Manuscripts." *Missouri Folklore Society Journal* 4 (1982):43–50.

Seeger, Peggy, and Ewan MacColl. *The Singing Island*. London: Mills Music, 1960.

Shay, Frank. *My Pious Friends and Drunken Companions*. New York: Macaulay, 1927.

Sherwin, Sterling. *The American Cowboy Sings Sherwin's Saddle Songs*. London: Francis, Day and Hunter, 1948.

Sherwin, Sterling. *American Cowboy Songs Old and New*. London: Francis, Day and Hunter, 1939.

Sherwin, Sterling. *Singin' in the Saddle*. Boston: Boston Music, 1944.

Sherwin, Sterling, and Henri F. Klickman. *Songs of the Roundup*. New York: Robbins Music, 1934.

Sherwin, Sterling, and Harry A. Powell. *Bad Man Songs of the Wild and Woolly West*. New York: Sam Fox Publishing, 1933.

Shirley, Glenn. "Daddy of the Cowboy Bands." *Oklahoma Today* 9 (Fall 1959):6–8.

Silber, Irwin, ed. *Songs of the Civil War*. New York: Bonanza Books, 1960.

Silber, Irwin, comp. *Songs of the Great American West*. New York: Macmillan, 1967.

Silverman, Jerry. *The Dirty Song Book*. New York: Stein and Day, 1982.

Silverman, Jerry. *The Panic Is On*. New York: Oak Publications, 1966.

Sims, Orland L. *Cowpokes, Nesters, & So Forth*. Austin: Encino Press, 1970.

Sinclair, John L. "Song of the Saddlemen." *New Mexico Magazine* April 1981, pp. 44–52.

Sires, Ina. *Songs of the Open Range*. Boston: C. C. Birchard, 1928.

Siringo, Charles A. *A Lone Star Cowboy*. Santa Fe: Privately printed, 1919.

Siringo, Charles A. *The Song Companion of a Lone Star Cowboy*. Sante Fe: Privately printed, 1919.

Siringo, Charles A. *A Texas Cow Boy*. Chicago: M. Umbdenstock, 1885.

Smith, T. R. [George Macy]. *Poetica Erotica*. New York: Crown Publishers, 1927.

Smith, William R. "Hell among the Yearlings." *Old Time Music*, no. 5, pp. 16–19.

Smyth, Willie. "Country Music in Commercial Motion Pictures (1933–1935)." *JEMF Quarterly* 19 (1983):103–5.

Smyth, Willie. "A Preliminary Index of Country Music Artists and Songs in Commercial Motion Pictures (1928–1953)." *JEMF Quarterly* 19 (1983):107–11; 19 (1983):188–96; 19 (1983):241–47; 20 (1984):8–18.

Songs of the Plains. New York: Belmont Music, 1938.

Songs of the Range. New York: Belmont Music, 1938.

The Songs You Hear No More. Privately printed [circa 1937]. This appears to be a songbook mailed by a border radio performer.

Spaeth, Sigmund. *Read 'em and Weep: The Songs You Forgot to Remember*. Garden City, N.Y.: Doubleday, Page, 1927.

Spaeth, Sigmund. *Weep Some More, My Lady*. Garden City, N.Y.: Doubleday, Page, 1927.

Stamps, Virgil O., ed. *Centennial Songs of Texas*. Dallas: Stamps-Baxter Music, 1936.

Stanley, Clark. *The Life and Adventures of the American Cow-Boy*. Providence, R.I.: C. Stanley, 1897. Reprints. No printing information.

Stanley, Clark. *True Life in the Far West, by the American Cowboy*. Providence, R.I.: C. Stanley, n.d.

Streeter, Floyd Benjamin. *The Kaw*. New York: Farrar and Rinehart, 1941.

"Symposium on Obscenity in Folklore." *Journal of American Folklore* 75 (1962): 189–265.

Taylor, Lonn, and Ingred Maar, eds. *The American Cowboy*. Washington, D.C.: American Folklife Center, Library of Congress, 1983.

Thomason, John W., Jr. *Fix Bayonets!* New York: Charles Scribner's Sons, 1926.

Thompson, Stith. *Motif-Index of Folk Literature*, 6 vols. Rev. and enlarged. Bloomington: Indiana University Press, 1955.

Thorp, N. Howard. "Cowboy Songs." *Poetry* 16 (1920):235–47.

Thorp, N. Howard. *Pardner of the Wind*. In collaboration with Neil M. Clark. Caldwell, Idaho: Caxton Printers, 1945. Reprinted, Lincoln: University of Nebraska Press, 1977.

Thorp, N. Howard. *Songs of the Cowboys*. Estancia, N.M.: New Print Shop, 1908.

Thorp, N. Howard. *Songs of the Cowboys*. Boston: Houghton Mifflin, 1921. Reprinted with an introduction by Guy Logsdon, Lincoln: University of Nebraska Press, 1984.

Thorp, N. Howard. *Songs of the Cowboys*. Edited by Austin E. Fife and Alta S. Fife. New York: Clarkson N. Potter, 1966.

Thorp, N. Howard. *Tales of the Chuck Wagon*. Santa Fe: Privately printed, 1926.

Thorp, N. Howard. "What's Become of the Punchers?" *Literary Digest*, August 21, 1920, p. 40.

Thorp, N. Howard, and Neil M. Clark. "Banjo in the Cow Camps." *Atlantic Monthly*, August 1940, pp. 195–203.

357 Songs We Love to Sing. Chicago: Hall and McCreary, 1938.

Tinsley, Jim Bob. *He Was Singin' This Song*. Orlando: University Presses of Florida, 1981.

Tinsley, Jim Bob. "He Was Singin' This Song." *Buckskin Bulletin* Summer 1984, p. 4.

Toelken, J. Barre. "The Ballad of the Mountain Meadows Massacre." *Western Folklore* 18 (1959):169–72.

Treasure Chest of Cowboy Songs. New York: Treasure Chest Publications, 1935.

Treasure Chest of Ranger Songs. New York: Treasure Chest Publications, 1942.

Trimble, Marshall. *Arizona Adventure*. Phoenix: Golden West Publishers, 1982.

Turner, Dallas. *"Cowboy" Dallas Turner's "The Roving Ranger,"* book no. 1. Chicago: M. M. Cole Publishing, 1950.

Turner, Dallas. *"Cowboy" Dallas Turner, "The Roving Ranger," Northwest Barn Dance Favorites*, folio no. 2. Chicago: M. M. Cole Publishing , 1950.

Turner, Dallas "Nevada Slim." *The Nevada Cowboy's Album of Songs*, folio no. 8. Reno: Republic Features Syndicate, 1977.

Turner, Michael R., ed. *The Parlour Song Book: A Casquet of Vocal Gems*. New York: Viking Press, 1973.

Wannan, Bill, comp. *Robust Ribald and Rude Verse in Australia*. Melbourne: Lansdowne Press, 1972.

Ward, Fay E. *The Cowboy at Work*. New York: Hastings House, 1958.

Ward, Grace B. "Cowboy Songs and Dances." *Pearson's Magazine*, January 1903, pp. 28–35.

Watson, Elmo Scott. "Colorado Springs Man Claims Authorship of Famous Old Cowboy Ballad." *Colorado Springs Sunday Gazette and Telegraph*, January 27, 1924, n.p.

Webb, Walter Prescott. "The Legend of Sam Bass." *Legends of Texas* 3 (1924): 226–30 (publication of the Texas Folk Lore Society).

Webb, Walter Prescott. "Notes on Folk-Lore of Texas." *Journal of American Folklore* 28 (1915):290–99.

Weissman, Dick. "Cowboy Songs from the Open Range to the Radio." *Colorado Heritage* 1 (1981):56–67.

West, John O. "Jack Thorp and John Lomax: Oral or Written Transmission?" *Western Folklore* 24 (1967):114–18.

Westermeier, Clifford P. *Man, Beast, Dust: The Story of Rodeo*. N.p.: World Press, 1947.

Westermeier, Clifford P. *Trailing the Cowboy*. Caldwell, Idaho: Caxton Printers, 1955.

White, John I. "A Ballad in Search of Its Author." *Western American Literature* 2 (1967):58–62.

[White, John I.]. "Bibliography of Articles on Cowboy and Western Songs." *JEMF Quarterly* 6 (1970):35–37.

White, John I. "A Busted Cowboy's Christmas." *American West*, November 1967, pp. 78–79.

White, John I. *Cowboy Songs as Sung by John White "The Lonesome Cowboy" in Death Valley Days*. New York: Pacific Coast Borax, 1934.

White, John I. *Git Along, Little Dogies: Songs and Songmakers of the American West*. Urbana: University of Illinois Press, 1975.

White, John I. "A Montana Cowboy Poet." *Journal of American Folklore* 80 (1967):113–29.

White, John I. "Rhyme on the Ranges." *American Speech* 2 (1927): 440–42.

White, John I., and George Shackley. *The Lonesome Cowboy: Songs of the Plains and Hills*. New York: George T. Worth, 1929.

White, Stewart Edward. *Arizona Nights*. New York: McClure, 1907.

Wilgus, D. K. *Anglo-American Folksong Scholarship since 1898*. New Brunswick: Rutgers University Press, 1959.

Wilgus, D. K. "The Individual Song: 'Billy the Kid.'" *Western Folklore* 30 (1971): 226–34.

Wilgus, D. K. "'Ten Broeck and Mollie': A Race and a Ballad." *Kentucky Folklore Record* 2 (1956):77–89.

Will, G. F. "Four Cowboy Songs." *Journal of American Folklore* 26 (1913):185–88.

Will, G. F. "Songs of Western Cowboys." *Journal of American Folklore* 22 (1909): 256–61.

Wister, Fanny Kemble, ed. *Owen Wister Out West: His Journals and Letters*. Chicago: University of Chicago Press, 1958.

Wister, Owen. *The Virginian*. New York: Macmillan, 1902.

Wolfe, Hewitt. *100 Old Songs*. No imprint information, probably Globe, Arizona, late 1970s.

Wright, Robert L. *Irish Emigrant Ballads and Songs*. Bowling Green, Ohio: Bowling Green University Popular Press, 1975.

WWVA World's Original Radio Jamboree Famous Songs. Chicago: M. M. Cole Publishing, 1940.

Yates, Mike. "The Pear Tree." *Folk Music Journal* 5 (1975):77–78.

INDEX

Note: Page numbers for the main discussions are given in **boldface**; for first lines, in *italics*.

A NOTE ON THE AUTHOR

For thirty years Guy Logsdon has collected songs and lore of cowboys, with a special interest in the bawdy songs to which other
collectors have alluded. His scholarly activities and writing interests
include such diverse personalities and topics as Hopalong Cassidy,
Woody Guthrie, western swing music, and the Dust Bowl. He has
been a public school teacher and a librarian, as well as a professor
at the University of Tulsa. Logsdon works as a public speaker and
entertainer and uses cowboy songs and poetry for his presentation.

Books in the Series Music in American Life

"Happy in the Service of the Lord":
Afro-American Gospel Quartets in Memphis
Kip Lornell

Paul Hindemith in the United States
Luther Noss

"My Song Is My Weapon": People's Songs, American Communism,
and the Politics of Culture
Robbie Lieberman

Chosen Voices: The Story of the American Cantorate
Mark Slobin

"The Whorehouse Bells Were Ringing" and Other Songs Cowboys Sing
Guy Logsdon